Dr and Mrs Frank Safran
One Melon Patch Lane
Westport, CT 06880 USA

ADULTS WITH
LEARNING DISABILITIES

ADULTS WITH LEARNING DISABILITIES

A practical approach
for health professionals

Edited by

Jean O'Hara and Anthea Sperlinger

JOHN WILEY & SONS

Chichester · New York · Weinheim · Brisbane · Singapore · Toronto

Other Wiley Editorial Offices

John Wiley & Sons, Inc., 605 Third Avenue,
New York, NY 10158-0012, USA

WILEY-VCH Verlag GmbH, Pappelallee 3,
D-69469 Weinheim, Germany

Jacaranda Wiley Ltd, 33 Park Road, Milton,
Queensland 4064, Australia

John Wiley & Sons (Asia) Pte Ltd, 2 Clementi Loop #02-01,
Jin Xing Distripark, Singapore 129809

John Wiley & Sons (Canada) Ltd, 22 Worcester Road,
Rexdale, Ontario M9W 1LI, Canada

Library of Congress Cataloging-in-Publication Data

Adults with learning disabilities : a practical approach for health
   professionals / edited by Jean O'Hara and Anthea Sperlinger.
       p.   cm.
   Includes bibliographical references and index.
   ISBN 0-471-97665-2. — ISBN 0-471-97664-4 (pbk.)
   1. Mentally handicapped—Medical care.   2. Mentally handicapped–
–Services for.   I. O'Hara, Jean.   II. Sperlinger, Anthea.
RC570.2.A38   1997
362.3'8—dc21   97–17410
                                                         CIP

British Library Cataloguing in Publication Data
A catalogue record for this book is available from the British Library

ISBN 0-471-97665-2 (cloth)
ISBN 0-471-97664-4 (paper)

Typeset in 10/12pt Palatino by Dorwyn Ltd, Rowlands Castle, Hampshire
Printed and bound in Great Britain by Bookcraft (Bath) Ltd, Midsomer Norton, Somerset
This book is printed on acid-free paper responsibly manufactured from sustainable forestation, for which at least two trees are planted for each one used for paper production.

CONTENTS

ABOUT THE EDITORS

Jean O'Hara MB BS MRCPsych is Consultant Psychiatrist and Medical Adviser with Tower Hamlets Healthcare NHS Trust, and the Department of Psychiatry, the Royal London Hospital. She qualified as a doctor in 1983 and became a member of the Royal College of Psychiatrists in 1988. She has worked in institutional and community settings, providing a range of specialist psychiatric services to adults with learning disabilities. From 1992 to 1996 she undertook additional managerial responsibilities as Head of Specialist Learning Disability Services in Tower Hamlets.

Anthea C. Sperlinger BA(Hons) MSc CPsychol AFBPsS is currently Consultant Clinical Psychologist in Learning Disability Services in the Ravensbourne NHS Trust, Bromley, Kent. She qualified as a Clinical Psychologist in 1971 and has worked in both mental health and learning disability services in a variety of settings and for both Social Services and Health Services. She has a special interest in staff training and development and her previous publications include *Making A Move*: a training resource pack for direct care staff in learning disability services.

ABOUT THE CONTRIBUTORS

Shulamit Ambalu BSc(Hons) MRCSLT
is Chief Speech and Language Therapist for Learning Disabilities Services in Tower Hamlets Healthcare NHS Trust, London.

Hilary Brown PhD
is Professor in Social Care at the Open University, Milton Keynes, and Chair of the Management Committee of NAPSAC.

Barbara Carmichael
is a member of the Fragile X Society and Genetic Interest Group. She has three siblings and two cousins affected with Fragile X.

Isabel C.H. Clare Bsc MPhil (Crim) CPsychol AFBPsS
is Clinical and Forensic Psychologist with Lifespan Healthcare NHS Trust, Cambridge, and with the Department of Psychiatry, University of Cambridge.

John Clements BA(Oxon) MPhil CPsychol
is a Chartered Clinical Psychologist with Applied Psychology Services in Surrey, Kent.

Heather Hogan RNMH CNMH
is Senior Nurse Manager for Learning Disabilities Services in Tower Hamlets Healthcare NHS Trust, London.

Gwyn Howells RD BSc DCH FRCGP
is a General Practitioner in Swansea, Wales. He is a former member of the All Wales Strategy.

Margaret Macadam MSc
is Research Fellow at the Norah Fry Research Centre, Bristol.

Peter Martin RNMH RMN CNMH DMS
is a community nurse with the Community Team for People with Learning Disabilities in Tower Hamlets Healthcare NHS Trust, London.

Sue McGaw BSc(Hons) MSc CPsychol PhD
is Consultant Clinical Psychologist and Head of Special Parenting Service, Trecare NHS Trust, Truro, Cornwall.

Glynis Murphy BA MSc PhD CPsychol
is Reader in Applied Psychology of Learning Disability at the Tizard Centre, University of Kent.

Zenobia Nadirshaw MA DipPsych CPsychol AFBPsS
is Consultant Clinical Psychologist and Lead Clinician for Learning Disabilities Services at Riverside Mental Health NHS Trust, London.

Jackie Rodgers BSc(Hons) PhD
is Research Associate at the Norah Fry Research Centre, Bristol.

Mohammed K. Sharief MD PhD MRCP
is Consultant Neurologist and Senior Lecturer at Guy's and St Thomas's Hospitals, London.

Sophia Thomson MB BS MRCP MRCPsych FRACP
is Consultant Psychotherapist at St Helier NHS Trust, Surrey.

David York Moore MB BS MRCGP DRCOG
is a General Practitioner in Barnstaple, Devon. He is a parent of a son with severe learning disabilities.

PREFACE

There is alarming evidence that the health care needs of adults with learning disabilities are not being met. The growth in the number of people with learning disabilities living in the community (as institutions continue to close) presents a major challenge to health care professionals, particularly those in primary care services and specialist learning disability services.

The aim of this book is to offer practical information and guidance for all health care professionals so that services to adults with learning disabilities are appropriate, responsive and accessible. We have tried to draw together authoritative and helpful information on key concepts, difficult issues, and practice guidelines which will be essential reading for professionals with limited experience of adults with learning disabilities, and for experienced, specialist staff. The choice of topics has been guided by concerns voiced by adults with learning disabilities about the services which they receive, and by recurrent themes and problems which colleagues and services raise.

We hope this book will be welcomed, in particular, by professionals in primary health care, specialist learning disability services and mental health services, including GPs, nurses, health visitors, midwives, psychiatrists, psychologists, social workers, community teams for people with learning disabilities (CTLDs), service providers, administrators and managers.

Part I
Chapters

1

INTRODUCTION

Anthea Sperlinger

Over one million people in the UK (1 in 50 of the population) have learning disabilities. There is evidence that this group has a higher burden of illness than the general population and that, to an alarming degree, their health care needs are not being met. Having learning disabilities should not mean that an individual has second rate health care. Between 1980 and 1993 the capacity of mental handicap hospitals in the UK was reduced by over 26,000 places. This change in the pattern of provision of residential services has resulted in many thousands of people with learning disabilities moving from such hospitals back to 'the community' (Emerson and Hatton, 1994). It is estimated that a further 10,000 people with learning disabilities will move out of long-stay institutions by the year 2000. The growth in the number of people with learning disabilities living in the community presents a major challenge to primary care services and to health care professionals. The general practitioner is now the primary provider of health care to adults with learning disabilities.

TERMINOLOGY AND DEFINITIONS

In this book the term *learning disability* will be used rather than the other terms in use—such as 'mental handicap' or 'learning difficulties' (United Kingdom), or 'mental retardation' or 'mental deficiency' (North America), or 'intellectual impairment' (Australasia).

There has been widespread disagreement and energetic debate over the past 10 years about how to best describe the users of 'mental

Adults with Learning Disabilities. Edited by J. O'Hara and A. Sperlinger.
© 1997 John Wiley & Sons Ltd.

handicap' services. On the one hand, there has been a search for a term which will accurately describe their real difficulties; on the other, there has been a search for a term which has no negative connotations. In England and Wales, the Department of Health has adopted the term 'people with learning disabilities'. The terms 'mental deficiency' and 'subnormality' are no longer used. This terminology reflects current practice within health and social services in the UK.

LEGAL DEFINITIONS

Legal definitions which cover people with learning disabilities tend to be different for different purposes (Ashton and Ward, 1992). There appear to be two broad types of context:

1. Definitions/assessment within criminal, civil, family and children's law—for example, fitness to plead, fitness to stand trial, ability to instruct counsel, ability to be a witness, Police and Criminal Evidence Act 1984.
2. Enabling legislation for various services and supports—for example, Mental Health Act 1983, Registered Homes Act 1984, Local Government Finance Act 1988.

The terms 'mental incapacity' or 'mental impairment' have specific legal meanings within the Mental Health Act 1983 and the term 'mental defective' has a specific legal meaning within the Sexual Offences Act 1956, but are not commonly used elsewhere to describe people in this client group.

DEFINITIONS OF LEARNING DISABILITY (MENTAL RETARDATION)

Learning disability (mental retardation) has been defined (Luckasson *et al.*, 1992) as referring to:

- significantly sub-average intellectual functioning (i.e. a composite score of two standard deviations below the mean on an accepted assessment of intellectual functioning); on the WAIS-R, a score of, or below, IQ 74 for the UK population (Crawford *et al.*, 1995);
- existing concurrently with related limitations in two or more of the following applicable adaptive skill areas: communication, self-care, home living, social skills, use of community resources, functional academic skills, health and safety, leisure and work;
- manifested before the age of 18.

People with a *severe* learning disability (severe or profound mental handicap/mental retardation), *will, in addition to the above general characteristics* (Emerson, 1995):

- score below IQ 50 on standardised tests of intelligence;
- show clear signs of significant disabilities in the acquisition of adaptive behaviours from early in life, and will need considerably more support than their peers to participate successfully in everyday activities;
- show (most of them) some evidence of damage to their central nervous system; and
- have (many of them) additional physical or sensory handicaps.

To clarify the definition further, *the following people are not included* in the accepted definition of learning disability:

- People who develop an intellectual disability after the age of 18.
- People who suffer brain injury in accidents after the age of 18.
- People with complex medical conditions which affect their intellectual abilities and which develop after the age of 18—for example, Huntington's Chorea, Alzheimer's Disease.
- People with some specific learning difficulties—for example, dyslexia, delayed speech and language development, and those with literacy problems.

There has been a major shift in emphasis away from measuring the psychological deficits residing within the person towards methods which focus on evaluating the social and environmental supports which a person will need in order to achieve success in his or her specific environments.

EPIDEMIOLOGY AND AETIOLOGY

Approximately 20 people per 1,000 in the UK have learning disabilities. Within this group, some 3–4 per 1,000 of the general population have severe or profound learning disabilities. Thus, in an average district of 250,000 people, 5,000 people will have learning disabilities and, of these, 750–1,000 will have severe or profound learning disabilities. The prevalence rates of severe and profound learning disabilities decrease with rising age (due to the increased survival rates of children with severe and complex disabilities), and it is estimated that between 18.75 and 22% of the total who have severe or profound learning disabilities are under 16 years of age (Audit Commission, 1987).

The corresponding figures for an average general practitioner, an average GP practice, and an average district are shown in Table 1. However, as Kerr *et al.* (1996a) point out:

Table 1:   Prevalence of learning disability

	Average GP	Average GP practice	Average district
Population	2000	7600	250 000
People with learning disabilities	40	150	5000
People with severe or profound learning disabilities	8	30	750–1000
Adults with severe or profound learning disabilities (age 16 and over)	6	24	600–800

- Variation is associated with a variety of factors such as the level of social deprivation within the practice area.
- Differential resettlement from hospitals to specific areas, patient or carer's choice of doctor, or birth cohort effects also account for considerable variation.
- Individuals with mild learning disabilities are difficult to identify.
- Identification is difficult as general service registers are not inclusive.

Table 2 shows, in summary form, the aetiology of learning disabilities, with some examples and estimated incidence (where this is available).

A HISTORY OF NEGLECT

The neglect and ill treatment of people with learning disabilities has probably one of the worst histories for any group in society. They remain among the most vulnerable members of society and, for the most part, cannot speak up for themselves. Until quite recently, people with learning disabilities were treated as 'substandard' or second-class citizens, segregated in large institutions in rural areas or isolated within their families, and discriminated against in almost every area of life. At times in our history people with learning disabilities have been (a) threatened by eradication because they were considered to be inferior, (b) exhibited for profit in freak shows, (c) considered not worth the cost to keep alive, or (d) put at risk "for the good of others", as in early trials of the measles vaccine.

In the UK there is a historical link between learning disabilities and health care/medical models. When the National Health Service was set

Table 2:   Aetiology of learning disability

Prenatal causes	Some examples	Estimated incidence
A. *Genetic disorders* Chromosomal disorders		
(i) Autosomal	Down's syndrome (Trisomy 21)	1: 660–700 births
Autosomal + Microdeletions	Prader–Willi syndrome (ch 15)	5–10: 100 000
(ii) Sex-linked	Klinefelter syndrome (47XXXY)	2: 1000 live male births
	Turner's syndrome (XO)	1: 4000 live female births
Single gene disorder (dominant)	Neurofibromatosis	1: 3000
	Tuberous sclerosis	1: 30 000 (60% have LD)
Single gene disorder (recessive)	Inborn errors of metabolism, e.g. Phenylketonuria	1: 14 000 newborns
X-linked	Lesch–Nyhan (hyperuricaemia)	
	Fragile X syndrome (Xq27) (most common inherited cause of LD)	1: 1500 male births 1: 2500 females
Multi-factorial	Neural tube defects	1: 500 births
B. *Infections*	Cytomegalovirus	0.4–2.2% all live births
	Toxoplasmosis	480 births per year in UK
	Rubella virus	Fewer since introduction of MMR vaccine
	Syphilis	Not available
C. *Physical/nutritional*	Irradiation, drugs, severe malnutrition, smoking, injury	Not available
D. *Maternal factors involving abnormalities in pregnancy*	Hypothyroidism	1: 4000 live births
	Placental insufficiency, diabetes, toxaemia	Not available
	Foetal alcohol syndrome	20–50% risk in alcoholic mother
E. *Others*	Cerebral palsy	1: 500 live births

Birth (Perinatal)	Some examples	Estimated incidence
A. *Early delivery or problems during delivery*	Prematurity	5–10% all births
	Birth injury, asphyxia, anoxia	Not available
	Infection at birth	Not available
	Intra-uterine growth retardation	Not available
B. *Immediate postnatal disorders*	Hypoxia	Not availiable
	Intraventricular haemorrhage	Not available
	Rhesus incompatibility	Not available

Following Birth (Postnatal) (Infancy, childhood and adolescence—up to age 18)	Some examples	Estimated incidence
A. *Severe physical injury*	Abuse (non-accidental injury)	Not available
	Accidents	Not available
	Neurotoxins (e.g. lead)	Not available
	Post status epilepticus	Not available
B. *Infections*	Meningitis, encephalitis	Not available
	Severe gastroenteritis (e.g. typhoid), brain abscess	Not available
C. *Progressive neurological disease*	Sturge–Weber syndrome	Not available
D. *Deprivation*	Maternal, sensory, cultural and environmental	Not available

up in 1948, the colonies or institutions which were built originally in the nineteenth century to segregate people with learning disabilities from the rest of society became 'hospitals' in which people were 'nursed' (all of their lives) and their problems were defined in medical terms. People with learning disabilities were seen as sick and in need of treatment, compared to other people of the same age who needed housing, education and social care. When families had difficulty coping with their son or daughter at home, they were advised to 'put them away' in an institution instead of being given support to enable them to cope at home. These hospitals publicised their 'cradle to grave' services, often had 'sick wards' providing medical (even surgical) services and had their own church, chaplain and cemetery.

We now know how damaging institutional life was for many people with learning disabilities. Because of their size, location and regimented routines, institutional services made people dependent, powerless and lacking in choice, privacy or social networks. They were often treated inhumanely and sometimes with deliberate cruelty or abuse. One factor which accelerated the pressure to close these large institutions was the evidence of maltreatment and abuse of the people who lived within them.

Although the last 15 years have seen major changes in attitudes towards people with learning disabilities, and this has been reflected in new patterns of service provision, many of the negative beliefs, a lot of the buildings and even some caring practices, remain as legacies of the past. When people with learning disabilities lived in large institutions, the staff there took responsibility for meeting their health care needs in a service based on the medical model. In spite of this, the medical care they received generally fell well below that of the general population. One legacy of this model has been a cautiousness about the 're-medicalisation' of learning disabilities and a suspicion that any emphasis on health care needs for this client group may lead to a return to the damaging overemphasis of the 'medical model' in the lives of people with learning disabilities. This cautiousness could again lead us to neglect them and their needs.

CITIZENS WITH EQUAL RIGHTS

The human rights movement of the 1960s, the work of Goffman (1961) on asylums and stigma, several scandals and public inquiries into hospitals, and the principle of Normalisation (Wolfensberger, 1972) and *An Ordinary Life* (King's Fund, 1980) led to a major change in attitudes towards people with learning disabilities and a radical shift in the planning and delivery of services to this group. The aim of services became to *enable people with learning disabilities to live an ordinary life in the community with whatever support and assistance they required to do so.*

In the UK three basic rights were identified:

• All people with learning disabilities, irrespective of age or disabilities, have the same human rights as non-disabled people.
• All people with learning disabilities, irrespective of age or disabilities, have a right and a need to live like others in the community.
• Service providers must recognise the individuality of people with learning disabilities and plan services accordingly.

The emergence of the consumer movement 'People First' was a significant development of the 1980s. Adults with learning disabilities are starting to have a voice in planning processes, in staff training and recruitment and in service evaluation. Self-advocacy groups are developing all over the country, and there is a growing awareness of the need to empower and enable people with learning disabilities to specify the services they need and to make complaints. However, most local services still lack teeth for planning at user level and most professionals have a service provider's view that self-advocacy is primarily about *commenting* on services. It is important to find out what kind of services users want and need.

COMMUNITY-BASED ALTERNATIVES TO HOSPITAL CARE

The Department of Health (DoH/SSI, 1992) estimated that 20% of adults with profound or severe learning disabilities lived in hospital and NHS community units; 28% lived in residential accommodation provided by local authorities or the voluntary or private sector; and 52% lived at home with family members. Hence, a very large number of adults with learning disabilities live at home with their parents or other family members who remain the largest group of carers. Support for family carers through respite care and home support is essential if care in the community is to be a reality for all concerned.

Epidemiological data suggest that increased life expectancy of people with learning disabilities, ageing family carers, and increased survival rates of children with severe and complex disabilities are likely to combine to *increase* demand for residential provision in the next two decades (Emerson *et al.*, 1996). While the majority of adults with severe learning disabilities live with their families, the provision of residential supports represents, and will continue to represent, a major component of the health and social care of people with learning disabilities.

Community-based alternatives to hospital care have gone through several changes in emphasis since the early 1980s. At first, de-institutionalisation involved the move of those individuals with the least severe disabilities largely into pre-existing services such as hostels, bed and breakfast establishments and independent living. Later, attention focused on the development of staffed houses in the community and the move of people who had more severe and multiple disabilities. Recently, there has been a shift, with less emphasis on services and more on providing supports in natural settings; for example, the development of 'supported living', 'supported employment', 'supported parenting' arrangements, planned and developed around the needs of each individual.

The early identification of 'care in the community' with hospital closure led to an emphasis on how best to close hospitals rather than how best to respond to the individual needs of people with learning disabilities, together with an assumption that 'living in the community' *would* guarantee a high quality of life. There have been many studies of the quality of life of people who have been resettled in the community. Research shows that people with learning disabilities, including those with more severe disabilities and those with additional needs, *can* be supported in the community in such a way as to improve their quality of life significantly. However, outcome measures also show that, in many domains (e.g. choice, income, employment, friendships), the quality of life of people with learning disabilities in *all* settings is impoverished when compared with the general population. *And 'for a significant minority of people life in the community would appear to be relatively indistinguishable . . . from life in hospital'* (Emerson and Hatton, 1994).

The goal of providing uniformly high-quality services in community-based settings remains elusive. The current challenge is how to develop and sustain a high quality of community care during times of economic recession.

The organisation of services for people with learning disabilities has undergone radical changes. It is government policy to close long-stay hospitals. There has been a move to create networks of providers based less on the resources of the statutory sector and more on an evolving independent sector. The NHS and Community Care Act 1990, the separation of purchasing and provision of services, the enhanced role of local authorities and the independent sector and the introduction of new procedures for assessment and care management have all helped to create new opportunities and new threats to the development of services for people with learning disabilities (Emerson and Hatton, 1994).

HEALTH STATUS OF PEOPLE WITH LEARNING DISABILITIES

Studies of the health status of community-based populations of people with learning disabilities have consistent findings, including a high prevalence of specific conditions. People with learning disabilities suffer from a similar range of morbidity as the general population, but some conditions are seen with greater frequency whether in general or within certain syndromes (Kerr *et al.*, 1996a). In addition, difficulties in identification are exacerbated by problems in understanding and communication. The OPCS (1988) showed that 48% of people with learning disabilities have impairment in one sensory domain and 18% are doubly impaired. Other significant issues are eating problems, nutrition, sleeping, respiratory function problems, foot care problems, skin conditions, pressure sores, bowel problems and heart disease.

Table 3 summarises the prevalence of medical and other conditions commonly seen in people with learning disabilities.

Table 3: **Prevalence of medial and other conditions commonly seen in people with learning disabilities** (Kerr *et al.*, 1996a; BPS, 1994)

Condition	Range of recorded occurrence
Additional mental health problems	10%–50%
Significant impairment of sight	12%–57%
Significant hearing problems	5%–60%
Dental disease	11%–29%
Epilepsy	16%–34%
Significant impariment in communication	50%–?

Meeting the primary health care needs of people with learning disabilities is clearly the responsibility of the general practitioner. The role of the GP is vital. Firstly, he or she is the only health care professional that most people see and, secondly, he or she is the gatekeeper to other services from which patients may benefit (Thornton, 1994).

PRIMARY HEALTH CARE AND ADULTS WITH LEARNING DISABILITIES

People with learning disabilities have a greater number and variety of health care needs compared to those of the same age and sex in the general population. Improved life expectancy is significantly increasing the number of people with learning disabilities who are elderly and, therefore, the number with the physical and mental illnesses and disabilities associated with old age. Over 60% of people with learning disabilities have one or more chronic physical or mental health problems sufficient to warrant ongoing medical intervention (Minihan and Dean, 1990).

The demands made of GPs by people with learning disabilities are less frequent than might be expected from the high levels of morbidity of this group. Recent research suggests that the primary health care needs of adults with learning disabilities are not being met. A number of research studies of health screening have revealed an alarming degree of unrecognised, undiagnosed, or unmanaged primary health care needs, including hypertension, heart disease, dietary problems, gross obesity, unmonitored treatment for epilepsy, sight and hearing impairment, chronic bronchitis, spinal deformities, skin disorders and mental health problems. *For many people, these physical difficulties were more limiting than the learning disability.* Several recent studies have emphasised that many people with learning disabilities have strong views on the quality of the health care they receive.

The general practitioner and the rest of the primary health care team have a central role in providing health care. However:

- To use a service, a person must recognise and report symptoms of ill health and ask for help. People with learning disabilities often have difficulty with this and their carers may not have the skills or knowledge needed to support them in obtaining health care.
- Many people with learning disabilities have a high threshold for pain, and, for some, disturbed behaviour may be a symptom of physical discomfort.
- Sometimes people with learning disabilities are offered different treatment for their illnesses from the rest of the population because of the perceived difficulties in obtaining consent and predictions about co-operation and reactions to treatment.

Surveys indicate that the majority of GPs have no idea of the number of people with severe or mild learning disabilities on their list, and consistently underestimate their number. A significant number of GPs do not feel that they should have the lead responsibility for dealing with the general medical problems of people with learning disabilities, but assert that it should be the role of medical staff from the specialist learning disability team. Since each GP will have only a small number of people with learning disabilities on his or her list, their particular health care needs require special emphasis or organisation to be dealt with effectively. Studies consistently show that primary health care team members acknowledge that they have only minimal education on the needs of this client group, yet only a minority welcome the possibility of further training.

HEALTH EDUCATION AND PROMOTION AND ADULTS WITH LEARNING DISABILITIES

The recent government publication *A Strategy for People with Learning Disabilities* (DoH, 1995) states that this client group should have access to all general health services, including health promotion and health education, programmes of health surveillance and maintenance, and primary and secondary health care with appropriate additional support as required to meet individual need. The strategy aims to encourage commissioners of services to address the particular needs of people with learning disabilities within the five *Health of the Nation* priorities (coronary heart disease and stroke; cancer; mental illness; HIV, AIDS and sexual health; and accidents). People with learning disabilities not only share many of the same risk factors relating to these five national priority areas. In addition, they face a range of other health problems which require continued surveillance and monitoring to optimise detection and treatment. Areas such as sensory impairment and dental health could easily be argued to be priorities for this group (Turner and Moss, 1996).

In contrast to *The Health of the Nation* strategy, the *Protocol for Investment in Health Gain* for people with learning disabilities, published by the Welsh Health Planning Forum (1992):

- recognises that people with learning disabilities not only have difficulties in learning, but that the way they are supported makes them even less able to make rational and consistent choices;
- highlights the link between socio-economic deprivation and learning disability;
- makes many recommendations on the way services are delivered rather than laying the blame on the individual—for example, by being more proactive, encouraging advocacy and fostering decision making (Standen, 1995).

If people with learning disabilities are to have the same opportunities for good health as the general population, it can be argued that the key issue is to ensure that health care services are accessible to them. For example:

1. People with learning disabilities have difficulties with *learning*, so health education needs to be provided in a form which they can understand.
2. Primary health care professionals often do not have the skills needed to overcome communication difficulties within a consultation and may not be aware of the need to provide information about health promotion in an accessible form.

3. For most people with learning disabilities, the role of their carers or relatives is crucial in encouraging and maintaining their health-related behaviour. Initiatives need to target the *carers* and their attitudes and beliefs.
4. The environments in which people with learning disabilities live may not support healthier lifestyles. For example, smoking has long been given as a 'reward' to some people with learning disabilities; dietary choice may not be available or taken up; adequate health screening or suitable facilities for physical activity may not be available.
5. There has been some interesting and relevant research (see McPherson *et al.*, 1995) on how best to give health relevant information to people with learning disabilities, how to effect change in their health-related behaviours, and the importance of establishing motivation for change. Such initiatives are in the early stages and the challenge will be to develop ways in which carers, families and primary health professionals can be helped to use such information.

Kerr *et al.* (1996b) conclude that some form of annual health check is necessary for people with learning disabilities (as advised by the Royal College of General Practitioners and the Welsh Health Planning Forum) to ensure regular health promotion and evaluation of health gain targets.

KEY POINTS

1. The use of the term 'learning disabilities' has been adopted by the Department of Health in England and Wales.
2. Legal definitions of learning disability tend to be different for different purposes. The definitions currently accepted in the UK are described.
3. There has been a fundamental re-thinking of the nature of learning disability which has moved the focus of concern from questions of competence to issues of citizenship, rights and supports required.
4. Over the last 20 years there has been a radical shift in public policy towards people with learning disabilities, from a policy of segregation and institutional care to one which is directed at integration and care in the community.
5. There are increasing numbers of people with learning disabilities living in the community and it is estimated that a further 10,000 will move out of institutions into the community by the year 2000. Some 50% of adults with learning disabilities continue to live at home with their parents or other relatives who remain the largest group of carers.

6. This group has a higher burden of illness than the general population, and the general practitioner and the rest of the primary health care team have a central role in providing their health care.

7. To an alarming degree, the health care needs of adults with learning disabilities are not being met. GPs and other primary health care professionals have minimal education on their needs or on how best to communicate with them (or their carers).

8. If people with learning disabilities are to have the same opportunities for good health as do the general population, the key issue is to ensure that health care services are accessible to them.

9. For most people with learning disabilities, the role of their carers or relatives is crucial in recognising and reporting symptoms of ill health and in encouraging and maintaining their health-related behaviour. Initiatives are needed to target the *carers* and their knowledge, attitudes and beliefs.

10. People with learning disabilities have strong views on the health care which they receive, but are usually not involved in any meaningful way in service planning.

REFERENCES

Ashton, G.R. and Ward, A.D. (1992) *Mental Handicap and the Law*. Sweet & Maxwell, London.

Audit Commission (1987) *Community Care: Developing Services for People with a Mental Handicap*. HMSO, London.

British Psychological Society (BPS) (1994) *Purchasing Clinical Psychology Services: Briefing Paper No. 3. Services for People with Learning Disabilities and their Carers*. Division of Clinical Psychology, Leicester.

Crawford, J.W., Gray, C.D. and Allen, K.M. (1995) The WAIS-R (UK): Basic psychometric properties in an adult UK sample. *British Journal of Clinical Psychology*, **34**, 237–250.

Department of Health and Social Services Inspectorate (DoH/SSI) (1992) *Guidance on Standards for the Residential Care Needs of People with Learning Disabilities/ Mental Handicap*. HMSO, London.

Department of Health (DoH) (1995) *The Health of the Nation: A Strategy for People with Learning Disabilities*. HMSO, London.

Emerson, E. (1995) *Challenging Behaviour: Analysis and Intervention in People with Learning Disabilities*. Cambridge University Press, Cambridge.

Emerson, E., Cullen, C., Hatton, C. and Cross, B. (1996) *Residential Provision for People with Learning Disabilities: Summary Report*. Hester Adrian Research Centre, University of Manchester.

Emerson, E. and Hatton, C. (1994) *Moving Out: Relocation from Hospital to Community*. HMSO, London.

Goffman, E. (1961) *Asylums*. Penguin Books, London.

Kerr, M., Fraser, W. and Felce, D. (1996a) Primary health care for people with a learning disability. *British Journal of Learning Disabilities*, **24**, 2–8.

Kerr, M., Richards, D. and Glover, G. (1996b) Primary care for people with an intellectual disability—a group practice survey. *Journal of Applied Research in Intellectual Disabilities*, **9**, 347–352.

King's Fund (1980) *An Ordinary Life. Comprehensive Locally-based Residential Services for Mentally Handicapped People*. Project Paper No. 24, King's Fund, London.

Luckasson, R., Coulter, D.L., Polloway, E.A., Reiss, S., Schalock, R.I., Snell, M.E., Spitalink, D.M. and Stark, J. (1992) *Mental Retardation: Definition, Classification, and Systems of Supports*. American Association on Mental Retardation, Washington, DC.

McPherson, F.M., Lindsay, W.R. and Kelman, L.V. (1995) Health promotion for people with learning disabilities: work in progress in Tayside. *British Psychological Society Health Psychology Update*, **21** (September), 12–14.

Minihan, P.M. and Dean, D.H. (1990) Meeting the needs for health services of persons with mental retardation living in the community. *American Journal of Public Health,* **80**, 1043–1048.

Office of Population Census and Surveys (OPCS) (1988) *The General Household Survey: Informal Carers*. HMSO, London.

Standen, P. (1995) 'The Health of the Nation: A Strategy for People with Learning Disabilities': So what's new? *Health Psychology Update,* **20**, 14–15.

Thornton, C. (1994) Primary planning. *Nursing Times*, 23 March, pp. 65–66.

Turner, S. and Moss, S. (1996) The health needs of people with learning disabilities and the health of the nation strategy. *Journal of Intellectual Disability Research,* **40**, 438–450.

Welsh Health Planning Forum (1992) *Protocol for Investment in Health Gain: Mental Handicap*. Welsh Office, Cardiff.

Wolfsenberger, W. (1972) *The Principle of Normalisation in Human Services*. National Institute on Mental Retardation, Toronto.

2

FAMILY ASPECTS

Sophia Thomson

Families are important. Families are particularly important to people with learning disabilities, whether they be nuclear families, extended families, the institutional 'family', the group home 'family', or the 'family network' involved in their care in the community. The person with learning disabilities may be the one who presents with problems and challenges, but attention to his or her environment—'his or her families'—is always worthwhile.

> People are much greater and much stronger than we imagine, and when unexpected tragedy comes . . . we see them so often grow to a stature that is far beyond anything we imagined. We must remember that people are capable of greatness, of courage, but not in isolation . . . They need the conditions of a solidly linked human unit in which everyone is prepared to bear the burden of others. (Bloom, 1969)

THE MEANING OF DISABILITY

There is a surprising amount of prejudice, suspicion and caution about people with learning disabilities. The meaning of disability to society, the family and the individual is changing and certainly differs across different cultures (see Chapter 9). Some societies feel that great shame accrues to the family where someone has learning disabilities. Others value their family member as special or blessed. It is important to

---

Adults with Learning Disabilities. Edited by J. O'Hara and A. Sperlinger.
© 1997 John Wiley & Sons Ltd.

understand the assumptions and beliefs which families and people with learning disabilities have. Different family members may also differ in their attitudes, especially across the generations. What does having a learning disability mean to the individual with the disability? How often does the person suffer from incomplete information and the stigmatised views of people around them and what do they make of it?

WORKING WITH FAMILIES

Families—not professionals—are the main providers of services to adults with learning disabilities. Over 50% of adults with profound or severe learning disabilities live at home with their families who provide a shadow welfare service, supporting their disabled offspring materially and practically (Mencap, 1994). Satisfaction with this varies, but in many cases there has had to be a difficult process of adjustment to lifelong responsibility for, and commitment to, the caring task (Flynn and Saleem, 1986). Historically, there were two options open to families with a son or daughter with learning disabilities: to take care of the person themselves, with little or no support; or to place their relative in an institution. Hopefully, this is now changing.

During the lifespan of a person with learning disabilities, his or her family will change. If such individuals stay with their biological family, it will progress through various life-cycle changes. There will be different professionals and paid carers involved. If they move to live with paid (or unpaid) carers, these will also change during their lifetime. Often there will be considerable discontinuity and confusion for the person with learning disability.

Intelligence is not just about cognitive ability. Emotional intelligence may actually be heightened in people with learning disabilities, but despite possible emotional appreciation of difficult situations, they rarely have the words to express this. It is more usual to present with a change in behaviour or biological symptoms such as a change in appetite, sleep or energy levels. These symptoms are often the clue that something is not going well in their world and we need to look at their 'family' (their nuclear family, their acquired family of paid carers, or both). If we see this person as the 'envoy' for a family in trouble, it can help to avoid colluding with the idea that it is the person who needs attention and not the whole context ('family') in which the person lives. Working with families in which there is a person with learning disabilities can, at first, be daunting, *but* most 'families' want to be involved, to be consulted and to help.

UNDERSTANDING FAMILIES WITH A MEMBER WITH LEARNING DISABILITIES

The Family Life-cycle

The sequence of life-events in families when a member has learning disabilities tends to be different from families without such disabilities. They may experience life-cycle transitions *in a different sequence* from that of the previous generation (Goldberg *et al.*, 1995). For example, the person with learning disabilities may leave home for residential school during childhood, returning as an adult to live in the family home for many years; the person's leaving home may be timed with transitions related to parental ageing and the prospect of death. Families may face a different range of issues when a child leaves home aged 40 rather than 20. These include anxieties about who will look after the aged parent(s) and what will happen to the person when the parent(s) die. For many parents, their reality is the lack of change in their son or daughter's life experiences and their own continuing responsibilities.

Transition to Adulthood

The transition to adulthood for people with learning disabilities is marked more by a shift in services and service agencies than in opportunities or social status and there are few specialist adolescent services to cushion the abrupt move from childhood to adolescence. Puberty and adulthood are usually characterised by major changes in the pattern and structure of family life but if there is a member with learning disabilities, the pressures on families at this time can be enormous:

- Families are faced with a move from the familiar service system to an unfamiliar and uncertain adult system.
- The subject of leaving home is often broached or reactivated with parents, on the assumption that it is one of the necessary criteria for a successful transition to adulthood.
- There can be a great deal of ignorance among young people with learning disabilities about the nature and cause of their disability.
- The effects of the disability on the young person's self-esteem and abilities can be considerable. Moving out of the parental orbit into a new older position means facing the fact that you will never be a normal adult (Sinason, 1992).
- During this transition, young people with disabilities can experience a high incidence of psychological problems, in particular depression,

anxiety, lack of self-confidence and fearfulness. Those who have complex disabilities and needs are most at risk.

- Acting out of threatening and aggressive behaviour peaks in the late teenage years and early twenties, and is more prominent in those with severe learning disabilities (Holland and Murphy, 1990). Mothers report greater stress and more negative effects on the family during adolescence (Brooks and Bouras, 1994).

Capacity to Grieve

The birth of a child with learning disabilities always comes as a shock to parents (Jupp, 1987) 'in essence, families have to come to terms with three separate impacts—changed expectations for the child, altered perspectives for the future, and acknowledgement of being a different family' (Manthorpe, 1995).

The family

Families with a member with learning disabilities know a lot about loss and their capacity to grieve is critical to their coping capacity. There are a series of griefs for all family members, starting with the parental grief about the perfect child who did not arrive. It is known that if the bad news is broken well, early and sensitively, families cope better in later years than if the diagnosis was fudged or incorrect. Families want to know the truth (which they often suspect) and to be given ample time to discuss their feelings, fears and hopes. Years later families often recall with clarity how they were informed. Talking about this difficult time with the family together can be healing in itself. The parents then also need to negotiate their grief about failed developmental milestones, social and academic achievements and all that being parents of fully independent children might mean.

The siblings

Siblings of people with learning disabilities have the loss of their 'normal' sibling to grieve. They have been found to be rated as more deviant by other parents or teachers (Gath, 1978) and to show increased anxiety and conflict with parents, lower sociability, and adaptation to life goals involving dedication and sacrifice (Farber, 1959). There may also be 'a diversion of feelings and scapegoating of the normal sibling, who can be rejected where the handicapped child cannot. Consequently he may feel it was his fault, expect punishment, provide it, or become anxiously depressed' (Bentovim, 1972). Clearly, life for a sibling of someone with learning disabilities is more complex than for his or her peers (see Chapter 3).

Paid carers

Paid carers also need to deal with loss; the loss of plans and expectations for the people they support, while maintaining realistic goals. One wonders how the life experiences of paid carers affect their work, how they deal with loss. If they are experienced in negotiating the stages of grief and loss, this can be an advantage. If they are not, what conscious and unconscious agendas do they bring to the life of the 'family' in which the person with learning disabilities lives? Professionals may express their own difficulties by:

- use of jargon to obscure the truth
- judgemental attitudes
- over-identification with the family, particularly the parents
- denial of extent of disability
- omnipotence in decision making
- collusion with the family's response.

It has been suggested that it is not the presence of a person with learning disabilities which leads to family distress, but rather the unmet service needs of the family.

The person

The person with learning disabilities must surely know, even if unexpected or inchoate, that he or she is different, that somehow he or she has not been what was wanted or expected, that there is something wrong. Bicknell (1983) and Sinason (1992) comment on the remarkable insight that some people with learning disabilities can show—if given the chance.

COPING AND POSITIVE ADAPTATION IN FAMILIES WITH A MEMBER WITH LEARNING DISABILITIES

Society as a whole tends to view the presence of a child with a disability as an unutterable tragedy from which the family may never recover. Service providers in learning disabilities have mirrored this perception, and tend to view the family as a whole as embroiled in a series of acute crises interspersed with chronic sorrow (Summers *et al.*, 1989). There is now increasing emphasis on *the coping processes and positive adaptation* rather than a continued search for signs of dysfunction.

Families in which there is a person with learning disabilities struggle with the same issues as other families, but have added stresses. Every family needs to negotiate the stages of beginning, working through problems, separations and endings. This can apply equally to a nuclear family, a group home or community family, or even an institution. How 'the family' negotiates each of these stages or potential 'crises' depends on a number of factors. The literature suggests that, where there is a person with learning disabilities in the family, the issues mentioned in Table 1 are important.

Most research has focused on young children and their parents. There is very little data about the characteristics of families whose child remains at home in adulthood, the characteristics of those adults who live with family members throughout their lives, or the cumulative effects of decades of caregiving on ageing parents.

PARENT–PROFESSIONAL RELATIONSHIP

These families may have had contact with local community services for many years (e.g. the Community Team for People with Learning Disabilities). Over this time, there will have been multiple team changes and transitions; families will often see team members arrive, mature and leave.

Relationships

A good relationship between the people involved in supporting adults with learning disabilities—parents, carers and professionals—is essential to good care. We underestimate how much hard work it takes to make the relationships involved workable. Good, shared caring between paid carers and parents may be like a good marital bond—it takes time to develop and needs constant care and respect. Without this solid relationship between mothers and fathers, children often suffer. Similarly, if the relationship between paid carers and parents breaks down, the person to suffer most is often the person with learning disabilities.

Partnerships

It is not an equal partnership, however—parents have more responsibility when their son or daughter is young. Paid carers and professionals can

Table 1: Coping in families

Physical health. Caring can be increasingly physically demanding, involving heavy lifting. Lack of sleep is often a significant problem. Long-term caring with few breaks may wear down the physical and health resources of some parents.

Spiritual or religious beliefs. There is evidence to suggest that families with firm religious views manage better than those without. A distinction is made between a personal belief and support gained through membership of a religious organisation, with some evidence of much less positive support gained from the latter (Fewell, 1986).

Specific views about disability. Views about disability usually manifest in the 'role' assigned to family members. Some common roles in families with learning disability include:

- Disabled person 'stupid' (denying any achievement or special talents).
- Disabled person 'special'.
- Disabled person as scapegoat or foil for other difficulties.
- Disabled person as family 'pet', or reason for staying together.
- Siblings who are not disabled may need to be 'special'—very successful. For example, the eldest girl in a family may be at particular risk of later behavioural problems as she may be coaxed too young into the caring role herself and hence not able to express her own needs (Gath, 1978).

Family therapists believe that all families have designated roles, but that there is some flexibility in these roles in healthy families, e.g. the 'good' one can make a few mistakes and the 'stupid' one has acknowledged achievements. There are also cultural variations in views about disability (see Chapter 9).

Social support. Social networks are often more limited, either because families are too busy or social attitudes are hostile or other people can be cautious about being helpful. Mencap and other voluntary agencies can be a great source of support.

Marital bond or carers' relationship. The literature is very mixed about what happens to marriages where there is a disabled son or daughter. Studies are only just beginning to appear. It is suggested that a good marriage may be strengthened by the stress of a child with learning disabilities, but the strain on a weak marriage may be too great.

Practical resources. Aids to living such as mobility assistance, continence pads, bathing aids, stair rails, special seating may be required and make an enormous difference to family quality of life.

Respite care. Using respite or just knowing that it is available, should the need arise, are both a source of support and enable everyone to 'recharge their batteries" and continue coping. Holidays away from the family can also be an opportunity for the person to develop more skills and make new friends.

feel it is their responsibility to provide care when the person is an adult. It must be very difficult for parents to cope with this changing role. The role of staff often involves many of the tasks and relationships which are associated with 'parenting'. It is not surprising that parents feel confused, displaced, or not even considered while they can still feel a lifelong commitment to their offspring.

Conflict

It can feel like a battleground for all concerned. It is a bit reminiscent of mothers and fathers arguing about how much responsibility their sons and daughters should or can take for themselves. The battle between parents and paid carers can take this form, with the eternally difficult question about *who* is responsible for the care, or for the life of a person with learning disabilities.

Disagreements

Problems can present when there are disagreements, e.g. over whether and when a person with learning disabilities moves house, has a sexual relationship or even when written consent is required for an operative procedure (see Chapter 11). Sometimes it isn't even clear what the tension is about. A good model for making decisions where decisions are difficult, is for all the people involved in the person's care, including the person with the disability, to meet to discuss the problem and come to some agreement. *'But,'* you may say, *'it's not that easy!'* Sometimes, agreement is not reached and tensions mount. Disagreements between professionals, carers (paid and unpaid) and nuclear family members can be intense, if subtle. It may be that this is where the unexpressed fears and anxieties, the hatred and envy, the disgust about disability is played out. It is difficult to be overtly angry with a person with learning disabilities, and anger and resentments may become displaced onto families and team members. The 'shadow' of learning disability may be expressed through these disagreements.

HELPING FAMILIES WITH A MEMBER WITH LEARNING DISABILITIES

It is worth remembering who the family is, as it will almost always involve more than the nuclear family. There is usually a carer (paid or unpaid), extended family members, a GP, and other professionals, as part of the 'system'.

Which Families Need Help?

The ones who present with problems need help. It would be very fruitful to know what the families who do not present with problems are doing, how they are coping and which coping strategies work well for them. There are some who do not present with obvious problems, but are struggling and suffering and not receiving the help they need. GPs are well placed to notice subtle changes, e.g. increased attendance at surgery for relatively minor complaints, increased serious illnesses, depression and anxiety in any or all family members. Increased sick rate among paid carers may also manifest worrying signals about coping difficulties.

Families in difficulty are often found to have these 'structures' (Berger and Fowler, 1980):

- Cross-generational alliance between disabled son and daughter and grandparents.
- Son or daughter in a role that detoured other conflicts in the family. (It is well recognised in traditional family therapy that children can behave in a way that keeps their parents 'busy'. It can be seen as a sort of sacrifice of their own development for the perceived relief from parental or other conflicts.)
- Over-involvement of one parent.
- Freezing of the family at an early stage of development. These frozen families can feel as if the mother–child bond is stuck at a very early stage when there is primary maternal preoccupation. Even when the son or daughter is middle aged, there is difficulty for the mother (or the carer in the mother role) in separating or allowing the person with learning disabilities to separate. The masculine (father) role of helping that separation has not been powerful enough to help. Often professionals can feel like an encouraging father, struggling to gain more independence for the person. Sometimes the roles are reversed. Sometimes there are similar tensions between groups of paid carers. But the re-creation of parental struggles over how much to let go and how much to risk, will feel very familiar to those sitting in case conferences over the years.

When do Families Need Help?

Families usually need help throughout the life-cycle of family life. They can present with changes in the behaviour of the person with learning disability or with overt breakdown of coping in other family members, usually parents. Their needs for help may actually increase when their son or daughter is a young adult, expressing desires for their own lives, their sexuality and for freedom to explore these issues. When parents get old, they may be more experienced, but often the whole family becomes increasingly concerned about the long-term future for the person with learning disabilities. It is not uncommon to hear parents quietly admit that they would prefer to die after their son or daughter with learning disabilities.

The GP is often the central figure. He or she may be the only professional who sees and knows all family members and is aware of their physical and emotional needs. The GP may also be seen as the most accessible person for help and has the advantage of longer contact with family members than any other professional. At times, he or she may be the only professional involved.

Table 2 shows the potential crisis periods for families with a member who has learning disabilities. At all these times, it may be possible to intervene briefly to make a positive contribution to the welfare of the family. All these potential crisis periods are additional to those normally experienced by every family and the likelihood of two or more hazardous times concurring is high.

Table 2:   **Potential crisis periods for families with a member who has learning disabilities (based on Rappoport, 1986)**

1. At diagnosis.
2. When parents realise the implications of the impairment for the child and family.
3. When a decision about placement has to be made (school, etc.).
4. When a decision about future pregnancies has to be made.
5. During subsequent pregnancies.
6. When the prospect of promotion or job change involves moving away from family, neighbourhood and professional supports.
7. When the child with disabilities goes to a primary school, and when he or she would have changed to senior school, had he or she not been disabled.
8. If there is a significant deterioration in the disability, so that it becomes life-threatening or terminal.
9. If the child dies.
10. When the child fails to negotiate a normal developmental stage (talking, walking, reading, etc.).
11. If another child in the family develops the same or another disorder.
12. At the onset of puberty and developing sexuality.
13. When leaving school and starting work (or not starting work).
14. If the person requires operations.
15. If the child goes into residential care or leaves home.

What can clearly be added to these are other crises, like moving house, leaving an institution, losing parents, losing carers, having an accident, losing mobility, becoming seriously ill.

What Help do Families Need and How can Help be Provided?

1. *Carers need*
   (a) Information and advice, practical help, opportunities for time off, financial assistance, emotional support, help with social networks, and a choice about whether to continue caring (Qureshi, 1996).
   (b) Early recognition of and early intervention for severe behaviour problems. The presence of such problems in people with learning disabilities has been widely demonstrated to influence both carer's levels of distress and the eventual decision to seek alternatives to family care (or existing residential care) (see Chapter 6).
   (c) To have a right to expect support, even if they are determined to provide care themselves. Carers' organisations have criticised the targeting of help on situations in danger of breakdown as 'rewarding failure to manage' (Qureshi, 1996).
2. *Tensions need to be acknowledged: e.g.*
   (a) The desire to avoid their relative using residential or respite care may result in unacceptable burdens for carers. Enabling carers to cease caring or to use respite services should themselves be valid goals.
   (b) A wish to enable independent living for the person with learning disabilities may conflict with the carer's wishes to continue to care, or their concerns about safety and protection.
   (c) The wishes and needs of the person with learning disabilities may differ from those of the parents or professionals involved.
3. *Professionals need*
   (a) To appreciate the potential stresses which they impose on families. It is not uncommon for a 'family' to have up to 10 professionals involved (e.g. GP, community nurse, physiotherapist, speech therapist, psychiatrist, neurologist, psychologist, social worker, occupational therapist, care manager, etc.). The need for a key worker or link person, who will coordinate services, is important.
   (b) To understand the 'family' as a system, and the people in it, and view the needs of the 'family members' as dynamic and changing as their situation changes.
   (c) To ask the right questions and be sensitive to cultural needs (see Chapter 9).
4. *Getting everyone together*
   (a) An *understanding of the difficulties* begins the process of help. A hypothesis (a 'diagnosis' based on looking with the family at the family structure, morale, coping skills and capacity to grieve) helps all involved to see where to begin.

(b) A *'family' meeting* may be convened to enable the people involved to meet and have the space or time to talk freely. Guidelines include:

- The *purpose* of the meeting must be clear.
- *Who should attend?* Some of these people may already be meeting regularly, and encouraging *all* people involved to attend may take some time. But all 'family members', including appropriate carers and professionals, should be present to express their views and suggestions.
- *Enabling people to attend.* It may take considerable negotiation to make it possible for all parties to attend, especially fathers. Family members may feel too anxious, too worried about blame, or too frightened to face what might seem insurmountable. Acknowledging these concerns may make it possible for them to come and participate.
- *Chairing the meeting.* The chairperson must follow some general principles, e.g. planning, thanking, setting boundaries, acknowledging confidentiality, setting realistic goals and planning actions with named people.
- *Strategies to use*
  - The chairperson needs a genuine belief that everyone has something to offer, both in understanding what is happening, *and* in helping to engage and bring out potential solutions to problems, so that each person has a role in the way forward. This may involve practical and social help as well as emotional support.
  - Engaging and acknowledging each person helps people to feel valued and hence less likely to argue. Keeping control of a meeting can be very demanding. Some people find it easier to work in pairs.
  - Watching non-verbal communications and responses to discussions can be very revealing. It also helps to see how the family group, carer group, or both are managing.
  - People with learning disabilities are often excluded from their own care planning for many reasons. This deprives them and their families of valued insights and information. People with learning disabilities are often in touch with important aspects of what is really going on.
  - Ritual can reach the parts that words cannot. They can provide a way that everyone in the 'family' can negotiate difficult times. Including people with learning disabilities in the normal rituals of life can help them negotiate crises even if they do not fully understand. *For example, David's*

family put him into care when he was 16 because his mother died. No one explained to him where she had gone, except to say she was now in heaven. Over the subsequent four years, his general health and behaviour deteriorated until he had to be admitted to hospital. Working with a behaviour programme helped to improve his challenging behaviour, but it was only when his own family were invited to come and talk through his mother's death with him that a genuine improvement came. A memorial service, where they all shared their grief, helped to confirm that David was not alone with his grief. A family meeting, including his social worker, was then able to work towards realistic plans for his future with him.

KEY POINTS

1. Over 50% of adults with profound or severe learning disabilities live at home with their families. Most professionals will have contact with people with learning disabilities and become part of their 'family' network.
2. The person with learning disabilities is often the 'envoy' for a 'family' in trouble. It is not just the person who needs attention, but his or her whole context ('family').
3. The transition to adulthood for people with learning disabilities is marked more by a shift in services and service agencies than in opportunities or social status.
4. Families with a member who has learning disabilities know a lot about loss and there is a need to understand and enable them to grieve. It is also important to look at the evidence on coping processes and positive adaptation.
5. There is a need for responsive support, especially at times of crisis throughout the family life-cycle.
6. Families usually want to be involved, to be heard, to participate and to be valued. Parents, siblings, extended families, paid carers, unpaid carers and professionals all have something to offer. The person with learning disabilities must be involved.
7. Professionals need to identify the 'family's' difficulties and needs, to ask the right questions and to have the courage to ask people to meet and discuss their problems. With careful assessment, planning and coordination, most professionals can help families negotiate their struggles and feel less alone with sometimes overwhelming situations.

REFERENCES

Berger, A. and Fowler, F. (1980) Family intervention project. A family network model for serving young handicapped children. *Young Children*, **51**, 23–32.

Bentovim, A. (1972) Handicapped pre-school children and their families. Effects on child's early emotional development. *British Medical Journal*, **3** (September), 634–637.

Bicknell, J. (1983) The psychopathology of handicap. *British Journal of Medical Psychology*, **56**, 161–178.

Bloom, B.L. (1969) Psychotherapy and the community health movement. *International Psychiatric Clinics*, **6**, 235–248.

Brooks, D. and Bouras, N. (1994) Adolescents with a learning disability. *Psychiatric Bulletin*, **18**, 606–608.

Farber, B. (1959) *Effects of a Severely Mentally Retarded Child on Family Integration*. Monographs of the Society for Research in Child Development, **24**, no. 2.

Fewell, R.R. (1986) Support from religious organizations and personal beliefs. In R.R. Fewell and P.V. Vadasy (eds), *Families of Handicapped Children: Needs and Support Across the Life Span*. Pro-Ed, Austin, Texas.

Flynn, M.C. and Saleem, J.K. (1986) Adults who are mentally handicapped and living with their parents: satisfaction and perceptions regarding their lives and circumstances. *Journal of Mental Deficiency Research*, **30**, 379–387.

Gath, A. (1978) *Down's Syndrome and the Family*. Academic Press, London.

Goldberg, K., Magrill, L., Hale, J., Damaskinidou, K., Paul, J. and Tham, S. (1995) Protection and loss: working with learning-disabled adults and their families. *Journal of Family Therapy*, **17**, 263–280.

Holland, T. and Murphy, G. (1990) Behavioural and psychiatric disorder in adults with mild learning difficulties. *International Review of Psychiatry*, **2**, 117–136.

Jupp, S. (1987) Breaking the news: a way of telling parents their new-born child is handicapped. *Mental Handicap*, **15**, 8–11.

Manthorpe, J. (1995) Service to families. In N. Malin (ed.), *Services for People with Learning Disabilities*. Routledge, London.

Mencap (1994) *Paying the Price: A Mencap Report on the Extra Costs of Disability*. Mencap, London.

Qureshi, H. (1996) Carers. In A. Nocon and H. Qureshi (eds), *Outcomes of Community Care for Users and Carers: A Social Services Perspective*. Open University Press, Buckingham.

Rappoport, R. (1963) Normal crises, family structure and mental health. *Family Process*, **2**, 68–80.

Sinason, V. (1992) *Mental Handicap and the Human Condition: New Approaches from the Tavistock*. Free Association Books, London.

Summers, J.A., Behr, S.K. and Turnbull, A.P. (1989) Positive adaptation and coping strengths of families who have children with disabilities. In G.H.S. Singer and L.K. Irvin (eds), *Support for Caregiving Families*. Paul Brookes Publishing Co., Baltimore.

3

PERSONAL PERSPECTIVES ON LEARNING DISABILITIES

Jean O'Hara with Barbara Carmichael and David York Moore*

While the emphasis in recent years has been on moving out of institutions, 40–60% of adults with learning disabilities live in the community with their families (Simons, 1992). Therefore, the family's views, expectations and experiences often mean the difference between (a) being allowed to participate in a range of social activities and relationships and (b) being denied services and opportunities. An important partnership must exist between families and service providers (be it school, social services, training centres, voluntary sector, employment agencies or the health service). This relationship must be handled with sensitivity and care, forged as it is at a time of considerable psychological trauma when families are told of their child's 'diagnosis'.

> Anyone who may try to convince you that being a parent of someone with learning disability is an easy road to tread, is positively misguided. Most of us are not exceptional people . . . many of us are considerably changed by our experience . . . As a result of years of dealing with the emotional and physical turmoil of rearing such a child, with the battles with authorities, with endless assessments and clinics and opinions, many of us will have

---

* The contributions by Barbara Carmichael and David York Moore are identified by their initials.

Adults with Learning Disabilities. Edited by J. O'Hara and A. Sperlinger.
© 1997 John Wiley & Sons Ltd.

become hardened and tempered and even a bit cynical. By the time the child has reached adulthood, the family—the parents, the affected child, and their siblings—will have been through many difficult times. By the time a 'health professional' comes into contact with such a family, the views of parents may be well moulded and ingrained by a series of previous experiences. [DYM]

Unfortunately, these experiences are often negative ones: insensitive, non-responsive, dismissive of parental concerns, impractical, full of broken promises and constantly changing personnel.

DISCLOSURE OF DIAGNOSIS—MAKING THE RIGHT START

The way parents are told that their child is 'not normal' can be a source of unnecessary emotional pain and distress (Quine and Rutter, 1994). Parents often remember this event with enormous clarity many years after, and can speak with a mixture of sorrow and anger. These concerns have led to 'good practice' guidelines on the 'breaking of bad news' (e.g. SCOVO, 1989; NWRHA, 1992) but it is still common to find clumsy and insensitive examples of bad practice.

'Your son's a mongol'—nothing leading up to it. I could have picked her [paediatrician] up and thrown her through the window . . .
(Herbert, 1995)

. . . All I could hear was the voice droning on in the background giving us information we did not need and could not hear. (Herbert, 1995)

I knew something was wrong. The staff were avoiding me . . . (NWRHA, 1992)

The doctor said, 'Your daughter has a very small head and brain. She will only ever be a vegetable . . .' (Quine and Pahl, 1987)

There is an extensive literature proposing a number of theories to help understand parental reactions (see Chapter 2). These include the ability to negotiate 'phases' similar to that of a bereavement, its non-sequential and cyclical nature, reactivated by transitional life crises (e.g. unemployment, major illness) or developmental milestones (e.g. starting school, statementing for special needs, puberty, leaving home), chronic sorrow and other factors such as religious and cultural beliefs, the severity of the disability, the ability of the child to respond, all of which impact on specific reactions and phases.

All parents . . . go through a grieving period when first told the diagnosis, whatever the cause. It is a grieving process which should not be underestimated as it may go on for a long time. It is grieving for the loss of the hoped for, normal child and all the lost potential. It is a different grief from that for a child that dies, as there is a substitute in that idealised child's place who is less than ideal, and who, in contrast to the wanted child, may never go away, at least not in the parents' lifetime. . . . Part of the maturation process allows the change of view from one of hopelessness to one of some sort of a vision of a future, but with a different set of aspirations.

All along the way there will have been painful reminders of the lack of normality of the growing child . . . through playgroups, peer groups, schools and inherent problems, social services and forms galore. . . . Ultimately the way forward comes through the resetting of sights and taking pleasure in lesser achievements. [DYM]

COPING WITH LIFE

Parents have an ongoing need for information about the meaning of their child's condition and the need for emotional support. Most find it difficult to tell other family members and friends, and experience negative reactions ranging from a denial of the problem to outright rejection. Interactions with professionals who so often display a lack of confidence and awkwardness, reinforce the family's sense of isolation and difference.

It is a tremendous advantage to have someone come to your home; most folk are more relaxed on home ground, and a truer perspective may be seen. If we have to go to someone's office for an appointment, we are aware of the uneasiness of the situation, the time constraints, the fact that other people are waiting, the fear of having shown emotion in public and being stared at as one tearfully leaves. [DYM]

My greatest need is to be able to talk to someone who knows exactly how I feel. (Beresford, 1995)

Happiness is like a butterfly . . . yet it is a different butterfly to each of us. I now realise that the one my son is after is not the same as the one I am chasing. I had thought that the one I was chasing was the right one for the rest of my family as well. . . . I have no idea what my son is thinking as he cannot communicate well, but I know that he only skips along if he is happy, as if he's not, he has to be dragged and cajoled. I know when he is happy as he has a wonderful mischievous smile which is often a delight to behold. However, against that there are all those things that I had really wanted to do with a son of mine which, because of his condition, we will never do together. Sadly, a great sense of frustration creeps in, and a feeling of disproportionate lack of reward for the amount of effort required in rearing and looking after him. Certainly my wife feels acutely the emotion of being trapped by our situation, as many aspects of our everyday life revolve around him. I am sure our other children have lost out as a result of the prolonged period of despair, grief and depression that we as parents both went through. [DYM]

Heaman (1995) found the extra time demands in caring for their offspring and being constantly worn out as major issues for mothers as compared to fathers who were primarily concerned about the problems of getting out of the house, their child's health and lack of time with their spouse. The extra costs of higher household bills; greater wear and tear on clothes, bedding, laundry equipment and furniture; and higher transport costs add to the financial burden of many families who have no income other than benefits (Beresford, 1995). Often they have to cope with unsuitable housing, difficult stairs, lack of space, toileting facilities and inadequate heating. How can they attend to the additional psychological and emotional needs, or support intensive interventions designed by a string of visiting professionals, when basic needs are not met?

> The nearest to an offer of help was a suggestion from a doctor that he [disabled brother] should be put into a home to enable my mother to cope better with the rest of us. Help with transport or laundry (we had no car or washing machine) would have been more welcome. [BC]

> We have received much more . . . than parents in similar situations in years gone by. This in many ways is a great advantage, yet it carries its burdens, as there is guilt just in having such a child, and this again is rubbed by the continuing use and need for use of the services. Every time we lift the phone to arrange for our son's differing care needs we feel the pain of guilt. [DYM]

> When I [sibling] left home it was with mixed feelings of relief and anxiety. It was a relief to be able to enjoy a social life without always feeling that I should be helping at home, but felt anxious about how my parents would cope with no help. [BC]

THE NEEDS OF SIBLINGS

For siblings, the need for information and discussion about their brother's or sister's disability, in an age-appropriate way, is often lacking. Many wonder if it is catching, if they are in some way responsible; they need advice as to how to deal with unusual or difficult behaviours, how to tackle questions and jibs from others; and that it is okay for them to have a life of their own, and to feel negative emotions too. While there are many similarities with having a non-disabled sibling, particular themes have emerged around the difficulties of taking on multiple roles (e.g. caregiver, child, surrogate parent), the feeling of deprivation (of parental attention), a sense of isolation and loneliness, the need for their own individual, non-disabled identity and a host of anxieties about growing up, the right to live their own lives, marriage and having children, and the future care of their disabled sibling (Fairbrother, 1988).

> I didn't know anyone else in a similar situation and although I don't recall feeling that I needed help, I do remember hoping for a sympathetic response from my English teacher after we were asked to write an essay on 'My Family' when I was about 13. I still remember the disappointment I felt when the essay was marked and returned with no comment. . . . [BC]

> By the time I was 9 or 10, I was aware that my brother (then aged about 5) was not the same as other children and I felt I had to prepare a friend who was visiting my house for the first time. I didn't know how to explain my brother's difficulties and said 'he can't talk'. That was interpreted as meaning that he was dumb and I knew that wasn't right but didn't know how else to explain his unusual behaviour. When I reached my teenage years it was clear that both my brothers were 'different', and for the first time I began to feel embarrassment, accompanied by guilt, about them. Embarrassment over the way my parents told every new acquaintance 'the boys are handicapped' (I realise now it was to pre-empt any comments about their behaviour), and because I hated being stared at while we were out, and guilt because I thought I shouldn't be embarrassed by my brothers.
> [BC]

> I remember many family outings when we spent ages choosing a suitable café. At the time I thought the choice was based on cost and cleanliness, but I have learned since that we were looking for one which was not too crowded, and where people looked understanding. We had once been asked to leave a café because my brother's continual rocking was annoying other customers. [BC]

> We were not encouraged to invite friends to play and so our social circle was small. . . . [BC]

> After my sister left home, there was no one to 'baby-sit' my brothers (now teenagers). My parents did not have a holiday alone from the time of their honeymoon until they celebrated their silver wedding anniversary, when I used some of my leave from my nursing post to care for my brothers for a week. . . . [BC]

PARENTAL DILEMMAS

In recent years discussion has focused on the need for the person with learning disabilities to know what such a label means for him or her and for others around them. It is painfully evident in clinical practice that people with Down's syndrome, for example, are acutely aware that this label is a reason for terminating a pregnancy, and that there are numerous prenatal tests to prevent such a birth. The literature suggests that parents often feel that telling their disabled offspring would have a devastating impact on them, and they go on to recall their own experiences when they were told. Others work to prevent their offspring from acquiring this knowledge; protecting them from situations and avoiding terminology, listening and contributing to unrealistic aspirations for jobs and marriage.

> I'm grateful she (daughter) doesn't know. She talks about getting married and having a job. . . . Why should I depress her? (Todd and Shearn, 1996)

> I (mother) think he might be becoming aware that he's handicapped. He started asking us if he was 'brain damaged'. I don't know where he picked it up from. . . . I just give him a hug and tell him, 'It's okay, love . . .'.
> (Todd and Shearn, 1996)

Many parents find it hard to allow their son or daughter to achieve full adult status, because, while they acknowledge physical maturity, their offspring's lack of involvement in a range of age-appropriate activities with peers outside the parental home and their perceived dependency makes them opt for an 'adolescent status'.

> He's not really an adult. An adult can reason out things . . . able to conceptualise various situations and self-awareness. It's about knowledge of life. There's an adult awareness because you've lived. . . .
> (Todd and Shearn, 1996)

Twigg and Atkin (1994, cited in Walmsley, 1996) point out that caring for adults with learning disabilities involves the complex task of fostering adult independence as well as providing emotional and practical resources. A particularly complex and challenging dilemma is that posed by developing sexuality and sexual identity and the important role it plays in society in the transition to adulthood. Denial of such development has significant consequences for the individual and his or her family. Several broad areas of parental and carer concern have emerged in the literature (Swain, 1996). Allowing such development means opening up many more issues: advocacy, the provision of privacy, the facilitation of sexual opportunities and experiences, the possibility of socially inappropriate sexual behaviours and vulnerabilities to abuse and exploitation (see Chapter 10). It may also fuel the image (and self-image) of producing something damaged as a result of 'bad sex' (Sinason, 1988). In addition, there are the practical implications of physical development and maturity, the onset and management of menstruation, and other needs for intimate physical care. It can be a particular source of conflict for the individual, his or her family, paid carers and the professionals involved. Sexuality needs to be seen within a broader context of communication, relationships, body awareness and the whole concept of self.

> Part of me, to be honest, thinks she'll never reach that stage. (Swain, 1996)

If it can be expressed . . . by masturbation, well it's really going to be the only outlet, the only way of expressing sexuality . . . and I think that's particularly important. (Swain, 1996)

GENETIC COUNSELLING

It is important that parents wishing to have another child, siblings and the extended family, and perhaps also the learning disabled individual, should understand whether or not there is a genetic basis for the disability. Genetic counselling and prenatal testing can be useful in allowing the individual or couple to understand their particular risks of having an affected foetus. Such counselling and procedures are emotionally and physically traumatic and not without their own risks.

When the cause of the disability is an inherited one, there are many potential causes of conflict in the family. Although many primary health care professionals lack a knowledge of genetics, they should understand and provide for psychological needs. [BC]

No one suggested that I should receive genetic counselling. When I was 24, married and hoping to start a family, I found my way to a geneticist. The consultation took place in a large room with the consultant seated behind a desk and several other people present, none of whom was introduced. I was told that there was a 50/50 chance that I was a carrier of the condition affecting my brothers, but that no carrier or prenatal tests were available. I was very distressed by this news. . . . As I left the room, a social worker pressed her card into my hand and said 'Never mind, you can always adopt'. There was no follow-up contact apart from a letter confirming the facts and noting that I 'seemed to have difficulty coming to terms with the situation'. [BC]

It was wonderful to have a name for the condition [Fragile X Syndrome], even if no one had ever heard of it, and to be in contact with a doctor who was interested in our difficulties and knew other families with the same problems. Even so, I still did not always feel that the professionals understood the desperately difficult decisions we had to make, nor the psychological impact of having a termination of pregnancy after foetal sexing, and the loss of another (unaffected) pregnancy at 17 weeks following a prenatal test. No support was ever offered to me or my husband after these events which put great strain on our marriage. The whole family suffered, and we were unable to support each other. [BC]

CONTACT WITH HEALTH SERVICES

Several studies have looked at the differing perceptions, attitudes, experiences and responsibilities of doctors and parents (e.g. Murdoch and

Anderson, 1990; Nursey *et al.*, 1990). They indicate that GPs often had considerable insight into the family situation, but tended to underestimate the problems parents faced in obtaining services. Parents, however, had more positive attitudes towards learning disabilities, the quality of life for their offspring and his or her place in society, except with regard to their potential for independence and autonomy. Nursey *et al.* (1990) emphasises that it is the professional's job to acknowledge these differences and work with them rather than see them as obstacles to be overcome.

> Most parents want to be given plenty of time to be heard. I [GP] have, as patients, some elderly parents of adults with learning disabilities whose greatest worry is what will become of their son or daughter once they die. Their lives have been interdependently entwined with that of their off-spring. . . . [DYM]

Much has been written about the health care needs of people with learning disabilities; the disadvantages and difficulties they face in a health system that is predominantly reactive and reliant on the individual seeking treatment; the low levels of recognition of basic and specific health needs, the perceived difficulties of consultation and treatment and the low uptake of preventative and health promotional activities (see Chapter 1). There are many different reasons for this. One is the fear of an unfamiliar situation.

> The thing about going to the doctor and being scared is because you don't know what's going to happen. . . . [Adult with learning disabilities]
>
> I would be frightened to get undressed. I wouldn't have the confidence. [Adult with learning disabilities]

Another is the feeling of being misunderstood, ignored and confused by the language that is used; not understanding either the explanations that may be given, if any, or the treatment that is being offered.

> Doctors say things, and I don't understand. I don't tell him. It's embarrassing. [Adult with learning disabilities]
>
> Gastro-enteritis. What's that? Is it something to do with the eye? [Adult with learning disabilities]
>
> I've got high blood pressure. I don't know what it is, just that I've got tablets for it. I don't know what the tablets are. He [doctor] told me to take one every morning. [Adult with learning disabilities]

Although the majority of adults with learning disabilities may appear verbally able, responding to instructions such as 'show me where it hurts', they find it increasingly difficult to answer more specific questions especially if it relates to the type of pain, or to the timing and sequencing of events (see Chapter 4). If their symptoms are of an emotional or psychological nature, many fear the doctor might get annoyed.

> He might say, 'You're wasting my time'. Doctors are there to help you when you are ill, or in an emergency. Sometimes for benefits or income. Not when you are well. When you are fighting fit, free from pain and can do sports.
> [Adult with learning disabilities]

While many adults with learning disabilities feel able to attend for an appointment by themselves, often they do not have the opportunity to do so, and admit that they rarely saw the doctor on their own. They experience difficulties negotiating a situation where they might wish to share more intimate details or where there is a need for a physical examination. Simons (1992) suggests that while some individuals who belong to self-advocacy groups have learnt to 'stick up for themselves' in peer groups, their increased assertiveness is rarely translated into the family situation. Unable to advocate for their own privacy, respondents would have liked the doctor to ask the accompanying carer to leave the room. Often carers are asked to give consent on their behalf (see Chapter 11).

> Doctors ignore me. They always speak to whoever is with me. Mum's there and he [the doctor] tells her about the medicine, and she gets it for me.
> [Adult with learning disabilities]

Many are anxious about making an appointment for themselves and find it impossible to contact the doctor by telephone. If left to their own initiative, such contacts are not made.

> I want the doctor to remind me. To call my name. I want the same doctor every time . . . to give me appointments for more time. About half an hour.
> [Adult with learning disabilities]

> He [learning disabled brother] is allowed to choose what to do with apparently very little guidance from his [paid] carers. This has resulted in him wearing scratched spectacles for some weeks because he didn't call in to the opticians to arrange a repair; failing to stick to a weight-reducing diet despite being over three stone overweight. . . . [BC]

Anxieties about their carer's failing health, how they would deal with an emergency, or if their parent got ill and they had to summon help are often not identified and addressed.

When my dad was in hospital, he stayed overnight. I visited him. They were sticking needles in his veins. I never talked to the doctor to ask what was wrong. I wanted to. I don't know why I never asked him.
[Adult with learning disabilities]

My dad, last Friday. I was there. I was upset. I saw him lying on the floor. I had to come to the Centre, but . . . he fell down twice. I didn't know what to do. . . . [Adult with learning disabilities]

Walmsley's interviews with learning disabled adults (1996) suggests that some individuals assume new roles as their parents age and become infirm. Her respondents welcomed the greater degree of mutuality and sense of reciprocity in the relationship and challenged the notion that such individuals are seen as merely being dependent on families.

PLANNING FOR THE FUTURE – IN PARTNERSHIP

Most parents want to be involved in the care of their disabled offspring. They want to be able to talk with the professionals and agencies involved, to provide information and their own perspective at planning meetings, and for their offspring to communicate as effectively as they can, to acquire and enjoy social and leisure activities. They also want to know that their son or daughter will be cared for in a 'home for life', adequately staffed and funded, and effectively managed so that his or her individual needs are paramount. Many clearly do not want their other children to be 'burdened' with the responsibility of caring for their learning disabled sibling, preferring instead to outlive him or her (Hand *et al.*, 1994).

I can only live in hope. . . . I still want the best for my son but now I have to weigh that against what the cost may be for me, for my wife and my family as a whole. I tend to live with the belief that something will always turn up that will help us on our way. However, for [my son] that really is not good enough, so we have to look ahead and plan for the future. . . . [DYM]

We still have anxieties about their [learning disabled brothers] care. One of the biggest issues is continuity of care. We accept that there will be a turnover of staff in care homes, but little effort seems to be made to minimise any problems this might cause. . . . Drawing up a 'care contract' between carers, the person with learning disabilities and the family can help minimise misunderstandings and could be combined with a 'personal portfolio' to which new staff could refer. There should be regular reviews with the opportunity for constructive discussion and the involvement of all relevant family members. [BC]

My parents feel that they should not always intervene, but find it hard to stand back and watch these things happening, especially after having coped with no help at all for so many years. Perhaps more trivial, but nonetheless upsetting, are instances when personal hygiene has been neglected, or cheap clothes bought so that he looks shabbily turned out. . . . [BC]

Despite high levels of contact with services and professionals, one in three families said they received little support (Beresford, 1995). Often there was a sense of being isolated from, instead of working with, professionals who, Maddon (1995) argues, all too often suffer from a mixture of prejudice, ambivalence and ignorance of the strengths, concerns and insights of parents. In order to work effectively with people with learning disabilities, services need to be willing to learn with and to work with them *and* their carers or families, despite the differing views and perspectives that will be around. Of course the challenge is to identify and meet the needs of the adult with learning disabilities, while also being mindful of the needs of the family. Issues of consent (see Chapter 11) and advocacy (or self-advocacy) must be addressed in all decisions. Key agencies must work towards avoiding unnecessary gaps in provision and duplication, simplifying and merging some access, assessment and review systems to embrace a model of service and planning based on the 'whole person' and 'the whole family'.

KEY POINTS

1. The partnership between family and service providers is an important one, and must be nurtured with care and sensitivity. It should be based on respect for the experiences and views of individual service users and their families.
2. The way parents are first told of the 'diagnosis' and the subsequent practical and emotional supports they receive will have a profound impact on their willingness and ability to work and plan with services for their future needs.
3. The needs of siblings are often ignored and must be catered for in age-appropriate ways.
4. Supporting an adult with learning disabilities in the family is a complex task and involves many conflicts and dilemmas, such as emerging sexuality and adulthood.
5. For adults with learning disabilities, self-assertiveness is rarely translated to situations outside the peer group. Service providers must be alert to the need for privacy, one-to-one consultations, and advocacy.
6. Specific strategies need to be in place to ease access to health care provision, and to ensure that consultations are more effective and responsive.

7. Both the individual with learning disabilities, and his or her family, must be empowered to contribute as equal partners with service providers, in shaping future services.

ACKNOWLEDGEMENT

The authors would like to thank Steve Cole, John Edwards, Jim Ferry, Paul Holmes and Peter Turrton from the men's group at the Kirkland Centre, for their contribution and for allowing their comments to be used.

REFERENCES

Beresford, B. (1995) Times they are a-changin'. *Community Care,* 14 Dec., 20–21.
Fairbrother, P. (1988) I was the lucky one: Information for siblings and parents of people with mental handicap. *Mencap and Sibs.*
Hand, J.E., Trewby, M. and Reid, P.M. (1994) When a family member has an intellectual handicap. *Disability and Society,* 9(2), 167–184.
Heaman, D.J. (1995) Perceived stressors and coping strategies of parents who have children with developmental disabilities: a comparison of mothers and fathers. *Journal of Paediatric Nursing,* **10**, 311–320.
Herbert, E. (1995) Parents reported responses to the disclosure of Down's syndrome. *Down's Syndrome Research and Practice,* 3(2), 39–44.
Maddon, P. (1995) 'Why parents: How parents': a keynote review. *British Journal of Learning Disabilities,* **23**, 90–93.
Murdoch, J.C. and Anderson, V.E. (1990) The management of Down's syndrome children and their families in General Practice. In William I. Fraser (ed.) *Key Issues in Mental Retardation Research.* Routledge, London.
Nursey, A.D., Rohde, J.R. and Farmer, R.D. (1990) A study of doctors' and parents' attitudes to people with mental handicaps. *Journal of Mental Deficiency Research,* **34**, 143–155.
North Western Regional Health Authority (NWRHA) (1992) *Breaking the News — A Resource for Developing Guidelines for Good Practice.* Procedures and Training in Informing Parents of Diagnosis of a Child's Impairment. Regional Advisory Group on Learning Disabilities Services.
Quine, L. and Pahl, J. (1987) First diagnosis of severe handicap: a study of parental reactions. *Developmental Medicine and Child Neurology,* **29**, 232–242.
Quine, L. and Rutter, D.R. (1994) First diagnosis of severe mental and physical disability. *Journal of Child Psychology and Psychiatry,* **35**, 1273–1287.
SCOVO (1989) *Parents Deserve Better.* A review report on Early Counselling in Wales. Standing Conference of Voluntary Organisations for People with a Mental Handicap in Wales.
Simons, K. (1992) *Sticking up for Yourself: Self-Advocacy and People with Learning Difficulties.* Joseph Rowntree Foundation, York.
Sinason, V. (1988) Richard III, Hephaestus and Echo: sexuality and mental/ multiple handicap. *Journal of Child Psychotherapy,* **14**(2), 93–105.

Swain, J. (1996) 'Just when you think you got it sorted . . .', Parental dilemmas in relation to the developing sexuality of young profoundly disabled people. *British Journal of Learning Disabilities*, **24**, 58–64.

Todd, S. and Shearn, J. (1996) To tell or not: parental dilemmas. *SCOVO, Llias* **39**, 3–7.

Walmsley, J. (1996) Doing what mum wants me to do. Looking at family relationships from the point of view of people with intellectual disabilities. *Journal of Applied Research in Intellectual Disabilities*, **9**(4), 324–341.

4

COMMUNICATION

Shulamit Ambalu

The ability to communicate is central if we are to take our place in the social world. Human communication extends beyond the simple signalling of basic needs to the powerful and sophisticated use of *language* . . . a symbolic and rule-governed system, which enables not only personal expression, but the ability to influence our environment and those around us. Disorders of communication in people with learning disabilities arise most commonly as a result of impairment in:

- cognitive skills
- hearing
- language
- speech
- social interaction

Estimates of the prevalence of communication disorders among adults with learning disabilities do not exist for some important reasons:

- The heterogeneity of the population, the broad range of conditions associated with learning disability and the range of ways they impact on the person.
- Studies look at different aspects of communication disorder (e.g. speech, language development, fluency, hearing loss).
- Most studies are developmental and focus on children.

Adults with Learning Disabilities. Edited by J. O'Hara and A. Sperlinger.

In this chapter four case studies reflecting common issues will be discussed, alongside the interventions that may be offered.

COGNITIVE IMPAIRMENT

People with learning disabilities may have communication problems, but this is not necessarily *because* they are learning disabled, although cognitive impairment does impact on communication. Cognitive *processes* likely to be affected include attention, memory and the ability to transfer recently learned material to new problems (Owens, 1989). Problems may include slow reaction times, difficulty sustaining attention, and long and short term memory deficits (particularly in people with more severe learning disabilities).

- Allowing more time to inspect new materials visually or by touch may help to focus attention.
- Use of pictures, together with short, simple sentences, may assist with understanding and recall.
- Breaking tasks down into steps and teaching them one step at a time is likely to facilitate learning.

HEARING LOSS

Many conditions associated with learning disability also result in hearing loss—a common and frequently undetected problem (Ellis, 1986). Estimates of prevalence vary widely, partly because many studies rely on questionnaire methods and carers are often unaware of the problem. Audiometric assessment of 500 adults with learning disabilities in one London district (Yeates, 1992) revealed that 39.6% had a hearing loss that was sufficiently severe to require amplification.

- The consequences of undetected hearing loss for the development and maintenance of speech and language are particularly serious for people with learning disabilities, who may have less ability to compensate for sensory loss and fewer opportunities to participate in rehabilitation programmes. Undetected hearing loss can be a cause of behavioural disturbance.
- A range of hearing tests are now available, including objective tests for people unable to follow verbal commands.
- The fitting of hearing aids can improve speech intelligibility and reduce reliance on gesture. Individuals with profound learning disability who

are unlikely to develop speech can receive stimulation and develop awareness of environmental sound.
- Careful introduction of the hearing aid through a programme of desensitisation prevents rejection of hearing aids.

PRE-LINGUISTIC DEVELOPMENT

Case Example

Christine is usually to be found sitting on the mat on the floor, rocking vigorously and shouting loudly. She stops when someone comes to sit close beside her, and holds her in their arms to gently rock with her. She also calms in response to loud music. Christine will hold large plastic rigid objects and explore them through taste and smell. She will hold and look very closely at fibreoptic tubes that light up, running them between her lips and rocking gently.

Christine was born with cerebral palsy and presents with spastic diplegia, visual impairment as a result of congenital cataracts, and a severe hearing loss. She has severe learning disabilities. Christine is unable to move around her environment independently. While her excellent carers attempt to include her in everything, life can carry on around her with very little real involvement. There seems to be little that she can literally get her hands on that makes any sense to her at all, although she is responsive to both people and things.

Since Christine's carers began to develop her existing responses to touch, sound and smell into essential pre-language skills, she has started to have some control over her world. Activities based on one-to-one games such as rocking, massage and sound-play with music are carried out every day. Christine is beginning to use rocking to stop and start the game and ask for 'more'. She has begun to reach out for sparkling lights or the plastic objects she likes to hold and will sometimes hand them back and forth in a simple turntaking game. She never rocks or screams when she is involved in such activities and seems even more aware of sound since she was fitted with a hearing aid, after objective testing confirmed her severe hearing loss. She has begun to experience the two-way, reciprocal nature of human communication.

Christine has no way of anticipating what will happen to her each day, so it is important that her routine is structured in ways that help her to know when events are beginning and ending, when she will be moving and when potentially invasive activities such as mealtimes and personal care will be happening. This is achieved partly through the use of sensory cues (such as certain types of music when an activity is ending and special types of touch to indicate that movement is about to occur). In time she will be introduced to symbolic communication through the use of Objects of Reference. A spoon placed into her hand, for example, will signal that a cookery class is about to begin. A piece of towelling on the door will indicate that she has reached the bathroom.

Comments

Early interactional skills such as mutual gazing, attending jointly with an adult and participating in turntaking games, which usually emerge in the first few months of life, may not have fully developed in people with profound learning disabilities. An individual is at a *pre-verbal stage* if the ability to use words or signs as symbols has not emerged, and is *pre-intentional* if he or she is not yet aware of a potential to influence the world through communication.

Pre-intentional adults can be enabled to recognise their impact on the world around them by building on their existing responses through the careful introduction of sensory experiences.

LANGUAGE DEVELOPMENT

An infant cries from the very beginning of life. Babbling develops around the sixth month and by the end of the first year the infant has a mixture of 'jargon', babble and perhaps the first word, although the infant can at this stage understand more than he or she can express. As words emerge they are used to refer to many more things than they do in adult speech. Vocabulary gradually increases to approximately 50 words by 18–20 months of age, followed by a 'burst' a few weeks later to around 350 words. Short two-word phrases are then likely to develop (Messer, 1994).

Language Development and People with Learning Disabilities

The core issue concerning researchers of language development in children with learning disabilities is whether their language skills are like those of a non-disabled child of an equivalent age (the delay hypothesis) or in fact develop differently (the deviance hypothesis). Although the link between language development and cognitive skills is generally accepted, in that speech and language disorders become more significant as IQ decreases, the precise nature of the relationship is controversial.

Many individuals with learning disabilities have a complex pattern of strengths and needs; the goal of communication assessment is to uncover them.

A 'delayed' pattern of language development will result in:

- Smaller vocabulary, receptively and expressively. *Kiernan (1982) reported that one-third of children in all special schools in the UK were unable to use more than three words to express their needs.*
- Limited syntactic (grammatical) skills, resulting in difficulties expressing and understanding the full range of tenses (e.g. the difference between 'will go out' and 'have gone out').
- Difficulties understanding and expressing abstract concepts such as time and number (e.g. not understanding 'before' and 'after').

Adults with a 'disordered' pattern of linguistic development may experience all of the above, together with difficulties of

- perception
- sequencing
- word finding
- understanding the precise meanings of words
- correct use of personal pronouns (i.e. I, you, me, he, she)
- echolalia (the repetition of utterances)
- social use of language.

These features are often seen in people with autistic spectrum disorders.

It should be noted that the relationship between language development and cognition is not straightforward. *Hyperlinguistic* people with Williams's syndrome (infantile hypercalcaemia) develop linguistic ability *in advance* of their cognitive skills. Some individuals with spina bifida together with hydrocephalus develop complex sentences, but have difficulties understanding and expressing meaning, resulting in 'Cocktail Party syndrome'.

INFORMAL COMMUNICATIVE BEHAVIOURS

Case Example

Aisha is 19 and has recently left school to join a local day centre for people with multiple disabilities. Aisha has a reputation of being challenging to work with and the workers at the centre are just beginning to believe they can allow her to stay there. Previous reports of hitting, biting, and scratching other children at school, an inability to spend longer than a few seconds at any activity and a tendency to rush up to people and scream into their ears turned out to be true, but they also discovered a charming person who clearly loves interacting with others, particularly adults. They learned that Aisha understood rather more in

Bengali, her first language, although she did understand simple English phrases such as 'dinner time' or 'want a drink?'. She had a few words, the most notably used of which was 'no', and her real words were interspersed with a mixture of 'jargon' and babble. Interestingly, these sounds seemed to develop as she spent longer at her new centre and now her vocalisations are heard throughout the day.

At school, Aisha had learned two Makaton signs—'toilet' and 'biscuit', which were both overextended—'toilet' being used for any activity outside the room, and 'biscuit' being used to request food, drink or indeed any desired object at all. Most troubling was her limited attention control; she only spent a few seconds in each activity and rushed from place to place, grabbing and even hitting staff from time to time to engage their attention.

Aisha has not been diagnosed as autistic, but professionals involved in supporting her suspect that elements of her communication impairment would place her within the spectrum of autistic disorders.

Aisha settled into the centre very well once the staff learned that she needed to experience very short, supervised, activities which had clear beginnings and endings. They use short, simple phrases accompanied by Makaton signs and have learned a few Bengali phrases. Activities and games based on copying movements and actions are used to develop her imitation skills. She is encouraged to use the relevant sign each time she has something to eat or drink, or uses the toilet. It has also become apparent that she can recognise photographs of common objects. Matching photographs to objects is a useful way of building her attention control, but more importantly these images are introduced into real activities, such as making a cup of tea. Eventually it is hoped that photographs will be a further source of symbolic language for Aisha and she will be able to use them to request activities and make choices.

Unfortunately, language and cultural differences have in the past made it difficult for professionals to share their ideas with Aisha's family, who experience considerable stress as a result of her behaviour at home, where she continues to rush from room to room, grabbing people and objects, screaming continuously. A support worker has been arranged to take Aisha out of the house for an afternoon each weekend, with the aim of reducing stress on the family and providing stimulation for her. Two of Aisha's older sisters have been identified as spending the most time interacting with her and a worker from the community team for adults with learning disabilities (CTLD) now works alongside each sister, together with Aisha, modelling how to carry out a short activity that will engage her attention, promote communication and have a satisfying result. Together they have made tea for all the family. Aisha loves anything to do with food and enjoys having the attention of her sisters.

A second member of the team has begun visiting, along with the specialist advice worker for Bengali families, to explore with Aisha's parents the possibility of setting boundaries around her behaviour. They will make many visits in the coming year to support them through the changes.

Comments

Aisha is at the stage where meaningful language has begun to emerge. She is generally reliant on *informal communication behaviours,* such as facial expression, use of her voice and physical contact. These are idiosyncratic and inconsistent and rely for effectiveness on the ability of others to recognise them and make accurate interpretations. As she begins to develop symbolic communication through signs and symbols, she will have access to a formal and therefore consistently interpreted form of communication.

DISORDERS OF SPEECH

Case Example

Bruce lives at home with his family, where he spends much of his time alone with his TV and extensive music collection. Bruce has cerebral palsy, presenting with spastic quadraplegia. He has mild learning disabilities. Bruce spent many years placed in the special care unit of the local authority day centre, because, as a wheelchair user, there was no other physically accessible placement available for him. Bruce, however, has a good understanding of language, can read at a basic level, and has some numeracy skills. He now attends college, where he is taking computer-based courses in basic academic skills.

Bruce, like many young men of 25, would like to have friends his own age, but his speech problems are a major barrier. Although his family understands him well, other people understand about 40% of what he says. Speech is very effortful and exhausting for him and he has difficulties planning longer exchanges, so that he often seems to 'lose his way' in a conversation or appears to interject irrelevant comments because the discussion has moved ahead without him. Other people are sometimes embarrassed by their difficulties in understanding him and many pretend to have understood him; Bruce sometimes suspects this, and is never really sure when he is making himself clear. His family would like him to become more independent, but have grown used to doing everything for him, even 'interpreting' for him in conversations, often quite unconsciously. From time to time his frustrations erupt in anger and he can become depressed.

Bruce has learnt to improve his intelligibility through controlling his posture and breathing for speech, slowing his pace and pausing regularly. He has also begun to use a communication aid outside his home. Consisting of written words and symbols arranged in a folder, it is used by him to cue his conversation partners when he has difficulty with pronouncing certain words, or signalling a change in topic.

Comments

Bruce has good language skills, but has dysarthria, a motor speech impairment affecting his respiration, voicing and articulation. Speech disorders can range in their impact on intelligibility, from mild problems (e.g. in being understood by strangers) to very severe, so that the person is rarely or never understood. Causes include:

- Cranio-facial anomalies, e.g. cleft lip and palate.
- Hearing loss.
- Dysarthria: motor speech impairment resulting from neurogenic dysfunction.
- Verbal dyspraxia: arising from impaired programming of articulatory movements.
- Dysphonia: voice disorder with organic/functional cause (e.g. differences in laryngeal anatomy).
- Stammering: fluency disorder.
- Phonological disorder: immature or deviant pattern of speech sounds.

ALTERNATIVE AND AUGMENTATIVE COMMUNICATION SYSTEMS

Both Bruce and Aisha are using communication aids to augment their spoken language. Aisha is being introduced to signs and symbols as a means to developing her symbolic communication skills. Bruce already has adequate language skills and is using symbols and the written word to promote his intelligibility. Some individuals use these systems as an *alternative* to speech. Box 1 summarises the alternative and augmentative communication systems used in clinical practice.

Communicative Competence

Communicative competence is the ability to influence the communication partner in order to meet one's needs. The competent communicator not only sends unambiguous messages but does it in such a manner that the listener understands not only *what* is conveyed, but *why*, because the listener has understood the speaker's intentions (Sperber and Wilson, 1995). Many adults with learning disabilities are effective communicators, particularly those who have developed excellent use of augmentative or alternative communication systems.

Box 1: Augmentative and alternative systems used by adults with learning disabilities

- **Objectives of reference**
  This approach enables the development of independence and language through the systematic use of special objects in daily routines, e.g. spoon placed in the hand to signify mealtimes, towelling attached to bathroom door.

- **Signs**
  Signs are discrete handshapes combined with movement and direction which, together with facial expression and body movement, transmit meaning. Language-teaching programmes such as Makaton and Signalong use signs taken from British Sign Language together with short, simple but grammatically normal spoken phrases.
  — Signs can be used to promote understanding and expression, as a temporary teaching tool or a permanent communication strategy.
  — Hand-over-hand signing can be adapted for people with dual sensory impairment.
  — Although many carers are concerned that using signs will result in the person never learning to speak, the evidence is to the contrary.

- **Symbol-based systems**
  Symbol systems include photographs, line drawings and commercially available symbol packages. Photographs or picture symbols are suitable if an individual has physical disabilities or requires a permanent visually based aid for cognitive or perceptual reasons.
  — They should be highly ideographic (i.e. look just like what they are meant to represent), and hence instantly meaningful.
  — Light technology aids present symbol material in the form of communication boards, books, files and personal organisers.
  — High technology aids require a power source, and range from simple pointer/scanner systems to sophisticated computers with speech output. Access is by means of keyboard or switches. Assessment is carried out by an occupational therapist and engineer, to ensure that the user can easily access the system.
  — 'High-tech' does not necessarily mean 'highly effective' and often simpler light-tech systems are more flexible, reliable and useful.

- **Total communication approach**
  — *Multi-modal communication* is the combination of visual channel modes such as signing, gesture, symbols, pictures and the written word, together with speech, the auditory channel mode. It enables access to a range of techniques that can be used as appropriate (e.g. signs can be used at the day centre and as a symbol-based organiser while out shopping).
  — Services wishing to enable their users to access every aspect of the programme can achieve this by ensuring that signs, symbols, objects of reference, speech and the written word are used in each and every activity and throughout the environment. This is known as the *Total Communication Approach*.

- **Facilitated communication**
  Facilitated communication training is a controversial technique which assumes that a disorder of motor planning underlies the communication impairment for many with learning disabilities, including those with autism. The individual is given physical support to type out messages on a keyboard, or point to letters or symbols on a chart. At this stage there is little evidence in most studies that these messages are coming from the communication impaired partner, although further research should indicate whether this technique is suitable for *some* individuals.

SOCIAL COMMUNICATION SKILLS
Case Example

Dave is in his early thirties and has lived in a large hostel since he moved from a long stay institution 10 years ago. He is proud of his part-time job at a garden centre, where his employers are satisfied with his work but a little concerned that he avoids contact with the customers. Dave never begins a conversation; he responds to others with one-word replies. If he has not understood an instruction or does not know how to fulfill a task at work he will not say so and, consequently, it is only when he has a frustrated outburst that his employer realises he has not understood. Dave is lucky that his present employer is sympathetic. He was fired from his previous gardening job because he would run away and hide if approached by a member of the public. Since then, he has been a member of a social skills group, which enables him to practise social communication skills such as greeting others and starting conversations. He has also started seeing a counsellor, who reports that Dave can express himself well within the session, but that this requires patient and unhurried listening. Dave needs medical investigation for a minor health problem, requiring a short stay in hospital. The staff at his home are worried that he has not expressed any feelings about the admission and that he will not be able to tell hospital staff if he has not understood them. They have been using the 'Books Beyond Words' series (Hollins et al., 1996) with Dave, to explain what will happen when he sees the doctor and when he eventually goes into hospital.

Comments

All human beings fail to understand what is said to them from time to time, but most can let their communication partner know when this has occurred; this is known as signalling *'communicative distress'*. Some adults with learning disabilities do not signal that they have not understood, or perhaps do, but in such subtle ways that the cue is not picked up. When a conversation 'breaks down' because of lack of understanding, one partner will pick up the topic to 'repair' it. The person who does this the most is likely to become dominant in the conversation; in practise, this is often the non-disabled partner. These experiences are likely to impact on the self-esteem of adults with learning disabilities.

- *Compensatory strategies.* Individuals may compensate for their difficulties by attempting to appear more competent than they are, perhaps by not signalling communicative distress, or avoiding situations where they anticipate difficulties in making themselves understood.
- *Withdrawal and control.* Others may have learnt to use withdrawal as a strategy for gaining control. Bedrosian and Prutting (1978)

demonstrated that the four adults with learning disabilities in their study could express control within conversations, but as a rule did not do so when interacting with their parents and clinicians. Control strategies were more likely to be used when interacting with peers and young children. While able to use strategies competently, their sensitivity to status differences prevented this.

• *Conversational skills.* There is a complex set of unspoken rules which govern participation in conversation (such as taking turns, being relevant, conveying information in a logical order). Failure to recognise and observe these rules can result in increased social isolation. Some adults with learning disabilities, for example, repeat the same topics, possibly a result of having very few new events to talk about, or because being involved in an interaction is more important than exchanging new information. They may repeat what has been said or continually fire questions as a means of continuing the conversation (Calculator and Bedrosian, 1988).

• *Language use in institutional settings.* Communicative competence can only be judged in relation to one's environment and, unfortunately, the environments in which many adults with learning disabilities spend the majority of their time—gathered in large groups and cared for by paid staff—are themselves highly atypical. An adult with learning disabilities resident in such an environment could expect to be interacted with for less than 3% of the time, for on average 105 seconds every 25 minutes (Thomas *et al.*, 1986). Interactions tend to be neutral, with very few consequences for either inappropriate or positive behaviour and mostly take place within the context of physical care. They are likely to violate conventions for normal conversation, consisting primarily of directives with frequent interruptions and unannounced changes (Landesman, 1988). Language ability is likely to deteriorate in those who move to institutional settings, perhaps because care staff do not recognise or respond to ambiguous messages together with a reduced need to communicate at all, as institutional settings anticipate and provide for all basic needs.

COMMUNICATION ISSUES FOR HEALTH CARE WORKERS

Interactions with health care providers have a somewhat unusual structure, being typically based around a series of questions asked by the professional. The professional is not, of course, seeking to dominate the patient, but is following convention so that he or she may gain the information needed. The risk is that the person with learning disabilities may withdraw—a reaction to years of intrusive questioning by professionals, perhaps exacerbated by the professional's higher social status.

- *Reliance on interviewing.* As a means of obtaining information, this has several important consequences. Although it is not possible to predict who will respond with accuracy, adults with mild or moderate learning disabilities can respond reliably. If the individual has profound learning disabilities, verbal questioning may be unsuccessful, leading the professional to depend on parents and carers for information. However, paid carers are often not the most reliable source of information, particularly where a large staff team is responsible for care. Parents may hold different views from each other and from their offspring. Professionals must ask questions but need to be cautious in their approach, and be mindful of the way the questions are phrased. Box 2 shows some strategies for enhancing communication.
- *Form of questions used.* Heal and Sigelman (1995) have shown that when asked a 'yes/no' question, an adult with learning disabilities is most likely to acquiesce in response and say 'yes'. In the few cases where the response to most questions is 'no', this is likely to be due to a taboo topic (such as institutional rules). There are ways of improving reliability of response. For example, by asking 'either/or' questions (e.g. 'Is the pain better or worse?'). There is a small risk that the individual will respond with the last option offered. However, if pictures or symbols (e.g. an uncomfortable looking face and a relaxed face) are used to accompany the question, the tendency to repeat the last choice is reduced. It does not, however, improve response accuracy. Questions requiring qualitative responses such as 'sometimes' or 'a lot' are particularly difficult. Simply phrased open-ended questions can be used, e.g. 'How have you been?'. However, many people with learning disabilities give limited and inadequate responses to this form of questioning which may be useful in establishing rapport rather than obtaining reliable information. Re-phrasing the question, and the use of probes such as 'How are you feeling? Tell me about your leg', may be helpful but should not be repeated more than once or twice. Repeating the question is likely to yield more information, but it is important to note that people with learning disabilities have difficulty in giving even known biographical data, such as age, date of birth and address, either with accuracy or indeed at all.
- *Recall and detail.* During more complex history taking, the more linguistically able person may be asked to describe a series of events. He or she may have coped well with simple short questions, but will experience difficulty in connecting sentences into a longer narrative. There may be omissions, inappropriate segments joined together and difficulty narrating events in their correct temporal sequence. The longer the time delay between the experience and its narration, the more problems with recall and omission of detail. There may, in addition, be the impact arising from uncomfortable or threatening topics.

Box 2:   Strategies for enhancing communication

Preparation

- Ensure adequate lighting and minimise background noise.
- Remove distracting or threatening equipment.
- Read notes before the person with learning disabilities arrives.
- Use an interpreter if English is not the person's first language and allow double the time: brief the interpreter before the session, and check that he or she understands you.
- Allow a break for the person to leave the room, if necessary.
- Allow extra time for discussion with carers.
- Prepare picture material (e.g. use a polaroid camera, commercially available materials, or simple line drawings).
- Avoid keeping the person waiting.

Making contact

- Arrange seating so that the participants can see and hear each other.
- Greet the person, make introductions, and explain the purpose of the meeting.
- Sit in front of, or to the 'better side' of a hearing impaired person.
- Seat the hearing impaired person with his or her back to any window.
- Find out from carers how best to communicate with the person.

The consultation

- Use short, simple sentences; speak more slowly; pause after each sentence.
- Replace jargon with commonly understood words.
- Check that the person understands you and/or the interpreter.
- Use gesture, mime, pointing and increased facial expression, if necessary.
- Enourage the person to use his or her communication aid, if one is used.
- Break explanations of procedures down into steps: use teaching models, photographs, or simple diagrams.
- Use open questions: e.g. 'Tell me about your foot'; use probes, e.g. 'What else can you tell me about your foot?'; repeat the question with small changes, if necessary, e.g. 'Your foot—tell me about it'.
- Use 'either/or' questions: e.g. 'Can you walk upstairs at home, or do you stay downstairs?'
- Avoid using questions which require a 'yes/no' answer.
- Be aware of difficulty in understanding the full range of tenses (e.g. 'did hurt', 'does hurt' and 'will hurt' may be heard and understood to have the same meaning).
- Be aware of difficulty in understanding time and number concepts (e.g. 'before' and 'after' may not be understood).
- Remember that reading skills may be very poor—adapt all written information so that the person can understand it (e.g. pictures, diagrams, symbols).
- If the person's speech is difficult to understand, do not pretend that you have understood. Ask him or her to:
  — say it again
  — say it more slowly
  — say it in different words
  — show you what he or she means.
- Watch the person carefully to check that he or she is not becoming anxious or distressed.
- Remember that parents' or carers' views may differ from those of the person with learning disabilities.
- Sum up at the end of the session and say what will happen next.

- *Basic pain behaviours.* Congenital insensitivity to pain is known in some conditions associated with learning disabilities, such as familial dysautonomia. Biersdorff's study (1994) of 125 adults with learning disabilities, showed that 25% had indications of pain indifference and insensitivity, with a higher prevalence in the more severely disabled. Some individuals presented with general hyperactivity, even when the pain was located very specifically. Others, who did not have spontaneous pain behaviours, seemed to have very deliberately learned to mimic the usual words and gestures associated with pain. They were able to use these effectively to summon help, but there was a danger that health care professionals would respond to their rather 'unnatural' communication style by assuming that the person was 'faking'. Clearly, the role of the carer is vital in detecting what can be very subtle changes in behaviour and arranging for medical attention.
- *Literacy.* Although there are some exceptions, most adults with learning disabilities have major difficulties with reading. Any written information (e.g. signs in a surgery or out-patient area; written instructions; medication labels) will have to be read and explained to the person by someone else (the health care professional, paid carer, family member or advocate). Any information given to the person about his or her health problems or about health promotion must be carefully planned and tailored to the person's needs. It may need to be available in several forms, and advance planning will be required. The use of pictures, photographs, diagrams, or books designed for adults with learning disabilities is helpful (see Chapter 11 and Checklists 3 and 4).

Adults with communication impairments demand a higher level of communication skill from their health care providers. However, it is not only they who will benefit from these skills, which are relevant in all circumstances that require higher levels of sensitivity in observation and listening, as well as clarity of verbal and non-verbal communication. When the professional develops the necessary skills to communicate with adults with learning disabilities, everyone benefits.

KEY POINTS

1. Communicative competence cannot be predicted from the level of language development, motor speech ability or degree of cognitive impairment.
2. Undetected hearing loss is a serious issue. Up to 40% of people with learning disabilities have a significant hearing loss.
3. Good functional communication skills are likely to develop if:

- there are real, regular and rewarding opportunities to communicate in the daily environment;
- the person with learning disability has developed the use of an augmentative or alternative system of communication;
- carers and services respond to these methods and incorporate them into their own communication behaviours.
4. Health care providers can structure their interviews to
   - establish and maintain rapport;
   - enable better understanding of the information they plan to convey;
   - avoid or minimise response bias, especially acquiescence, by using 'either/or' questions with accompanying pictures.
5. Any written/visual and health promotional material needs to be carefully planned so that it will be understood by people with no or poor literacy skills.
6. Unconventional ways of reporting symptoms can lead to problems accessing appropriate treatment. Carers may have detailed knowledge of the person's typical behaviours, as well as their responses to pain.

REFERENCES

Bedrosian, J.L. and Prutting, C.A. (1978) Communicative performance of mentally retarded adults in four conversational settings. *Journal of Speech and Hearing Research*, **21**, 79–95.

Biersdorff, K.K. (1994) Incidence of significantly altered pain experience among individuals with developmental disabilities. *American Journal of Mental Retardation*, **98**(5), 619–631.

Calculator, S.N. and Bedrosian, J.L. (eds) (1988) *Communication Assessment and Intervention for Adults with Mental Retardation*. Taylor & Francis, London and Philadelphia.

Ellis, D. (ed.) (1986) *Sensory Impairments in Mentally Handicapped People*. Croom Helm, London.

Heal, L.W. and Sigelman, C.K. (1995) Response biases in interviews of individuals with limited mental ability. *Journal of Intellectual Disability Research*, **39**(4), 331–340.

Hollins, S., Bernal, J. and Gregory, M. (1996) *Going to the Doctor*, illustrated by B. Webb. Books Beyond Words, St George's Mental Health Library, London.

Kiernan, C.C., Reid, B.D. and Jones, L.M. (1982) Sign and symbols: a review of literature and survey of use of non-vocal communication systems. *Studies in Education*, No. 11. University of London Institute of Education, London.

Landesman, S. (1988) Preventing institutionalization in the community. In Janicki, M.P., Wyngaarden Krauss, M. and Mailick Seltzer, M. (eds), *Community Residences for Persons with Developmental Disabilities. Here to stay*. Brookes, Baltimore.

Messer, D.J. (1994) *The Development of Communication: From Social Interaction to Language*. Wiley, Chichester.

Owens, R. (1989) Cognition and language in the mentally retarded population. In M. Beveridge, G. Conti-Ramsden and I. Leuder (eds), *Language and Communication in Mentally Handicapped People*. Chapman & Hall, London.

Sperber, D. and Wilson, D. (1995) *Relevance, Communication and Cognition* (2nd edn). Blackwell, Oxford and Cambridge, Mass.

Thomas, M. Felce, D., de Kock, U., Saxby, H. and Repp, A. (1986) The activity of staff and of severely and profoundly mentally handicapped adults in residential settings of different sizes. *British Journal of Mental Subnormality*, 32(2), 82–92.

Yeates, S. (1992) A district project for the identification and rehabilitation of people with severe learning difficulties and hearing loss. Paper presented at New Directions Conference on Audiology Services for People with Learning Difficulties. Guy's Hospital, London.

5

A GENERAL PRACTICE PERSPECTIVE

Gwyn Howells

Adults with learning disabilities often have additional health problems. As children, they benefited from community and hospital based paediatric services. As adults, they find no comparable body of expertise available. GPs then become the professionals to whom they most consistently turn. How can we fill this service gap and meet their diverse needs? We can do so by adopting positive attitudes and exploiting our basic clinical skills to the full. If we also see ourselves as part of a local network of services, we can close the gap between what is expected of us and what we currently provide.

Our difficulties are that we lack training, and the opportunity to learn by experience is limited by the small numbers of people with learning disabilities on our practice lists (see Chapter 1). Yet these small numbers give us the opportunity to get to know and understand their special problems and become part of the network of family relationships. It is this understanding that matters most and for which no amount of expertise can substitute.

THE IMPORTANCE OF WORKING WITH FAMILIES

Working with families is the cornerstone of general practice, and nowhere is this more apposite than in the care of people with learning disabilities. Many families are unable to accept the full implications of disability, and

Adults with Learning Disabilities. Edited by J. O'Hara and A. Sperlinger.
© 1997 John Wiley & Sons Ltd.

this results in the development of inappropriate coping strategies or signs of dysfunction. These emerge as marital or sexual difficulties, problems in a sibling, drug or alcohol abuse or increased susceptibility to illness. When learning disability is due to a hereditary cause there are additional stresses encircling perceptions of guilt and blame. These families benefit from sensitive counselling as well as genetic screening and advice.

GPs are in an unrivalled position to assess family dynamics: an impromptu home visit after the evening surgery is a good time to see how family members interact. To be able to do this an alliance must already exist between the GP and the family. Caring for people with learning disabilities necessitates alliances—not only with the family and their friends but with community nurses, social workers and other helping professionals. As the GP will normally be caring for the whole family, it is not surprising that conflicts of interest can arise.

DEFINING THE PROBLEM

Grouping together people with learning disabilities because they share a history of developmental delay is a questionable concept as no two people are alike and generalisations about their medical needs are fraught. We can achieve more by focusing on specific diagnostic groups. Many problems, even the cause and timing of death, relate directly to the underlying aetiological condition (Shepard et al., 1991). People with learning disabilities experience a greater number and variety of health problems than most people, as well as being susceptible to the special risks of any underlying syndrome.

BARRIERS TO CARE: HOW THEY CAN BE OVERCOME

People with learning disabilities are entitled to all general health services including health promotion and health education. Box 1 summarises some important barriers to health care (see also Howells, 1986).

Only part of the explanation lies in the way in which cognitive deficits and poor communication mask early symptoms. Additional reasons are detailed below.

Discrimination

Discrimination against people with learning disabilities leads to exclusion from care and screening that are available to others. Frequently they have

---

Box 1:   Barriers to health care

1. Physical barriers—e.g. wheelchair accessibility.

2. Administrative procedures—e.g. appointment times, waiting rooms.

3. Communication difficulties—e.g. an inability to describe symptoms clearly.

4. Attitudes of health professionals—e.g. lack of confidence, limited experience, negative attitudes and assumptions.

5. Recognition of ill health may be difficult or delayed because:
   (a) symptoms may not be easily identified;
   (b) family members/carers may not have the skills and knowledge to support individuals with learning disabilities to obtain health care or to maintain health-related behaviour;
   (c) 'problematic' symptoms (such as aggression) may be brought to the attention of services earlier; others that are equally significant (such as withdrawal, loss of interest) may not.

6. Reluctance to consider and provide the same range of treatment options as for the rest of the population, because of:
   (a) 'diagnostic overshadowing'—the inability to see beyond the disability;
   (b) perceived difficulty obtaining consent;
   (c) assumptions and negative predictions about how patients might react or cooperate.

---

negative experiences of primary care services which contribute to lowered expectations. Because reception staff are not always helpful and reassuring, visits to the surgery become stressful. This results in a disinclination to keep essential follow-up appointments. Difficulties in understanding advice contribute to feelings of disaffection. Members of the primary care team must appear unhurried and sympathetic if they hope to gain the trust necessary to provide care of acceptable standards. Carers can help by anticipating any problems that might arise. For example, with the help of a book designed for this purpose (Hollins *et al.*, 1996), they can try to explain to the patient the purpose of visiting the doctor, what might happen and how it can benefit. Simple measures, such as the choice of easily removable or loose clothing, facilitate a more relaxed examination by reducing levels of anxiety.

Lack of autonomy

Few people with learning disabilities have chosen their GPs. Only a minority are able to negotiate medical, dental or personal social services. Decisions to seek medical advice devolve to carers who may see common treatable complaints as trivial and, as a result, do not solicit care. Although they may seek advice when behavioural changes occur, they are more likely to bring to our attention those behaviours causing problems to others.

Inadequate medical records

Central to optimal medical care is good record keeping. People with learning disabilities are rarely able to give adequate accounts of their previous medical histories and their medical notes are usually incomplete. Records should include a patient profile, problem list, current medication, adverse drug reactions and 'at risk' details. The database must include a list of all other professionals involved.

Communication

It is salutary to imagine ourselves in the predicament of patients with learning disabilities. We would wish our GPs to look directly at us and speak clearly in language that we can understand. Non-verbal cues like tone of voice and body language would be especially important. Because people with learning disabilities have difficulty in describing symptoms, physical problems often appear as changes in behaviour. *Maladaptive behaviour may be their only means of communicating mental or physical discomfort* and we should always see this as a non-specific clue that something might be physically amiss.

Failure to recognise mild learning disability

There is an unwillingness to recognise mild learning disabilities as a distinct entity. Instead it is seen as a socio-cultural problem. Yet people with mild disabilities are particularly vulnerable and need special help. We can misconstrue their social clumsiness and misreading of social situations, adopt negative attitudes and compromise the provision of optimal health care.

Reluctance to provide treatment

People with learning disabilities do not invariably receive the same medical care for their illnesses as the general population. Occasionally this represents *diagnostic overshadowing:* our inability to see beyond the obvious cognitive and psycho-social deficits. Often, however, it is because we make unnecessarily pessimistic predictions about their ability to cooperate.

Uncertainty about consent

Currently there is no mechanism in English law for anyone to authorise consent to treatment on behalf of an adult unless that treatment is thought 'necessary' or provided on an 'emergency' basis. Treatment can be given only if the patient understands its nature and is able to communicate consent (see Chapter 11).

For adults incapable of giving informed consent, difficulties arise from the lack of an appropriate framework within which such decisions can be made on their behalf. The purpose of existing legislation is not to deprive such patients of treatment but to protect them. It should rarely be necessary to apply to the court for the everyday practice of medicine. *Whatever treatment we offer must accord with a responsible body of medical opinion and demonstrably be in the best interests of the patient.* Normally treatment is 'necessary', but if there is doubt we should seek the opinion of another appropriately qualified doctor. Although their relationship gives no legal authority to make proxy decisions on behalf of patients, it is also sensible to consult relatives.

Behavioural disorders

About 15% of adults with severe learning disabilities show associated behavioural disorders of sufficient severity to complicate diagnosis and treatment. These behaviours make it difficult to carry out essential clinical procedures and prejudice treatment. The use of adequate sedation can overcome this problem, but potential risks must be balanced with the perceived advantages to the patient. Even phlebotomy can be difficult, and it is useful to remember that most laboratory tests, for example thyroid function, require only a small amount of blood obtainable from a heel prick.

Agreeing not to intervene

When potentially dangerous medical or surgical treatment is necessary, medical advisers will explain the risks. They are usually sanguine and offer the chance of a better quality of life. For people with learning disabilities the experience can be different. We tend not to act unless carers are actively in favour of intervention. We frequently represent beneficial but potentially hazardous interventions from only a negative perspective (Silverman, 1985). Before reaching a decision about treatment, the individual's capacity to consent must be assessed. If he or she does not have the capacity to consent, no one can consent on his or her behalf. Family and carers will need help in understanding the law, and where conflicts arise it may be necessary to seek judicial review (see Chapter 11).

CLINICAL STRATEGY FOR THE GP: THE FAIL-SAFE APPROACH

People with learning disabilities suffer, not simply because we are unfamiliar with the complexities of their various syndromes, but because we do not take sufficient time to listen to them and to examine them (see Checklist 1). Our best approach is the adoption of a fail-safe strategy to minimise the margin for clinical error (Murtagh, 1994). Table 1 summarises potentially life-threatening conditions which need to be excluded, as well as commonly overlooked conditions which cause avoidable suffering.

Common Life-Threatening Illness

Severe infections

The commonest cause of death among people with learning disabilities is respiratory disease, particularly pneumonia. Difficulties in describing early symptoms lead to delays in localising the site of infections. Endocarditis is also a constant threat because of the high incidence of congenital heart disease. Antibiotic prophylaxis prior to dental treatment reduces this risk.

Heart disease

Heart failure due to complex anomalies is common in Down's syndrome. Although myocardial infarction is unusual in this syndrome it commonly strikes people with learning disabilities as a whole and is often due to a modifiable lifestyle. Difficulties in describing cardiac pain can lead to delay in diagnosis.

Table 1: A clinical strategy for minimising errors

Exclude common life-threatening illnesses	Check for commonly overlooked conditions
• Severe infections	• Sensory impairment
• Heart disease	• Side-effects of drugs
• Malignancy	• Epilepsy
• Asthma	• Depression
	• Urinary tract infections
	• Faecal impaction
	• Incontinence
	• Foreign bodies
	• Diabetes
	• Abuse (physical, sexual, emotional)

Malignancy

People with learning disabilities share, with everyone else, the morbidity and mortality caused by breast, lung, cervical and skin cancers. *Additionally they often have chromosomal anomalies which are risk factors for malignant diseases.* The incidence of leukaemia in Down's syndrome, for example, is over ten times that of chromosomally normal people. Undescended testes, common features of several genetic syndromes, predispose to malignancy.

Asthma

Among people with learning disabilities, who are always at risk of developing severe or fatal attacks, asthma is under-diagnosed and under-treated. Faulty inhalation technique is one factor preventing adequate treatment. Large volume spacing and breath-actuated devices or electric nebulisers help to overcome the problem and reduce mortality.

Commonly Overlooked Conditions

Sensory impairments

Sensory impairments can distort the perceived potential of an individual. Impaired vision reduces stimulation, and loss of eye contact limits the ability to build personal relationships. Unrecognised deafness often leads to behavioural disorders or even features confusable with psychotic disorders. A golden rule is that assessments of sensory function should precede assessments of mental ability. It is unwise, in the absence of this, to label any person with visual and hearing deficits as having learning disabilities.

Side-effects of drugs

People with learning disabilities are one of the most medicated groups in the community. Their responses to psychotropic and anticonvulsant medication are less predictable than in the general population. Differential or unexpected responses to treatment are most striking in people with profound disabilities. Their inability to describe unexpected responses to medication affects our capacity to evaluate side-effects (see Checklist 4).

Epilepsy

Undiagnosed, untreated or under-treated epilepsy are common among people with learning disabilities. In a study in Colorado more than 70% of

people referred for mental health assessment had other medical problems. The commonest of these was unmanaged epilepsy (Ryan and Sunada, 1992). They frequently have more than one type of epilepsy and may
take several different anticonvulsants. Newer and more specific anticonvulsants can be more effective, have fewer side-effects and provide a
better quality of life (see Checklist 5).

Depression

There is often difficulty in diagnosing depressive disorders in adults with
impaired verbal ability, conceptual thinking and cognitive functioning
(see Chapter 7). Classic symptoms are easily recognisable, including biological features such as loss of appetite, loss of weight and sleep disturbance, but often hypochondriasis, apathy, clinging behaviour, aggression,
or self-injury may be the presenting features.

Urinary tract infections

People with learning disabilities may not complain of the usual symptoms of infection: frequency of micturition, dysuria and loin pain. Instead
they may have only constitutional symptoms or show confusion or behavioural changes.

Faecal impaction

Faecal impaction due to an atonic bowel, dietary factors, drugs or poor
mobility is common among people with learning disabilities. It results in
overflow diarrhoea or in discomfort causing unexplained mental irri-
tability. Carers and nurses working in the community seem less alert to
this common problem than hospital nursing staff.

Incontinence

People with learning disabilities may fail to develop continence or lose
already acquired control. As the incidence of incontinence increases with
the severity of the cognitive deficits, there can be an erroneous assumption that it is totally attributable to the disability, with the result that
instead of promoting continence we make efforts only to contain the
incontinence. We overlook the evidence that behavioural programmes
can be successful. The effective management of incontinence not only
enhances self-esteem and quality of life but reduces the levels of
dependency.

Foreign bodies

Foreign bodies in the nose and ears sometimes cause pain and discharge. Occasionally we find them in the bowel producing pain or diarrhoea, or in the urethra where they cause unexplained discharge or persistent urinary infections.

Diabetes

In the general adult population the prevalence of diabetes is about 3%, and of these 1% is undiagnosed. Among adults with learning disabilities the prevalence rate is higher because of the high incidence of diabetes in syndromes such as Down's and Prader–Willi. Obesity, which predisposes to diabetes, is also more prevalent in this group. Detection rates are lower because adults with learning disabilities are less likely to complain of symptoms which often suggest the diagnosis, such as tiredness and fatigue.

Abuse (physical, sexual, emotional)

An awareness of the possibility of abuse is as important when dealing with adults with learning disabilities as it is when dealing with children. Sexual abuse may present to the GP as a change in behaviour which is sometimes sexualised. Where there is a suspicion of abuse our obligation is to involve the social services department, the lead agency in the processes of investigation and decision making. The primary concern when following the recognised procedures must be the welfare of the person with learning disabilities (see Chapter 10).

MEDICAL HAZARDS OF SPECIFIC SYNDROMES

GPs should be confident that their understanding of general medical principles will help in the management of any condition. Nonetheless, it is vital that we familiarise ourselves with the medical risks of the specific syndrome with which we happen to be dealing and that we formulate our own checklists and management plans. The following examples of relatively common syndromes illustrate the heterogeneous nature of their challenges and how we can respond.

Down's Syndrome (DS)

The frequency of DS varies with maternal age (1 : 2,000 for babies born to mothers aged 25 years to 1 : 40 for those aged 40 years). People with DS are susceptible to a wide range of conditions such as respiratory disease, diabetes, sleep apnoea, bone and joint problems such as atlanto-axial instability, dental problems and behaviour disorders. A number of other conditions are so common that they need to be looked for routinely.

- Hearing loss affects more than 50% of people with DS. Carers notice that they have to speak louder or that the person does not seem to understand what they say. The removal of a build-up of wax may be all that is necessary but referral to an audiologist is always desirable.
- Disorders of the eye, particularly blepharitis, errors of refraction, squints, cataracts, keratoconus and poor visual accommodation are common. Visual impairment should be suspected when we learn that patients move around less, lose interest in television or activities or appear to be anxious when walking on uneven surfaces.
- Hypothyroidism affects about 40% of adults, so annual thyroid function checks are necessary. The common presentation of weight gain, lethargy or cognitive decline can be confused with dementia. Hyperthyroidism is also much more common than in the general population.
- Congenital heart disease is 50 times more common than in the general population. Symptoms of lethargy, shortness of breath or cyanosis may not be obvious to carers. Subacute bacterial endocarditis is an ever-lurking threat. No dental work should proceed without antibiotic prophylaxis.
- People with DS are remarkably prone to depression which often presents as loss of interest, appetite, weight or disturbed sleep. Frequently it follows a move or change in daily living patterns, which are features of care in the community.
- The incidence of epilepsy is the same as in the general population until the fifth decade when it increases to 12% at the age of 55 years. Although we invariably suspect epilepsy when patients are found unconscious, we tend to miss the diagnosis when someone has 'fallen', 'been found on the floor' or has become incontinent.
- People with DS show an accelerated ageing process (Martin, 1982). A quarter of those over the age of 50 years will develop Alzheimer-like dementia. The task is to make certain that there is no treatable cause for reported functional decline.

Fragile X Syndrome

This is the most prevalent familial cause of learning disabilities. It affects 1 : 1,500 males and 1 : 2,500 females. The X-linked mode of inheritance is unique in that it is neither dominant nor recessive. Of the males who inherit the fragile X gene (FMR1), 20% are unaffected (*normal transmitting males*). One woman in 500 is a carrier. Of the heterozygous females, 50% have some features of the disorder and as many as 30% have learning disabilities. Unlike other X-linked disorders the mothers of all affected offspring are obligate carriers. The affected offspring may have the full syndrome or become carriers. Consequently, grandchildren and not children may develop the disorder. As the sons of unaffected male carriers receive only the Y chromosome they are normal.

GPs are in a pivotal position to identify affected families. But the provision of genetic counselling is an infinitely complex issue. Even for the professionals, Fragile X syndrome remains the most recondite of concepts in medical genetics.

There is a characteristic but subtle phenotype with a largish head, a rather long thin face, large ears and macro-orchidism. This accompanies a characteristic profile of abnormalities of behaviour, learning, language and memory which suggest temporal lobe dysfunction. Autistic spectrum disorder, particularly of the Asperger type, is common and set against a background of attention deficit disorder in childhood. Among females, excessive shyness and poor eye contact are common behavioural features. Our checklist would highlight the following risks:

• Dilatation of the aortic root, hypoplasia of the aorta and mitral valve prolapse affect about one-third of males, and are responsible for the high mortality rate.
• The nervous and urogenital systems are vulnerable to cancer.
• 20% have epilepsy.
• Joint laxity, awkward gait and flat feet affect about one-third.

The majority of adults with learning disabilities will not have had any genetic testing. We should suspect the possibility of this syndrome when assessing anyone with learning disabilities or behavioural disturbance.

Klinefelter Syndrome (KS)

The underlying chromosomal abnormality is the presence of one or more extra X chromosomes (XXY) and affects 2 : 1,000 males. The hallmarks are small firm testes, long legs, a short trunk, broad feminine-type hips, gynaecomastia, poor musculature and poorly developed secondary sexual characteristics. Frequently there is a delay in diagnosis until after puberty when the sexual characteristics fail to appear. Those affected show apathy, lack initiative, have personality problems and poor social adaptation with varying degrees of learning disability.

Our checklist should focus on:

- Obesity—a common and severe problem in older people with KS who may develop sleep apnoea syndrome.
- Chronic pulmonary disease including asthma.
- Varicose veins are troublesome and often associated with ulceration. Interestingly, varicose ulcers are comparatively rare in normal males. When they do occur, and if there is any other suggestion of KS, it is worth while arranging a karyotype.
- An increased incidence of diabetes.
- A predisposition to neoplasia, particularly extragonadal germ-cell tumours.
- When there is androgen deficiency, testosterone replacement is necessary. This can produce a transient increase in gynaecomastia with nipple tenderness.

Prader–Willi Syndrome (PWS)

PWS has an incidence of about 1 : 10,000. The clinical features of learning disability, hypotonia, obesity, hypogonadism and small hands and feet are unmistakable. Two-thirds of sufferers have an abnormality of their paternally derived chromosome 15, a small interstitial deletion of bands q11–13.

PWS presents several important medical challenges.

- Obesity begins in early childhood and relates to at least three factors: an unusual inability to vomit, an insatiable appetite and a reduced caloric requirement. Those with continuous hunger may steal food from shops or scavenge in gardens or rubbish bins, exposing themselves to the risk of poisoning. It may become necessary to fit locks on kitchen, refrigerator and food cupboard doors. Consistent dietary and behavioural management can be combined and are successful, but this imposes considerable strain on families and carers.
- Behavioural problems, particularly temper tantrums or rages involving crying and screaming, are common. The frequency and intensity of rages increase during the late teen years. Obsessional behaviour, talking about the same thing continually (perseveration) and stubbornness are commonly reported features which add to family or carer stress.
- Non-insulin dependent diabetes can resolve as a result of weight reduction.
- The combination of reduced circulation and skin picking predisposes the legs to infection, usually by streptococci. This condition, which

responds well to penicillin, sometimes presents with high fever. It may be only a day or so later that the cellulitis on the leg is noticed.
* People with PWS often have dental problems related to abnormalities in saliva. Oral hygiene and meticulous dental care are essential.
* There are often altered responses to potentially painful conditions such as ear infections or appendicitis. In sharp contrast there may be hypersensitivity to light touch. These unusual responses complicate the diagnostic process.

Women with PWS are infertile with hypoplastic ovaries and low oestrogen levels. There is a case for the use of replacement therapy. To protect the uterus from the adverse effects of unopposed oestrogen it is convenient to give this as a contraceptive pill of the combined type. This can also prevent osteoporosis and heart disease and produce a feeling of well-being. The advantages of testosterone in males are less clear.

Williams Syndrome

This sporadic congenital syndrome has an incidence of 1 : 20,000 births and is due to a microdeletion of chromosome 7. Classically there is a history of transient hypercalcaemia in infancy with a triad of mild learning disability, supraventricular aortic stenosis and characteristic facial features. The phenotype includes peripheral pulmonary artery stenosis and dental hypoplasia. Associated features are attention deficit disorders, hypersensitivity to sound and aberrations of both fine and gross motor activities. Language is reminiscent of the 'cocktail party chatter' of hydrocephalus.
There are several medical challenges, including:

* Subacute bacterial endocarditis (SABE). Antibiotic prophylaxis is always necessary before dental procedures. Whenever there is unexplained fever, repeated blood cultures are necessary to exclude SABE.
* Hypertension is a common complication and because of the anomalies in the aortic root it is important to check the blood pressure in both arms.
* In adults the serum calcium is usually normal but recurrence of hypercalcaemia is always a risk.
* Nephrocalcinosis, nephrolithiasis and recurrent urinary tract infections, which are often persistent, are common complications.
* Hyperacusis affects 90% of patients and can be uncomfortable when, for example, a dental drill is being used.
* Bone and joint problems including scoliosis are common.

Good liaison between members of the primary health care team and other professionals predicates adequate care of this often complex condition.

Rett Syndrome

This puzzling disorder appears in females and has a prevalence of 1 : 10,000. Following a period of normal development lasting 6–18 months the child loses purposeful use of the hands. Stereotypic hand-wringing movements appear, often with distressing hand-mouthing, followed by severe learning disability, seizures and microcephaly. The variability of presentation can lead to a misdiagnosis or delay in diagnosis until the patient reaches adulthood (Hagberg, 1989).

The following frequently complicate the disorder:

- Epilepsy can be severe and of several types.
- Scoliosis is a frequent early onset complication. Curve progression which causes pain or loss of function will require surgical correction to maintain posture and mobility.
- Undernutrition may result from difficulty in feeding due to a de-synchronisation of swallowing.
- Episodes of intense hyperventilation are common and cause respiratory alkalosis, sometimes with tetany. It is possible to abort these attacks by breathing into a paper bag. Apnoeic pauses may follow these episodes but they occur independently and cause hypoxaemia.
- Air swallowing can cause abdominal distension. In a minority this gives the abdomen the appearance of late pregnancy.

Despite all their difficulties, women with this syndrome can expect to reach the fifth decade. In those dying younger, the cause of death is often unexplained.

Tuberous Sclerosis (TS)

TS is characterised by benign growths in multiple organ systems. Involvement of the brain results in learning disability and persistent seizures. Skin involvement includes characteristic facial angiofibromas, subungual fibromas and hypomelanotic patches. About 60% of cases are sporadic. In families it shows autosomal dominant inheritance with 95% penetrance. About half of the familial cases show linkage to chromosome 9q34 and half to chromosome 16p13 (Kwiatkowski and Short, 1994).

TS is clinically complicated. Main problems include:

- Seizures of various types occur and may be the only manifestation of the disorder. CT scans are essential to establish the presence and extent of intracranial lesions. Giant cell astrocytomas may appear. Retinal examination may show asymptomatic astrocytomas (phakomas).
- Renal angiomyolipomas appear in 80% of cases and renal cysts in 50%. They may constitute the only lesions of TS and may be asymptomatic. Catastrophic bleeding into these lesions may be the cause of unexplained sudden collapse.
- Although they decrease in frequency with age, cardiac rhabdomyomas can present in adults who may develop cardiac failure, murmurs or arhythmias.

The most severely affected patients have a shortened lifespan. Status epilepticus, brain or visceral tumours, renal failure and infections are the common causes of death.

Cornelia de Lange Syndrome (CdLS)

CdLS is a dysmorphogenic disorder characterised by learning disability, growth retardation, limb reduction abnormalities and characteristic facial features. The incidence is about 1 : 20,000 live births. Deafness is always present.

The variety of physical anomalies produces a range of medical challenges, including:

- Two gastrointestinal anomalies which are critically important: gastro-oesophageal reflux, a lifelong problem sometimes occurring as 'silent reflux' and complicated by pneumonia; intestinal obstruction due to caecal volvulus. If carers are aware of these potentially lethal anomalies earlier diagnosis and treatment becomes possible.
- Cardiac anomalies occur in over 25% of patients and may not produce symptoms until adult life when cardiac failure supervenes.
- Myopia, ptosis and blepharo-conjunctivitis are common. If ptosis is severe it will restrict vision and require surgical correction.
- Poor jaw development, crowded teeth, poor oral hygiene and erosion of teeth caused by gastric acid from reflux, demand regular dental care.

Many people with CdLS are medically fragile, but if we provide good medical care and a safe environment, they can enjoy years of adult life.

HOW CARE CAN BE IMPROVED: THE PREVENTIVE ATTITUDE

Although people with learning disabilities have higher rates of illness they use fewer services than the general population. Frequently, treatable illness is undetected until it reaches a stage when treatment is less effective. We can improve this situation by moving away from a crisis-led pattern of work to one of strategic prevention involving the whole primary care team.

The Health of the Nation Policy

GPs are in an unrivalled position to provide opportunistic health promotion and health surveillance as well as good care if illness is present. *The Health of the Nation* policy (DoH, 1995) defines five key areas which set GPs priorities and specific targets.

Heart disease and stroke

Obesity is more prevalent than in the general population. Lack of exercise and a high consumption of 'junk food' are contributory factors. Because of the extra time needed for explanation or perhaps to gain cooperation, we may not offer screening for major risk factors like hypertension, or advice on smoking. People with learning disabilities, like others, can be encouraged to stop smoking by example and by persuasion.

Cancers

It is difficult for people with learning disabilities to make healthy lifestyle choices about such risk factors as smoking or sunbathing. They are less aware of the evidence that diets high in animal fats or low in fibre predispose to cancers of the bowel. Those exposed to passive smoking may have their complaints ignored. Women with learning disabilities need encouragement to have screening for beast cancer and, those who are at risk, for cervical cancer. Maldescent of the testes, a risk factor for carcinoma, is common among men with learning disabilities.

HIV/AIDS and sexual health

People with learning disabilities may not understand the link between sexual activity, pregnancy and sexually transmitted diseases. Their sources of information—reading magazines and learning about safer sex practices from their peers—are also less available. GPs can help by refer- ring patients for appropriate sex education organised by suitably qualified community learning disability teams.

Accidents

Due to difficulties in evaluating risks, people with learning disabilities are especially prone to accidents. Those with sensory deficits, poor coordina- tion or impaired mobility are particularly susceptible. Prescribed medica- tion can impair attentiveness and lead to accidents. A valuable cognitive shift occurs when we substitute the word 'accident' by 'preventable oc- currence'. This emphasises their often preventable nature among people with learning disabilities.

Mental illness

Mental illness is common among people with learning disabilities. This may relate to abnormal brain function, impaired cognitive processes or the experience of educational failure. Often it follows major life events. Brain injury, epilepsy, the adverse effects of drugs and low socio-economic status also predispose to mental illness. Furthermore, a disadvantaged lifestyle coupled with lack of contact with non-disabled peers restricts emotional development. They have few opportunities to exercise choice, their expec- tations are low and they suffer from overprotection. Little scope exists to develop social networks beyond the family and paid carers. The result is too great an emotional investment in too few people. This, in turn, increases the significance of loss through bereavement and changes in staff.

WORKING TOGETHER FOR PEOPLE WITH LEARNING DISABILITIES

Nowhere is there greater opportunity for inter-agency working than in the field of learning disabilities. On the one hand, we have to ensure that we do not overlook their medical needs. On the other, we have to ensure that our adoption of the clinical perspective will not isolate them from other professionals and voluntary agencies. The advantages of working closely with other clinicians, for example consultants in learning dis- abilities, are clear. Less obvious, but equally important, is the advantage of extending our alliance to include social services departments, housing authorities and vocational training organisations.

Inevitably there will be differences between what GPs recommend and what carers or people with learning disabilities feel they need. Here the roles of key workers or care managers can be helpful. They are able to act as advocates for their clients and as advisers to family carers struggling to decide what is best. The hope is that carers feel that their GPs are always working with them and not against them. When asked what quality they most value in their GPs, almost invariably carers will reply that it is the ability to listen and explain.

KEY POINTS

1. People with learning disabilities should have access to all health services including health promotion, health surveillance, primary and secondary health care, with additional supports as required to meet individual needs.
2. Their relatively small numbers should allow the individual GP the opportunity to understand their special problems and become part of the support network.
3. Recognition of ill health may be difficult or delayed because:
   - symptoms may not be easily identified or communicated;
   - family/carers may not have the necessary skills and knowledge to support the person with learning disabilities to obtain health care, or maintain health-related behaviour;
   - discriminatory practices and negative experiences lead to poor attendance.
4. Maladaptive behaviour should be seen as a non-specific clue that something physical might be amiss.
5. GPs can improve health care by involving the whole primary health care team; providing opportunistic health promotion and surveillance; and drawing up individual checklists and management plans.

REFERENCES

Department of Health (DoH) (1995) *The Health of the Nation: A Strategy for People with Learning Disabilities*. HMSO, London.
Hagberg, B.A. (1989) Rett syndrome: clinical peculiarities, diagnostic approach and possible cause. *Paediatric Neurology*, **5** (Part 2), 75–83.
Hollins, S., Bernal, J. and Gregory, M. (1996) *Going to the Doctor* (illustrated by B. Webb). Books Beyond Words, St George's Mental Health Library, London.
Howells, G. (1986) Are the medical needs of mentally handicapped adults being met? *Journal of the Royal College of General Practitioners*, **36**, 449–453.
Kwiatkowski, D.J., and Short, M.P. (1994) Tuberous sclerosis. *Archives of Dermatology*, **130**(3), 348–354.
Martin, G.M. (1982) Syndromes of accelerated aging. *National Cancer Institute Monogram*, Vol. 16, pp. 241–247.

Murtagh, J. (1994) *General Practice*. McGraw-Hill, Sydney.

Ryan, R.M. and Sunada, K. (1992) *Medical assessment of persons with developmental disabilities and mental health needs.* Presentation at the National Association of the Dually Diagnosed. Ninth Annual Meeting. Data published in Synopsis of the 9th Annual Meeting NADD, Kingston, New York.

Shepard, C., Gomez, M., Lie, J. and Crowson, C. (1991) Causes of death in patients with tuberous sclerosis. *Mayo Clinic Proceedings*, **66**, 792–796.

Silverman, D. (1985) Agreeing not to intervene: doctors and parents of DS children at a paediatric cardiology clinic. In D. Lane and B. Stradford (eds), *Current Approaches to Down's Syndrome*. Holt, Rinehart & Winston, London, pp. 363–381.

6

CHALLENGING NEEDS AND PROBLEMATIC BEHAVIOUR

John Clements

Adults with learning disabilities who have problematic behaviour are likely to present to GPs as acute management problems (often with requests for sedation). Families and carers are often highly stressed and there is a temptation to use medication as the only intervention. Problematic behaviour is functional: it may be, for example, an indication of physical discomfort, pain, emotional distress, mental illness, or conflicts in the person's environment. Usually, there are many contributory factors. This chapter provides a framework for understanding and responding to people who have problematic behaviour and Checklist 6 gives a brief guide to the steps involved.

Behaviour can be said to be problematic in the mind and heart of the beholder. A person's behaviour will be defined as challenging or problematic when it is judged by another to be socially unacceptable and when it evokes significant negative emotional responses in the other (fear, embarrassment, despair). Identification is not a matter of clinical diagnosis and has strong subjective elements. However, there are certain behaviours which are commonly identified as challenging.

Adults with Learning Disabilities. Edited by J. O'Hara and A. Sperlinger.
© 1997 John Wiley & Sons Ltd.

COMMON EXAMPLES AND A GUIDE TO IDENTIFICATION

The behaviours most often labelled as problematic are: physical and verbal aggression; sexually abusive behaviours; self-injury; property damage; and stealing. However, strong feelings may also be evoked by more passive behaviours such as not eating or not participating in offered activities.

For a behaviour to merit active consideration, it should be:

• unacceptable by the social standards relevant to the person's age, class and cultural background;
• imposing (or threatening to impose) a significant cost on the person himself (e.g. physical damage, social rejection, limiting opportunities for learning);
• imposing (or threatening to impose) a significant and unreasonable cost on the lives of others.

Subjective elements remain, but *unless at least two of these criteria are met* there seems little justification for seeking to effect change.

How Many People with Learning Disabilities would Meet Such Criteria?

Although definitions vary, at any one time between 15 and 20% of those in contact with services for people with learning disabilities will present significant, active challenges to those who live and work with them—with most engaging in more than one type of behaviour (Keirnan and Qureshi, 1993). Although the number who present in seriously dangerous ways is much smaller, it is misleading to think that problematic behaviour is a question of 'a troubling few'.

Why Identify?

Identifying someone as presenting their needs in challenging ways does no more than indicate that the status quo should change. Two issues should inform responding:

• *The relationship of behaviour to need.* The reason for one person's aggression is not necessarily the same as another's. Similarity in behaviour does not mean similarity in need. In addition, an individual may use the same behaviour to express different needs—self-injury may reflect an attempt to gain social contact on some occasions and to be left alone on others. The needs of people who behave in problematic ways are no different to the needs of people who do not behave in these ways—they are just expressed differently. Their needs are about being able to understand and to influence the world, to experience social support, personal well-being and general quality of life. These are universal needs, not special needs unique to those who challenge. Identifying behaviour as problematic gives no guide to the appropriate intervention which might reduce the behaviour. One purpose in identifying is to inaugurate the process of assessment to pinpoint individual needs.

● *The issues around dangerousness.* Identification does not indicate the risk posed to the person or to others by the behaviour. Risk assessment is very relevant in some cases and the outcome may indicate the degree to which the individual's liberty should be restricted. (This is a major topic in its own right and will not be covered fully in this chapter.) A second purpose in identifying someone as challenging is to indicate the need to consider carefully the risks that the individual presents.

Thus labelling a behaviour as problematic is not in any sense a 'diagnosis' indicating need or a judgement indicating risk. It is a starting point for further exploration.

FROM BEHAVIOUR TO NEED: MAKING SENSE OF OTHER PEOPLE'S BEHAVIOUR

About Human Behaviour

There are a number of important ideas relevant to making sense of behaviour:

● Most behaviours are functional—they achieve an important, immediate outcome for the individual . . . at least some of the time.
● Most behaviours reflect the operation of many different contributory factors, not single causes.
● Some of the contributory factors will be unknown, others beyond control. Change is about altering probabilities, not complete/permanent elimination.
● Contributory factors include both environmental and individual variables, with a dazzling array of combinations and interactions. Factors also vary in the time of operation—some influences come from past experience and history, some from current life and personal circumstances.

- The most powerful understanding comes when two perspectives are combined: professional analysis (the gathering and integration of objective information) and empathy (access to the internal experiences of the person whose behaviour is of concern).
- There are active blocks to the identification of someone else's needs.

Active Blocks to Understanding

- *Everyday language* about behaviour suggests simple cause and effect based upon closeness in time (correlation = causation) and/or hierarchical relations ('the underlying cause'). It does not reflect the notions of multiple contributors, interacting and operating in probability relationships.
- *Personal attitudes and values: prejudices and stereotypes.* Interpretations of behaviour can reflect *stereotypes* about class or cultural background, or sexual orientation. Such stereotypes often amount to *prejudice* and are oppressive in their implications. They are particularly dangerous when applied by powerful people to the powerless. These judgements (of others) largely determine what happens to the person with learning disabilities, who can rarely challenge them. Professional judgements about other people's needs are vulnerable to (prejudicial) stereotypes (Scotti *et al.*, 1991) and active steps are needed to counter their influence.
- *Attribution errors.* Interpretations will be influenced by a range of other distortions. For example, stories told may reflect: the quality of the relationship between the judge and the person judged (the less close the more likely to attribute to causes internal to the individual); the emotional state of the judge (more anxious, more likely to attribute hostile intent); projections of the feelings of the judge to the person judged; the power relationship and level of contact (the greater the imbalance and the less the contact, the greater the likelihood of dehumanisation and prejudicial stereotypes).

Thus, making judgements and interpretations about other people and their needs is not a simple, scientific matter. It is a social process of construction and can be seriously flawed.

A FRAMEWORK FOR UNDERSTANDING

As behaviour may be multiply determined, it is important to gather wide ranging information. An organising framework helps to ensure a comprehensive analysis (Clements, 1992). Such a framework will need to consider:

- The immediate influences over behavioural incidents (results and triggers).
- Short-term influences, close in time to incidents (environmental and personal contexts).
- Longer term influences (background factors).

The Immediate Influences over Behavioural Incidents (Results and Triggers)

Behaviour is developed and maintained because it achieves an immediate change which is meaningful to the individual. *Results* may be gains— access to a favoured material reward, social response and/or form of sensory stimulation. They may also be things escaped or avoided— withdrawal of others to a preferred distance, withdrawal of a task or demand, escape from unpleasant stimulation (including offset of pain). Such reinforcement processes show large individual differences and powerful reinforcers do not have to occur every time for behaviour to be maintained. Even when other behaviours (actions) will achieve the same result, challenging behaviour will persist if it works more reliably and with less effort or cost.

Triggers may indicate the availability of a favoured result—*there's a cup full of tea, now I can produce that wonderful effect when I tip it over*. They may also increase motivation—*it is when you get close that I feel uncomfortable and need to act*. Triggers may be positive occurrences or events not happening for a given period of time—*it is when no one has looked my way for two minutes that I need to regain contact*.

Short-term Influences, Close in Time to Incidents *(Environmental and Personal Contexts)*

These do not directly trigger behaviour. They may be environmental or personal factors (see Table 1).

These factors reduce tolerance to situations and increase motivations which may then be dealt with by behaving in a challenging way. *The noise is getting me down and when you ask me to do something, I snap and get sent out.*

Longer Term Influences *(Background Factors)*

These affect both the motivations that an individual experiences and the options available or seen as relevant for dealing with these motivations.

Table 1: Examples of context influences over behaviour

Environmental contexts	Personal contexts
Noise level	Mood
Lighting	Level of agitation
Temperature	Tiredness
Crowding	Blood sugar level
Movement rate (busy-ness)	Pain (e.g. ear/sinus infections, dental problems)
Unstructured periods	

They include environmental and personal characteristics and personal history (see Table 2).

Table 2: Long-term influences over behaviour

Environmental characteristics	Personal characteristics	Personal history
Social system variables	Information processing	Life events
Organisational variables	Emotional functioning	Role models (core
Activity options	Skill level	messages)
	Physical functioning	

Environmental influences

• *Characteristics of the social systems* of which the person is a part will affect behaviour. A family or service with unresolved serious conflicts will create many uncomfortable interactions, frequently demonstrated anger, inconsistency and the need to find a scapegoat for the system's discomfort. Sadness and anger in one person may reflect a lack of fondness, warmth and respect from others around him or her. Lack of consistent limits may lead an individual to believe that anything goes. A system which allows individuals little control in their lives will generate frustration and anger for some, passivity for others. (Who will get identified as challenging?).

• *Organisational characteristics.* The extent to which experiences are structured or unstructured, the level of predictability of events, the work systems in place for planning and problem solving, are important. For example, an unstructured environment is likely to create boredom for those who are not good at thinking up what to do for themselves. It may also generate anxiety if it means that an individual cannot predict what will happen or when.

• *Activity options.* The types of activities available (their interest level, perceived value), the timing of their availability and the general pace of life are important. Some people like a life of continual action and high stimulation; others a slower pace and more gentle stimulation. Many people will be frustrated by being kept in 'disability world'—they want to be doing the things that their family members and staff do. If access to these is not created, then their anger and frustration may be expressed in ways seen as challenging.

Personal characteristics

- *Information processing.* Difficulties in decoding speech, in reading the feelings of others, in keeping up with the rate of input, in judging what a situation is about, will make it difficult to understand what is going on, what is required and how other people are feeling. The blocking of current information by dominant ideas (obsessions) may mean that important information is missed or expectations are set up which are disappointed: (e.g. *if I believe that every outing should include a visit to a well-known fast food restaurant, then a failure to include this element in a trip will provoke strong reactions*). The presence of hallucinations or delusions may mean that I believe people mean me harm or that I am told how to behave. It is easy to see how these factors might contribute to situations which result in challenging behaviour.
- *Emotional functioning* will contribute to behavioural challenges. Sustained general emotional states (such as sadness, anxiety, anger and excitement), lower tolerance to demands or intrusions, alter interpretation of everyday situations and generate needs for relief. More specific difficulties such as fears, panics and flashbacks may create high levels of emotions in certain situations. Complex difficulties such as obsessive-compulsive phenomena may generate strong conflict if others try to interfere with the completion of a ritual.
- *Lack of skills* in key areas will make behaviour challenges more likely as the person has fewer means of getting needs met. Difficulties in communicating, in making relationships, in managing high levels of emotion, in occupying oneself, will all increase vulnerability.
- *Physical functioning.* General and specific health difficulties will reduce tolerance and generate needs for relief in their own right. There are also speculations about the role of brain biochemistry (serotonin, dopamine and the endogenous opiates) in problematic behaviours.

Personal history

- *Life events*—loss, abuse and trauma can impact upon many areas of personal functioning over extended periods of time. They may create

negative emotional states and lower the individual's sense of self-worth and value.
• *Role models and 'core' messages* to which the person has had sustained exposure (e.g. about what it takes to be a 'good' person).

Thus, to understand a behaviour requires the gathering of information on a range of variables (assessment).

DEVELOPING THE UNDERSTANDING OF THOSE WHO CHALLENGE

Gaining insight into the reasons underlying behaviour requires two distinct types of activity followed by a clear formulation:

Developing Empathy with the Individual

This is hard to pin down to specific techniques. It means getting to know the person as a unique individual, how he or she views the world and the issues experienced by him or her as important in his or her life. It will mean spending time with the person and reflecting upon all the information available about him or her. But there remains an element hard to operationalise—the leap of imagination that may enable one to glimpse the world from the other's point of view.

The Assessment of Behaviour

The more technical process of assembling good quality information about the behaviour(s) of concern, will require:

• *Defining a specific behaviour (action) of concern.* Individuals identified as challenging may do several things that cause concern. A productive outcome is more likely with *one* specific concern as the starting point.
• *Assessing the immediate circumstances that surround specific incidents of the behaviour.* This may be done by interviewing those involved (including the person him or herself if possible), getting them to keep structured records of incidents, using an external observer to record incidents and circumstances, setting up mini experiments that structure the environment to test for the effect of specific variables on behaviour (O'Neill *et al.*, 1990).
• *Assessing characteristics of individual's living environments,* usually by observation and discussion with the person him or herself and others with whom he or she lives and works. (There are also more structured questionnaires and interviews that can be used.)

- *Assessing the individual.* A detailed personal history will be required. Assessment of the key areas of individual functioning is likely to involve detailed observation and a range of specialist assessments (speech therapist, psychologist, psychiatrist).

The Process of Formulation

Box 1: **Summarising assessment information: a job aide for reaching a coherent formulation**

(Sample analysis of Sandy's pinching and biting others)

From the assessment information gathered, the following contributors were identified as relevant to explaining the behaviours (lines can be drawn to indicate links between specific contributors).

BEHAVIOURS OF CONCERN: Pinching and biting others (occur together)

1. **Immediate influences**

Triggers	*Results*
Asked to do tasks	Demand withdrawn (sometimes)
In group situations with no attention from staff	Taken to a quiet area

2. **Short-term influences**
   - *Environmental contexts*
     — Mornings
     — Noisy environments
   - *Personal contexts*
     — Low mood
     — 3 days before period

3. **Longer term influences**
   - *Environmental Characteristics*
     — Recent staff turnover
     — Inconsistent expectations
     — Winter
   - *Personal characteristics*
     — Lack of communication skills
     — Lack of understanding about other people's feelings
     — Determined 'my way' personality
     — Sustained low mood state
   - *Personal history*
     — Moved from family home to full-time residential care 2 years ago

---

Information gathering and empathy building need integration—a 'story' about why the person engages in a specific behaviour, which summarises, out of all the information gathered, the potential key contributors to the behaviour of concern. Such a formulation will guide action planning.

How such a formulation can be arrived at has not been well articulated. The true test of a 'story' is whether the insights it affords generate action plans which yield gains in personal well-being and behaviour functioning. Box 1 shows a sample assessment summary.

INTERVENTIONS FOR CHANGE: A REVIEW

The aim of intervention is to create and sustain the conditions under which the individual is most likely to be able to function well. A range of skills are necessary to maximise the understanding of individual needs and to effect the interventions that meet these needs. The input of a range of disciplines and agencies must be integrated. The specific areas of intervention will be determined by the results of the assessment process, but the test will always be: does an intervention yield a measurable gain for the individual? Table 3 summarises the intervention options outlined below.

Table 3:   Areas for intervention

Environmental	Personal
Basic prevention (remove triggers)	Enhance emotional well-being
Change attitudes	Enhance physical well-being
Resolve conflicts	Teach relevant skills
Redistribute power	Enhance motivation to function
Structure time better	positively
Improve self-esteem	
Improve engagement levels	
Adapt communication systems to needs of users	

Basic Prevention

If there are obvious conditions (activities, people, approaches, situations) which trigger the challenging behaviour and these can be avoided without serious cost to the individual or to others, then these conditions should be avoided or removed.

Interventions within the Social System of which the Person is a Part

Change attitudes

If an individual's behaviour reflects the negative attitudes of those around him or her, then the focus of change is upon those attitudes—for example, building empathy, identifying individual strengths and positive characteristics, or finding an alternative placement for staff who do not like the individual.

Resolve conflicts

The individual's behaviour may reflect tensions and conflict within the social system. Resolution of these tensions and conflicts will reduce the likelihood of challenging behaviour itself and the need for a system (family or staff group) to have a scapegoat for its discomforts. There may also be a need for intervention at the more micro level of interactional style. *If the individual has a lot of difficulty processing spoken language, does not like noise and is very sensitive to people being close and touching, then having somebody with him or her who talks a lot, is noisy and hugs a lot is a nightmare.* Those who are paid to work for people may have to adjust their style of relating according to the individual needs of the person.

Redistribute power

Behaviour difficulties can arise when the person is unable to exert *control or choice* over key areas of his or her life. Empowering the individual to choose over matters of food, clothing, activities and companions may reduce frustration levels. On the other hand, if choice is presented in a way that the person cannot handle, or if the system is failing to set *clear limits* on behaviour, it may be necessary to restrict choice, present it in a more user friendly format and develop ways of communicating about limits.

Structure time better

There may be a need to alter the way a system is organised. If behavioural difficulties are more likely at unstructured times, it will be necessary to introduce more structure—for example, schedule leisure activities rather than just leave the person to sort something out for him or herself. If meal times are a situation in which behaviour difficulties are likely to present, it will be necessary to look at factors such as crowding and noise, seating arrangements, waiting time, choice of food or drink.

Improve self-esteem

People who are identified as disabled are often confined to spend much of their time with other people so labelled and often limited in the roles allocated to them (perpetual learners, receivers of care). Supporting the person into more valued roles and relationships will be a route to enhancing self-esteem and reducing challenging behaviour. This might involve developing employment opportunities (independent or supported), developing friendships, the chance to care for as well as be cared for, or the chance to take a leadership role.

Improve engagement levels

One of the most replicated findings in the research literature is that the more time people spend *without engagement* in the world around them, the more likely that challenging behaviour will occur. Therefore, it is important to look at what opportunities for engagement are available in the social system. This may mean looking overall at the individual's general lifestyle. It may mean looking at the moment to moment activities available—the waiting times, the times when carers are busy elsewhere, time on transport—to ensure that at all times the individual does have the opportunity to access something that he or she finds involving.

Adapt communication systems to the needs of users

Difficulties in understanding can be strongly implicated in challenges. When the individual is confused, disappointed or uncertain, difficulties arise (see Chapter 4). Social systems need to pay close attention to the information needs of their members. The guiding principles are:

- *Need to know.* People need to know what is happening when in their lives, who they will be doing things with, and what is expected of them in specific situations.
- *User friendly media.* Information needs to be available in an accessible form. If the spoken word is not a useful medium, then switching to visual media may provide an alternative (pictures, symbols, written words, timetables, rotas, cue cards). Tactile or olfactory media can also be used.
- *High salience.* Information needs to be made obvious to those who need to know. It is not sufficient to have a visual timetable on the wall; it must be referred to whenever a change of activity or personnel is about to occur.
- *Just in time delivery.* As a general rule, the information needs to be brought into focus at the time it is actually needed.

Interventions to Effect Change within the Individual

Enhance emotional well-being

Negative emotional states and moods are implicated in many challenging behaviours. These may be addressed through:

- *Lifestyle interventions.* For example: use of fitness building exercise to counteract anxiety; increasing 'fun' activities to lift mood; systematic use of positive mood induction to pre-empt the drift to negative mood states.
- *Specific therapies.* A number of therapies can be beneficial if offered by a skilled therapist. For example, psychotherapy, counselling, cognitive therapy, music, dance and art therapy, aromatherapy, massage.
- *Drugs.* Medication may assist in the reduction of anxiety and the lifting of mood. Given the risk attached to most drugs, they should only be used where a clear need has been identified which it is known that a specific medication can address. Their effect should be monitored objectively and, in general, the guideline should be the lowest dose for the shortest period of time. Medication should be withdrawn when either improvement has been maintained or the drug has been shown to have no measurable impact.
- *Diet.* Dietary intervention may assist emotional as well as physical well-being.

Enhance physical well-being

Physical discomforts and dysfunctions can be a contributory factor in behavioural difficulties. Interventions at this level will include:

- *Specific treatments* for diagnosed difficulties.
- *Lifestyle interventions.* Some people have difficulty in sustaining positive health and it may be that intervention at the lifestyle level will assist with this. Exercise and good nutrition may complement some of the interventions at the social system level to decrease stress and enhance positive well-being.
- *Non-specific treatments.* Some people's behaviour seems to reflect internal discomfort even though no diagnosable condition can be found. Judicious use of pain killers, under medical supervision, may prove a useful approach in some of these situations.
- *Brain chemistry alterations.* There is much speculation about the role of brain chemistry in behaviour and some drugs are held to have a very specific effect at this level (opiate antagonists such as naltrexone and

naloxone, serotonin reuptake inhibitors such as fluoxetine). The use of diets and supplements (gluten/casein-free diets, high doses of vitamin B with magnesium) may also have an effect at this level (Shattock, 1995).

Teach relevant skills

Challenging behaviours, on some occasions, will lead to needs being met (needs for social engagement, to be left alone, for stimulation). These are legitimate things for people to want. An important component of working constructively with those who challenge is to teach skills which enable people to get their needs met in ways that are *not* seen by others as challenging. *For example, if I scratch and pinch to get people to move away from me for a time, teaching a word/sign/symbol to communicate this message may enable me to get my needs met without being identified as challenging.*

There are other skills which, while not achieving the same results as the challenging behaviour, may enable the individual to function constructively in situations associated with challenging behaviour. These include learning how to choose, learning how to reduce anxiety/upset for oneself, learning how to solve problems, learning how to ask for assistance.

Enhance motivation to function positively

In many ways the real story about challenging behaviour is how rarely it occurs, given the situations that people have to cope with. It is a reminder that the people identified as challenging can function in different ways. This opens up the possibility of increasing the *incentive* to function in non-challenging ways as a means of decreasing the behaviour of concern. There are a number of ways to enhance motivation in this way. Many of the interventions mentioned earlier contribute. (The texts starred for 're-commended reading' in the References section will give details of how to design these interventions using specific reinforcement tactics.)

Box 2 illustrates the intervention implications of 'Sandy's' formulation. This constitutes a 'menu' of relevant options. In practice these would need to be *prioritised* in terms of judgements about importance and feasibility.

INTERVENTIONS FOR CHANGE: WHAT CAN BE EXPECTED

The impact of an intervention will be determined by:

- *Knowledge limitations.* There is much that is not understood about the causes of human behaviour.

Box 2: Intervention implications of Sandy's formulation (see Box 1)

This constitutes a 'menu' of relevant options which, in practice, would require prioritising in terms of judgements about importance and feasibility.

BEHAVIOURS OF CONCERN: Pinching and biting others (occur together)

1. **Immediate influences**
   - *Summary of contributors.* Sandy's pinching/biting are more likely to occur when demands are made and in group situations. The behaviour is effective sometimes in getting rid of pressure or gaining support.
   - *Intervention implications.* Review quality of activities provided. Review specific demands made and agree a limited, consistent number of requests. Look at how requests are presented (better as a choice or in visual format?). Teach Sandy a means of saying 'No' (gesture, symbol, sign?). Use timer to indicate when activities will end. Increase reinforcement for agreeing to requests.

     Adopt a room management approach to group activities. Teach Sandy a communication skill for requesting support (button activated tape loop, gesture, symbol, sign?).

2. **Short-term influences**
   - *Summary of contributors.* Sandy's pinching/biting are more likely to occur in the mornings, in noisy environments, when her mood is low and three days before a period.
   - *Intervention implications.* Look at how mornings are managed to emphasise gentle approaches and limited pressure. Schedule mood enhancing interventions to the morning. Avoid exposure to noisy environments, especially in the morning. Seek medical advice for reducing pre-menstrual discomfort.

3. **Longer term influences**
   Environmental characteristics
   - *Summary of contributors.* High staff turnover, inconsistency and the winter seem to be contributory factors at this level.
   - *Intervention implications.* Look at reasons for turnover and either work with service provider to deal with these (or consider an alternative provider). Establish guidelines for supporting Sandy. Provide winter sun holiday, consider access to special lighting in the winter or use of antidepressant medication.

   Personal characteristics
   - *Summary of contributors.* Sandy's behaviour is made more likely by her lack of communication skills, her lack of understanding about the effect of her behaviour on others, sustained low mood and the fact that she is a very determined woman.
   - *Intervention implications.* Work on communication skills as outlined above. Include in conversation with Sandy comments about feeling states (ours and hers) and how these link to experiences. Address her emotional difficulties through lifestyle interventions (quality of activities, friendship building, holidays), everyday activities (scheduled mood lifting) and possible medication. Celebrate her personality ('true grit'!).

   Personal history
   - *Summary of contributors.* The major life event of moving from the family home is seen as a contributor to Sandy's behaviour difficulties.
   - *Intervention implications.* Help all those who work with Sandy to understand what she is going through. Develop a means of maintaining family links that is satisfactory to all concerned. Develop a 'life book' for Sandy. Work to develop Sandy's social network (friends and acquaintances).

- *Control limitations.* It is not possible to control all the things that might influence human behaviour towards its more challenging manifestations—loss and trauma occur, biological systems malfunction, relationships break down, motivation drops.
- *Competence limitations.* Services do not have a uniform and sustained standard of functioning. The capacities to assess, comprehend and intervene outlined in this chapter are not therefore always available to the person regarded as challenging. This is, of course, remediable.
- *Resource limitations.* Any system (family or professional) has a finite amount of resources to allocate to an area of concern. It may not be possible at any one moment in time to do all the things that need to be done. Prioritising will always be a core skill.
- *Personal choice.* People make lousy decisions. They eat the wrong things, take no exercise, smoke and drink, engage in dangerous sexual practices, stick with lousy jobs and lousy relationships, refuse help offered. This is part of ordinary life. Therefore, it is no surprise if people identified as disabled say 'no' to help—refuse therapy, medication, anger management training, sexual counselling. What is most disturbing about this is not that it occurs, but that one only becomes aware of the possibility when people articulate their refusal verbally. That leaves those who cannot articulate in favoured ways vulnerable to compulsory intervention without due legal process (see Chapters 10 and 11).

INTERVENTIONS FOR SAFETY: THE ISSUE OF DANGEROUSNESS

Some behaviours regarded as challenging will threaten the physical safety of the person him or herself or other people. Thus, one element in the work with people who challenge in dangerous ways will be to develop approaches to incident management which minimise the risks to the person or to others. *Behaviour management in this sense must be clearly distinguished from behaviour change.*

Behaviour management plans will include details of how to:

- *Prevent behaviour occurring.* This will include situations to access and those to avoid, ways of working to practice/avoid.
- *Respond to incidents.* The response must be planned, practised, written up, recorded and reviewed. Planning is based upon what is known about the person and the behaviour, the resources available in the situation(s), and a risk–benefit analysis of the options for responding.

Acknowledging the reality of working with those who challenge has implications for services at a number of levels. These will include policy (the need for policies on behaviour management, risk management and ethical dilemmas), training (basic prevention, diffusion and possibly physical management) and staffing levels.

SUPPORT FOR CARERS

Those who live and work with people who present themselves in challenging ways will experience considerable stress. Stress may come from the behaviour itself (some behaviours are very frightening, some are very provocative), from the emotions of the individual concerned (mirroring of the person's distress), from the impact of sustained but (perceived as) unsuccessful attempts to resolve the behavioural issues. The sources of stress may lie quite outside the challenging behaviour, arising from other areas of carers' lives.

Unless this stress is managed constructively it will, over time, reduce the capacity of carers to deliver quality support to the person and add factors that will increase the likelihood of the behaviour occurring. Constructive management means carers having timely access to people who can offer:

• social and emotional support (listening, reflecting, empathising)
• problem-solving support (questioning, brainstorming, offering ideas)
• competent specialist advice.

According to the situation, this may come from one person or, more likely, several (each fulfilling separate roles). It may come from informal (friends, relatives, colleagues) or formal (supervision, counselling, access to specialist behavioural services) sources. The local community team for people with learning disabilities (CTLD) and/or any specialist 'outreach' team for people who have challenging behaviour may be useful resources. Without this support, quality work is not possible, no matter how many pairs of hands are used to manage the situation. With this support, not only is quality work possible for the individual, but there is the chance for positive growth in the carers (knowledge, competence, confidence, self-esteem).

There are no grounds for congregating those who challenge or for removing them from their everyday lives (unless they present such a danger as to require legal detention). There is every reason to take services to people, not people to services, and to ensure that the major investment of resources should go to supporting people into high-quality everyday lives. The offer to remove or cure a source of social discomfort becomes, in reality, a mechanism for sustaining the social status of those who make the offer and for relieving the embarrassment of those who take it up. It sacrifices the needs of the relatively powerless to the needs of the relatively powerful.

KEY POINTS

1. Challenging behaviour is a social construct, not a clinical diagnosis. Behaviours commonly identified include aggression, self-injury and property damage.
2. At any one time, 15–20% of people using learning disability services show such behaviours, but only a small number to a severe degree.
3. Behaviour is multiply determined and change is about altering probabilities, not cure. An organised framework for developing understanding is necessary.
4. Assessment involves professional analysis, building empathy, and reaching a formulation of the factors contributing to the observed behaviour of concern. Active steps are needed to counter the influence of prejudiced judgements.
5. Effective interventions for change may target environmental and/or personal variables, the exact mix depending upon what the assessment process identifies as important contributors to the behaviour of concern.
6. Positive change is always possible, but the amount of change is influenced by available knowledge, amount of control, competence of service providers, resources and personal choice.
7. When the behaviour of concern is dangerous, it will be necessary to develop behaviour management procedures which are about effecting safety, not behaviour change.
8. The stress of supporting those who challenge must be acknowledged and managed.
9. Services for those who challenge need to focus upon delivering needs driven, high quality, everyday lives—not removing people for 'treatment'.

REFERENCES

Starred entries indicate recommended reading

Clements, J. (1992) I can't explain . . . 'challenging behaviour': towards a shared conceptual framework. *Clinical Psychology Forum*, **39**, 29–37.

*Donnellan, A.M., LaVigna, G.W., Negri-Shoultz, N. and Sassbender, L.L. (1988) *Progress without Punishment: Effective Approaches for Learners with Behaviour Problems*. Teachers College Press, New York.

*Durand, V.M. (1990) *Severe Behaviour Problems: A Functional Communication Training Approach*. The Guilford Press, New York.

*Emerson, E. (1995) *Challenging Behaviour: Analysis and Intervention in People with Learning Difficulties*. Cambridge University Press, Cambridge.

*Jones, R.S.P. and Eayrs, C.B. (eds) (1993) *Challenging Behaviour and Intellectual Disability: A Psychological Perspective*. BILD Publications, Avon.

Kiernan, C. and Qureshi, H. (1993) Challenging behaviour. In C. Kiernan (ed.), *Research to Practice? Implications of Research on the Challenging Behaviour of People with Learning Disability*. BILD Publications, Avon.

O'Neill, R.E., Horner, R.H., Albin, R.W., Storey, K. and Sprague, J.R. (1990) *Functional Analysis: A Practical Assessment Guide*. Sycamore Publishing Company, Sycamore, Illinois.

Scotti, J.R., Evans, I.M., Meyer, L.H. and Walker, P. (1991) A meta-analysis of intervention research with problem behaviour: treatment validity and standards of practice. *American Journal on Mental Retardation*, **96**(3), 233–256.

Shattock, P. (1995) Back to the Future: an assessment of some of the unorthodox forms of biomedical intervention currently being applied to autism. In *Psychological Perspectives in Autism*. A collection of papers from the conference held at the University of Durham, 5–7 April 1995. Autism Research Unit, Sunderland.

*Zarkowska, E. and Clements, J. (1994) *Problem Behaviour and People with Severe Learning Disabilities*. Chapman & Hall, London.

7

MENTAL HEALTH ISSUES

Jean O'Hara and Anthea Sperlinger

The mental health of adults with learning disabilities has become an important issue over the past 20 years as their vulnerability to emotional distress has been increasingly recognised. It is now generally accepted that adults with learning disabilities are at risk for the development of mental illness and prevalence rates as high as 50% have been reported in the literature. There are real difficulties in accurate diagnosis and assessment, particularly in people with severe learning disabilities (see Checklist 7) and a comprehensive multi-disciplinary assessment is most important—followed by a comprehensive, multi-disciplinary approach to treatment. In recent years, issues of funding and poor service provision for this population led to the concept of 'dual diagnosis' and the acknowledgement of co-morbidity. People with learning disabilities who have mental health needs now have the right to access the same range of mental health services available to everyone else, as well as to local specialist mental health services, if required. Guidelines for considering and offering drug treatment are offered in the light of the historical tendency to overprescribe medication with little evaluation of effectiveness. Examples of a variety of psychological treatments are described, with some specific guidelines for their use with adults with learning disabilities.

Adults with Learning Disabilities. Edited by J. O'Hara and A. Sperlinger.

VULNERABILITY TO MENTAL HEALTH PROBLEMS

There is a growing tendency to move towards an integrative model to explain the relationship between learning disabilities, behavioural disorders, mental illnesses and various pathogenic factors. Many possible explanations have been proposed for the increased prevalence of mental health problems in people with learning disabilities:

• Syndromes associated with learning disabilities may predispose to mental health problems; associated brain damage and epilepsy, motor abnormalities and sensory impairments.
• Repeated losses/separations.
• Communication and language disorders (see Chapter 4).
• Low intelligence and cognitive impairments, leading to poor coping mechanisms and vulnerability to exploitation.
• Family difficulties, parental ill health, marital discord.
• Failure to acquire social, interpersonal and recreational skills may impair relationships.
• Low self-esteem from repeated failure, perceived/true rejection, perceived unattractive/dysmorphic appearance.
• Social isolation (a significant risk factor for depression).
• Labelling, adverse environmental factors, adverse life events.

Many services routinely fail to recognise the internal emotional life of people with learning disabilities. Extreme manifestations of distress and anger are commonly not even conceptualised as rooted in emotional difficulties and internal conflict, but are characterised as behavioural problems, or are attributed to some spurious syndrome (Pemberton, personal communication). Adults with learning disabilities have repeated, profound losses, deprivation, rejection and abuse to deal with, in addition to bearing the burden of the original learning disability. It is not surprising that emotional problems or behavioural disturbances are very common. What is surprising is that these problems have only recently been widely recognised as having an emotional origin in people with learning disabilities. Grief, loss and conflict have been significantly associated in adults with learning disabilities with problematic behaviours of new onset and admission to a psychiatric hospital. 'Transition shock' has been observed in adults with learning disabilities when they move from a large institution to a community unit.

> Every move, even if explained, must be seen as a potential psychological trauma, minimised only by using the utmost care, such as the use of photographs and mementoes, and never by medication. (Bicknell, 1994)

Struggling with these emotions and experiences, many people with learning disabilities find defensive ways of surviving. These can involve both a denial of and/or an exaggeration of disability (secondary handicap) to foster the illusion of control (Sinason and Stokes, 1992). Repeated 'life events', losses and bereavements, financial and social struggles, lack of control within their own environment and lives, and the inability to react adaptively to stress and social demands, lead to an increased vulnerability to the entire range of mental health problems.

BEHAVIOURAL DISTURBANCE AS A PRESENTING SYMPTOM

Behavioural disturbances may be due to any mental health problem and these problems may present as any, or all, of the behaviour disturbances commonly seen, i.e. aggression, mood disturbances, withdrawal, anti-social behaviour, idiosyncratic mannerisms and self-injurious behaviours (Fraser and Nolan, 1994).

Over 52% of referrals to one specialist mental health services for people with learning disabilities were for 'behavioural problems' (Bouras *et al.*, 1988). In evaluating such a presentation (see Chapter 6), not only is it important to assess the frequency and severity of the problematic behaviour, but also the possibility of underlying psychopathology (e.g. depression, paranoid states, psychosis, anxiety states, acute confusion). *Clearly, people with learning disabilities can suffer from mental illness without behavioural problems, and equally can show behavioural problems without being mentally ill.* Different theoretical approaches may be required to gain an understanding of the factors which cause and maintain a particular behaviour, including possible biological, developmental, environmental and psychological factors, as well as sensory impairments, underlying physical problems (such as pain, pyrexia, infection or epilepsy) and genetic syndromes associated with particular clusters of behavioural symptoms (Berg and Gosse, 1990).

Particular skill deficits are often found in people with mild learning disabilities who present with behavioural disorders. Typically, they come from disorganised early family backgrounds, and have acquired relatively good basic self-care skills and adequate communication. However, they often show major deficits in interpersonal skills, finding it difficult to control and express their emotions in an acceptable way (Holland and Murphy, 1990).

DIAGNOSTIC ISSUES

Psychiatric diagnostic criteria (e.g. ICD-10, DSM-IV) may be appropriate for people with mild learning disabilities, but are inadequate for those with more severe disability. Rigid adherence to strict criteria in a group of people whose limited language may impair their ability to describe abnormal mental phenomena (Holland and Murphy, 1990) may result in failure to diagnose and treat an underlying mental health need. On the other hand, there are some behavioural patterns, especially self-injurious behaviours, which may constitute new psychiatric syndromes, yet to be included.

Difficulties in diagnosis include: the traditional reliance on self-reported symptoms; the need for reliable reports from informants; disentangling those features which may be part of the person's learning disability from those which are not; the need to rely on direct observation; and the need to consider symptoms within a developmental and environmental context.

Sovner (1986) describes four factors which affect the diagnostic process:

- *Intellectual distortion.* The influence of cognitive deficits on the person's ability to label his or her experiences and communicate them to the interviewer.
- *Psychosocial masking.* Relatively impoverished social skills and life experiences leading to 'simple and naive' symptoms which go unrecognised and undetected as psychopathology.
- *Cognitive disintegration.* Disruption of information processing as a non-specific stress response, leading to a misdiagnosis of psychosis or schizophrenia.
- *Baseline exaggeration.* Increase in severity of pre-existing cognitive deficits and maladaptive behaviours that may cloud the diagnostic process.

Reiss (1994) describes the phenomenon of *diagnostic overshadowing,* when the presence of learning disabilities overshadows the diagnostic significance of an accompanying behavioural or emotional disturbance usually considered indicative of psychopathology.

PRINCIPLES OF ASSESSMENT

One of the challenges in diagnosis and assessment is how to decide when a behaviour is symptomatic of a mental illness. Reiss (1994) suggests four principles of assessment:

- The symptom should be one in an *overall pattern of symptoms* that is described as a mental illness.
- *Principle of change.* There is a history of change in behaviour, with periods of onset and deterioration from a premorbid state and level of functioning.

- The *impact of learning disability on the expression of symptomatology*. Symptoms may be expressed in concrete, simple or physical ways. Consider them within the context of the person's developmental level and life experiences.
- *Admit limitations of knowledge*. In people with severe learning disabilities it is often not possible to make a diagnosis with any confidence, and it is best to acknowledge this and not make any diagnosis at all.

MENTAL HEALTH PROBLEMS

Schizophrenia and Psychotic States

The prevalence of schizophrenia is at least three times that of the general population (3% vs 1%), and this is thought to be an underestimate. The age of onset is earlier in the learning disabled population but the reasons are unclear (Fraser and Nolan, 1994). Chronic schizophrenia in the general population may produce a deterioration in intellectual functioning as assessed on psychometric tests. At times, this leads to inappropriate referrals to learning disabilities services. It is generally accepted that the presentation of schizophrenia in people with mild learning disabilities is similar to that of the general population.

- However, they may also present with withdrawal, fearfulness and sleep disturbance.
- Typical first-rank symptoms may be present (such as auditory hallucinations in the third person or as a running commentary, delusional perceptions and primary delusions and passivity phenomena) but:
  — it may not be possible to elicit the nature or content of hallucinatory experiences;
  — delusions often lack the complex and elaborate systems found in the general population though simple paranoid ideation may be expressed;
  — formal thought disorder may be difficult to elicit;
  — often people with learning disabilities have very little control over their lives or their environment and will answer affirmatively to questions about being controlled by others, or outside influences ('passivity');
  — some people with learning disabilities have problems separating fact from fantasy, and their mental state may be considered psychotic and medication given (Bicknell, 1994).

In people with severe learning disabilities, or limited verbal skills, it is not possible to diagnose the presence of schizophrenia or psychotic states.

This does not mean that they do not suffer from these illnesses, and therefore there is a risk of inadequate treatment.

Negative symptoms (such as poverty of speech, emotional blunting, avolition, psychomotor retardation, attentional impairments) are considered to be primary factors in the high social morbidity associated with schizophrenia. They pose particular diagnostic difficulties in people with learning disabilities, as many of the problems can be seen as an inherent part of the learning disability itself. It is vital that a developmental and longitudinal perspective is taken when considering these symptoms, and that the principles of assessment outlined above are applied.

Possible differential diagnoses include:

- *Autistic spectrum disorders.* Autism is a pervasive and life-long disorder, characterised by profound deficits in communication (including failure of speech development, mutism, echolalia, reversal of pronouns, neologisms and 'irrelevant utterances') and social understanding, together with ritualistic and obsessional behaviours, and a general resistance to change. Although usually associated with cognitive impairments, autism can occur in individuals at all levels of ability, and around 20% have an IQ score within the normal range (Howlin, 1997). Some authors argue that the existence of autism with learning disabilities should be considered as a 'dual diagnosis'.
- *Temporal lobe epilepsy.* Behavioural or mood disturbances and patterns of abnormal thoughts and feelings may be associated with an aura preceding the seizure, the seizure itself, or post-ictally. There is a complex relationship between different types of epilepsy, psychotic illness and behavioural disorders (Holland and Murphy, 1990). The importance of establishing such a link in diagnosis is that it offers the possibility of improved control, for the seizures themselves as well as the behaviours.
- *Other mental health problems* such as depressive illness, organic states.
- *Non-specific responses to stress* resulting in 'cognitive disintegration'.
- *Drug-induced psychosis:* e.g. anticonvulsants such as vigabatrin.

Mood Disorders

The reported prevalence of mood disorders in adults with learning disabilities ranges from 0.9 to 6.0%. There is a genetic loading for bipolar illness (i.e. recurrent episodes of hypomania or episodes of depression and hypomania) with no specific link to learning disability. Unipolar depression probably goes undiagnosed for a variety of reasons, including diagnostic overshadowing and the often non-disruptive nature of symptoms. Reiss (1994) has found that depression in adults with learning disabilities is strongly associated with both low levels of social support and poor social skills. People who became depressed were not necessarily those who faced the most adversity in their lives: the people who became depressed were those who were isolated and alone with no one to support them through adversity.

The manifestation of mood disorders is not different from that of the general population. The diagnosis is made on the basis of a sustained mood change in addition to disturbances in sleep, appetite, psychomotor activity, energy and cognition (pessimistic thoughts of past, present and future). In severe forms, there may be hallucinations and delusions, but these are mood congruent (e.g. delusions of guilt and worthlessness in depression, delusions of grandeur in hypomania). The traditional diagnostic process may be hampered by the person's inability to recognise and describe feelings, and problems with limited vocabulary and concrete thinking. Changes from premorbid levels of functioning (e.g. in work performance, self-care) may be less obvious as adults with learning disabilities are often denied social roles and responsibilities. However, a clinically useful diagnosis can still be made on the basis of behavioural or biological changes (Holland and Murphy, 1990). The major issue is recognising the patterns that suggest the presence of a mood disorder, especially depression, such as:

- sleep disturbance (including early morning wakening)
- significant weight loss, changes in appetite
- hypochondriacal and somatic symptoms
- social withdrawal, decreased interest
- tearfulness, observed changes in mood, irritability/agitation
- decrease in skills of daily living and self-care, reassurance-seeking behaviour
- increased pre-existing maladaptive behaviours.

Possible differential diagnoses include:

- Pseudodementia.
- Drug-induced akinesia (such as neuroleptics): presenting with psychomotor retardation, apathy and decreased facial expressivity.
- Other mental health problems: psychotic states, schizophrenia, anxiety disorders.

Suicidal and Self-injurious Behaviours (SIB)

From a historical perspective, ritualistic self-inflicted pain is not confined to people with learning disabilities. Today, in the general population, it is thought of as a key feature in borderline personality disorders, and can present in depression, schizophrenia and as a result of the toxic effects of stimulant drugs (Thompson *et al.*, 1993). SIB can serve multiple functions (see Chapter 6) and some stereotyped actions found in people with severe learning disabilities, such as body rocking, eye poking, self-biting, can be severely self-mutilating and involve complex components. There is little literature on suicidal ideation and suicidal behaviour in adults with learning disabilities, which may be a reflection on their supervised environment and lack of opportunity. Deliberate self-harm and suicidal ideation must always be taken seriously and assessed with care.

Dementia

As life expectancy of adults with learning disabilities increases, identifying and meeting the mental health needs of an ageing population become more important. It has long been known that Alzheimer-like neuropathological changes (neural plaques, neuro-fibrillary tangles, reduced brain weight, increased ventricular size and neurotransmitter changes) are found at autopsy in most adults with Down's syndrome over the age of 35. More recently, genes coding for the beta-amyloid precursor protein (amyloid is found in neural plaques) and the enzyme implicated in premature ageing, have been located on the long arm of chromosome 21.

Clinically, dementia is found in 8% of adults with Down's syndrome between the ages of 35 and 49, but this increases to 60% in those over the age of 60. In those without the diagnosis, specific cognitive impairments (such as reduced visuospatial skills and loss of orientation) have been found on neuropsychological testing and may be an early indication of dementia. Epilepsy, relatively uncommon in Down's syndrome, increases to 30% in adults over the age of 30, perhaps reflecting the development of Alzheimer neuropathology (Holland, 1994).

Diagnostic criteria include the presence of a number of cognitive impairments sufficient to interfere with social functioning:

- Memory—and at least one of the following: impaired thinking, judgement, higher cortical functioning (e.g. dyspraxias, dysphasias) and/or personality change.
- Evidence of organic rather than a functional cause (e.g. depression).

- The absence of fluctuating levels of consciousness (i.e. acute confusional states).
- A global deterioration from premorbid levels of functioning.

Differential diagnoses include:

- *Hypothyroidism* (occurs in up to 30% of adults with Down's syndrome).
- *Sensory impairments*, such as hearing loss, cataract formation.
- *Depression*—by itself or in conjunction with early dementia.
- *Acute confusional states.* Adults with learning disabilities are already compromised with structural brain abnormalities and cognitive deficits. They are often more sensitive to systemic illness (including minor infections) and side-effects of medication. Problems of delayed presentation and diagnosis can lead to prolonged symptoms of an acute confusional state.
- *Other causes/types of organic psychosis*, such as multi-infarct dementia, space-occupying lesions, Vitamin B12 and folate deficiency.

It is often difficult for carers to accept the additional 'label' of dementia, and its progressive deteriorating nature. Management involves not only treatment of any other medical problem such as sensory impairments, epilepsy and infections, but also strategies to maintain skills that have not been lost, reality orientation, and greater care given to the design of the person's routine activities and safety. The person's environment can be managed to reduce confusion (e.g. lighting at night, special markings, colours or textures on bedroom door and toilet, etc.)

Anxiety States

Adults with learning disabilities often have a history of personal adversity, repeated life events, traumas, vulnerability, abuse (see Chapter 10), failures, lack of control and stigmatisation which cause considerable distress and anxiety. Collectively, studies suggest that 10–30% of the institutionalised learning disabled population have generalised anxiety states (Ollendick *et al.*, 1993), and that the problems, which are equally prevalent in both genders, are obvious during childhood and adolescence. Sometimes psychological mechanisms are insufficient to contain feelings of anxiety, and depression and somatisation occur. In people with learning disabilities, these are often copies of a particular disability such as hemiplegia, epilepsy or blindness, or may take the form of the magnification of normal aches and pains (Bicknell, 1994). Generalised anxiety disorder, panic attacks, agoraphobia, specific phobias, post-traumatic stress, hysterical conversion and obsessive-compulsive disorders have all been described. The diagnosis is based on:

- physical symptoms and signs: such as nervousness, sighing, shortness of breath, palpitations, tachycardia;
- motor symptoms of anxiety: and its evaluation compared to repetitive behaviours associated with stereotypies or habit disorder commonly seen in this population;
- observed behaviours, such as
  — repetitive, ritualised behaviours and its functional consequences, as in obsessive-compulsive disorders. The most common compulsion is that of ordering (e.g. always turning right, or a particular sequence/ ritual when washing) compared to handwashing in the rest of the population. It is often difficult to elicit the subjective anxiety required in the strict adherence of diagnostic criteria, but in practice this makes little difference to the treatment options available;
  — observed low mood, withdrawal, sleep disturbance, self-injury or acting out behaviours in those unable to verbalise their feelings;
  — exacerbation of pre-existing behaviours, somatic symptoms such as headaches, vomiting, disturbances of mobility and gait;
- corroborating self-statements: feelings of unease, discomfort, fear.

Sleep Disorders

Disturbances in sleep often present to health professionals. It can be persistent and distressing, resulting in sleep deprivation and additional stress to carers. Such chronic problems can reduce one's tolerance and abilities to cope with everyday pressures, leading to aggressiveness, misperceptions and behavioural problems. Sleep disorders are of four main types: (a) sleeplessness, (b) sleep/wake cycle disorders, (c) excessive daytime sleep, and (d) parasomnias, such as hypnogogic imagery, sleep walking, sleep talking, nightmares (Stokes, 1995). It is important to recognise these, and to look for physical and psychological causes which may be amenable to intervention.

Physical causes include:

- sensory deficits (for example the person may not be aware of night and day);
- respiratory problems, obstructive sleep apnoea (associated with Down's syndrome);
- nocturnal epileptic seizures.

Psychological causes include:

- poor sleep habits and settling problems;
- mental health problems such as mood disorders, anxiety states, hyperactivity.

Inappropriate Sexual Behaviours

This often precipitates a referral to local specialist services. Behaviours include: public masturbation, exhibitionism/stripping, inappropriate sexual advances towards children or less able adults, and non-consenting sex (see Chapters 10 and 11). Often they are part of a normal developmental process, but within a relatively impoverished environment with: lack of privacy; little formal education on sexuality or personal relationships; limited opportunities to learn appropriate sexual behaviour; restricted social networks; and a denial of sexuality. Given the background of increased vulnerability, the presentation of sexualised behaviours should alert professionals to the possibility of sexual abuse. Assessment and management must take into account all these factors, as well as the person's sexual and developmental history, contributing psychological, physical and social factors, and an assessment of risk to themselves and others.

Other Mental Health Problems

Although relatively little is written about *alcohol and substance abuse* in adults with learning disabilities, individuals are presenting to community teams and specialist psychiatric services as the closure of large residential institutions and 'ordinary life principles' may lead to increased opportunity and access, vulnerability to exploitation, and exposure to additional social pressures.

Eating disorders often associated with learning disabilities such as *picas* (the ingestion of non-food substances), *dysphagias* (due to neuromuscular dysfunction) and *obesity* (due to Down's syndrome or Prader–Willi syndrome) have long been recognised, but the existence of eating disorders such as *anorexia nervosa* and *bulimia nervosa* remains controversial, despite a growing literature.

Other mental health problems such as abnormal grief reactions, functional disorders in later life (e.g. paraphrenias), conditions associated with the puerperium (childbirth) and gynaecological factors (such as premenstrual and menopausal problems) are gradually presenting to health professionals as awareness of the mental health needs of this group increases.

MANAGEMENT AND TREATMENT OPTIONS

The emotional and behavioural disturbances of adults with learning disabilities are often the result of a complex interaction between biological and psychosocial factors. Therefore, a comprehensive, multi-disciplinary approach to treatment—preceded by a comprehensive multi-disciplinary assessment—is most important. All interventions which are typically used in mental health treatment should be considered for adults with learning disabilities, including environmental change, behavioural strategies, psychotherapy, family interventions and drug treatments (Bregman, 1991).

Drug Treatments

Until the fairly recent past, the mental health 'treatment' of people with learning disabilities consisted largely of sedation and restraint. There has been little research into the efficacy and potency of medication acting on the brain in a population already cognitively compromised, and the increased risks of side-effects such as the development of tardive dyskinesia (Holland and Murphy, 1990). Historically there has been a tendency to overprescribe medication with little evaluation of effectiveness.

In considering drug treatment, there must be a clear indication for its use, and due consideration given to: issues of consent (see Chapter 11); the recognition, reporting and monitoring of side-effects and efficacy; constant review; the choice of drug based on sound pharmacological principles; and an awareness of potential interactions and side-effects. (see Tables 1a and 1b.)

Psychological Treatments

The following is not a comprehensive list, but an example of the range of psychological treatments which may be offered to adults with learning disabilities, together with some specific guidelines for their use with this client group. The central question remains: *'What treatment, by whom, is most effective for this individual, with that specific problem, under what set of circumstances?'* (Paul, 1967).

Behavioural therapies

Behavioural therapies have undergone major changes in the last decade, moving beyond symptomatic relief and 'behaviour modification' to a functional approach to analysis and intervention (Emerson, 1995). These changes are evident in:

- the decline in the use of various punishment procedures;
- an increased emphasis on the use of functional diagnosis;

Table 1a: Drug treatments

Drug group	Main uses	Some common side-effects (see British National Formulary)	Comments
NEUROLEPTICS			
Phenothiazines	Control of	Anticholinergic—include:	Remember pharmacokinetics:
Aliphatic—e.g. chlorpromazine	– disturbed behaviours	dry mouth, confusion, urinary retention, blurred vision, constipation, sexual	induction of liver enzymes, plasma protein binding and *drug interactions*—e.g.
Piperidine—e.g. thioridazine	– hyperactivity states	dysfunction, ECG changes	anticonvulsants
Piperazine—e.g. trifluoperazine	– severe anxiety states schizophrenia and psychotic	Noradrenergic—include: postural hypotension, impotence	Blood dyscrasias—esp. with clozapine
	states		Neuroleptic Malignant syndrome
Butyrophenones	stereotypic behaviours	Extrapyramidal (EPSE)—include:	Early diagnosis and hospital treatment is crucial
e.g. Haloperidol		1. *Parkinsonism* (dose related) tremor,	Mortality rates up to 25%
		slowing of movement and stiffness	Symptoms include: hyperthermia, muscular
Thioxanthenes		2. *Acute dystonias*: involuntary	hypertonicity, delirium, autonomic instability
e.g. Clopenthixol		contraction of skeletal muscle	Affects 0.5–1% of patients on neuroleptics
		3. *Oculogyric crises*: hyperextension of	Oculogyric crisis can be dramatic and
Newer 'atypical' drugs		neck, opening of mouth and rolling of	distressing.
e.g. Sulpiride		the eyes	Rapidly alleviated by an injection of procyclidine
Clozapine		4. *Akathasia* (dose related): inner feeling	
Respiridone		of restlessness	Akathasia is often mistaken for a behavioural
			disturbance in people with learning disabilities
			Increasing neuroleptic medication makes it worse
			Responds best to either beta-blockers or
			anticholinergics if Parkinsonian symptoms are
			present
		Tardive dyskinesia	
		Abnormal movement of face, tongue and	Tardive dyskinesia is thought to be the result of
		occasionally trunk and limbs	compensatory supersensivity of dopamine
			receptors.
		Others—include	There is no consistently effective treatment
		Lowering of seizure threshold	available.
		Rashes and Photosensitivity	Requires judicious use of drugs, at the minimum
		Prolactinaemia—irreg. menstrual cycle,	effective dose for the shortest period of time.
		ammenorrhoea, gynaecomastia,	Avoid concurrent use of anticholinergics purely
		galactorrhoea	for prophylaxis of EPSE. The newer 'atypical'
		Sedation	drugs appear to cause fewer problems.

Table 1b: Drug treatments

Drug group	Main uses	Some common side-effects (see British National Formulary)	Comments
ANTIDEPRESSANTS **Tricyclics (TCA)**—e.g. amitriptyline **Related TCAs**—e.g. trazodone	Depressive illness Phobic anxiety states Obsessive-compulsive disorders Chronic pain	Anticholinergic effects (see Table 1a) Sedation Cardiac effects: heart block and arrhythmias Gastrointestinal disturbances	Selection of an antidepressant is based on personal history, the side-effect profile of the drug, administration issues and need for monitoring as well as the likelihood of overdose.
MAOIs and Reversible MAOIs **(RIMA)**—e.g. moclobemide			MAOIs are seldom used now because of their dangerous side effects with foods containing tyramine. RIMAs are said to be safer.
SSRIs and related—e.g. fluoxetine			SSRIs have fewer sedative and cardiotoxic effects and are preferable in many cases.
MOOD STABILISERS **Lithium**	Mood disorders (Prophylaxis) Control of mania Chronic hyperactivity Aggression and self-injurious behaviours	**Lithium** *Early:* related to peaks in blood level gastrointestinal, tremor, slight thirst **Toxicity:** serum levels > 2.0 mmol/l *Long term:* Nephrogenic diabetes insipidis Hypothyroidism—3% per annum	**Lithium** Excreted by the kidneys, unchanged. Altered fluid and electrolyte states (e.g. vomiting, diarrhoea, parturition can precipitate toxicity) Lithium should only be used if the potential benefits clearly outweigh the risks Need to monitor serum lithium levels 12 hours after the last dose, renal and thyroid function on a regular basis
Carbamazepine (also an anticonvulsant)		**Carbamazepine** Maculopapular rash—15% Can progress to severe exfoliative dermatitis and requires stopping the drug Aplastic anaemia—rare	**Carbamazepine** Serum levels do not correlate well with clinical response In rare cases, carbamazepine causes **aplastic anaemia**. Monitoring of blood counts and platelets is important
ANXIOLYTICS/HYPNOTICS Long acting—e.g. Diazepam Short acting —e.g. Temazepam	Anxiety disorders Sleep disturbance Muscle relaxant Anticonvulsant	Side-effects are uncommon Relatively safe in overdose **Dependency: psychological and physical**	Be aware of active metabolites Should only be used as *short-term treatments* given problems with dependency Convulsions on abrupt withdrawal

- the expansion of the model to include psychological, biological and socioenvironmental contributors to behaviour;
- and a focus on teaching coping skills as replacements for problematic responses (Gardner and Cole, 1990).

Nowadays, in clinical practice, there has been an increase in the use of complex, multimodal intervention strategies and in special multi-disciplinary 'outreach' teams using this approach. Chapter 6 gives a comprehensive outline of this approach.

There has been increasing emphasis on improving the living circumstances and adaptive capabilities of adults with learning disabilities as a means of enhancing the quality of their lives and ameliorating emotional and behaviour disturbances. Improvements in functioning can be achieved by: responding to individual needs and preferences; providing greater opportunities for engagement; and enhancing personal competence and independence through skill development. Behavioural interventions, which used to be limited to developing self-help skills (such as dressing and toileting), are now used to teach adults with learning disabilities to cope with anxiety. Educational programmes often include vocational skills, improving communication, self-management/self-monitoring skills, and social skills training (Bregman, 1991).

Box 1 summarises some of the key points and strategies of several behavioural or cognitive-behavioural approaches.

Individual, group and family psychotherapy

Bender (1993) has documented the history of therapeutic disdain towards people with learning disabilities. There is a small, but growing literature on psychotherapy with this client group, but, until recently, much of it has focused on process rather than outcome. Positive evidence and case examples of psychotherapy are to be found in Brandon (1989) and Waitman and Conboy-Hill (1992).

Practitioners emphasise:

- The need for many things usually taken for granted to be underscored, verbally stated and clearly contracted with the carers (staff or family) present.
- The difficulty of ensuring consent to treatment, or to individual sessions, when the person is so dependent that he or she has to be escorted (or even pushed in a wheelchair) to sessions.
- The problems of confidentiality and the negotiation of the appropriate distance carers might need to maintain during therapy.
- The need to effectively integrate psychotherapy into a plan for the whole life of the person. There may be a need to provide several

Box 1:   Some examples of behavioural and cognitive-behavioural strategies

Intervention	Key points and strategies
Social skills training	• Typically in a group setting. Treatment phases involve: active instruction, modelling, role play and rehearsal, performance feedback, reinforcement, and real life exposure. • Social skills are enhanced and can generalise to neutral settings, but it is not clear which components of training are most effective or whether underlying motivational and social cognitive processes are altered as a result of training (Bregman, 1991).
Self-management	• Increased emphasis on teaching self-management skills as alternatives to the external management procedures which have dominated behavioural interventions. • Adults with learning disabilities have been taught to use behavioural strategies to control their own behaviour. • There is some evidence that self-monitoring alone may reduce some aggressive or self-injurious behaviours. • The relationship between the development of language and the emergence of behaviour such as self management is important, but not yet clear (Emerson, 1995).
Anger management	• Benson (1994) has developed training in anger management (using cognitive-behavioural techniques) for adults with mild to moderate learning disabilities. • Uses group therapy format (but has been used with individuals) and includes 15 weekly sessions for 6–8 participants with 2 group leaders. Individual training is offered to people who are less verbal, or who have psychotic symptoms. • The 4 components of the programme are: identification of feelings, relaxation training, self-instructional training and problem-solving skills. • Daily monitoring of moods is done as homework. • Initial research has established the effectiveness of the programme. Future planned developments include training in perspective taking (attribution) and empathy.
Systematic desensitisation	• Systematic desensitisation has been offered for a wide range of phobias and anxiety states with adults with learning disabilities. • Successful in treating a range of fears (e.g. of travelling on buses, of dogs, of heights, of physical examinations), often using *in vivo* procedures combined with imagined ones, and positive reinforcement procedures for performing the approach responses.
Progressive relaxation (PR)	• PR and abbreviated progressive relaxation have been used with some success with adults with learning disabilities for a range of behavioural and cognitive difficulties, but results have been disappointing with adults with severe learning disabilities. • Lindsay *et al.* (1989) have used Behavioural Relaxation Training (BTL) with some success in both individual and group treatment for adults with moderate and severe learning disabilities with anxiety and agitation. • BLT differs from other forms of relaxation in that there are no paradoxical instructions to induce tension before relaxation and it does not require a conceptual understanding of internal states. It concentrates on observed behaviour (modelling both relaxed and unrelaxed behaviours in 10 areas of the body), and on encouraging the individual to imitate the relaxed positions (using manual prompting). • Studies suggest BLT can produce general reduction in anxiety in the person's life.
Anxiety management	• Traditional anxiety management techniques, using a cognitive-behavioural approach, have been used successfully with adults with learning disabilities. • Success enhanced by these strategies: pictorial examples of concepts; practical exercises for relaxation; repetition of information; reduction of focused time in sessions; finding practical ways to involve people fully (Turk and Francis, 1990).
Cognitive therapy	• Lindsay *et al.* (1993) describe the adaptation of cognitive therapy for adults with mild learning disabilities. The essential components are maintained, but the methods are simplified and considerably revised. • They report the use of isolating negative thoughts through role play, and reversing roles with the client as the 'doctor' to find out what the 'patient' is thinking. • Daily monitoring of feelings, worries and depression is done using an analogue scale, aided by descriptive histograms and 'happy' and 'sad' faces (Lindsay, 1991)

interventions, of which individual psychotherapy is only one (e.g. support to staff, support to the family, short-term use of medication, etc.).

• The need for the adult with learning disabilities to have a social worker or keyworker (e.g. from the CTLD) to limit the responsibility which therapists could otherwise feel for his or her daily problems.

• Being alone with one person and being given that person's undivided attention is such a foreign experience for some individuals that they reject the intensity of the relationship.

• The need to consider the ethics of offering psychotherapeutic help when the individual has an 'uncontaining' or adverse environment, and is repeatedly thrown back on depleted resources.

• The need for appropriately qualified and experienced therapists who have skilled supervision available. 'Working with people who, by definition, have more complex needs than average, demands *more* highly trained staff, not less' (Hollins *et al.*, 1994).

Guidelines for adapting *individual psychotherapeutic* methods to adults with learning disabilities, to compensate for their cognitive and developmental limitations, include the following (see Box 2):

Group analytic therapy

This approach has been eloquently described for adults with learning disabilities by Hollins (1992). Many of the above guidelines apply. In addition, since it is likely that many of the group members will know each other from special schooling, day services or social clubs, and group discussion will often reflect this ongoing social contact, time and place boundaries have to be strongly established. This approach is not seen as appropriate for people who have aggressive acting out behaviour or psychosis.

Family therapy

Family meetings, including key professionals who are part of their network, have been found to be fruitful (see Chapter 2 for a full description of this approach).

Counselling

Before counselling can be effective, the adult with learning disabilities must want to communicate (whether through words, movement, play or actions), and must feel good enough about him or herself to feel that he or she can do this. The individual also needs to know his/her world sufficiently

Box 2: Guidelines for adapting therapeutic methods for adults with learning disabilities (based on Hurley, 1989)

Recommendation	Example
Match technique to cognitive and developmental level	• Modify language: be concrete • Consistently check that person understands • Use child therapy techniques (art and music therapy) • Use non-verbal techniques • Ensure visual contact (few can manage the lack of contact of lying on a couch
Need for a directive approach	• Structure topics • Structure sessions (use role play, etc.)
Need for flexibility	• Use alternative techniques (tapes, life books) • Shorten session length
Involve family and staff	• Negotiate to enable attendance but to guard confidentiality • Consult, on the person's behalf, within his or her home and day services, but guard your relationship with the person
Carefully manage transference/ countertransference issues	• Treat transference as a manifestation of an early developmental stage (idealisation) • Control reactions to learning disability (rescue wishes, fear of setting limits, becoming a 'parent')
Address disability counselling areas	• Explore the person's understanding of his or her disability and define learning disability • Address ability areas (help the person to see his or her abilities)

well to see the importance of working on problems, even if these are identified by someone else. Much preparation by the therapist may be needed to both identify the problems and to raise the self-esteem of the client before work can begin. With adults who have little speech, considerable time is devoted to developing communication tools, e.g. role play, pictures, drawings, music, etc. (Bicknell, 1994). Some practitioners recommend a direct, practical, problem-solving approach rather than a non-directive approach, particularly with adults who have severe learning disabilities and have difficulty with abstractions and generalisations or with separating fact from fiction. The use of books designed for adults with learning disabilities—for example, on bereavement (Hollins and Sireling, 1994) and depression (Hollins and Curran, 1995)—can be very helpful.

Reminiscence groups

These groups have been used not only with older adults with learning disabilities, but also with adults managing transitions, such as the move from an institution to a supported house. The use of group processes and of concrete and practical objects, music and mementoes are an integral part of the approach. As a technique, it relies on the individual as the expert in his or her own unique history and promotes a sense of identity and self-esteem.

Adults with learning disabilities have an increased vulnerability to emotional distress, behaviour disturbance and mental illness. There remains a disturbing tendency to ascribe these difficulties to their learning disability. We have a responsibility to ensure that assessment, treatment and prevention are offered to this vulnerable group of people

> . . . by modelling dignified interactions with clients, addressing the possibility of emotional roots to problems, offering interventions which are humane and developmental, and arguing at all levels for services in which respect, dignity, value and emotional growth are of paramount importance.
> (Bicknell and Conboy-Hill, 1992)

KEY POINTS

1. Adults with learning disabilities are at risk for the development of mental health problems and for behavioural disturbance. Prevalence rates as high as 50% have been reported.
2. There is a move towards an integrative model to explain the relationship between learning disabilities, behavioural disorders, mental illnesses and various pathogenic factors.
3. Repeated 'life events', losses, lack of control within their own environment and lives and a difficulty in reacting adaptively to stress and social demands, leads to an increased vulnerability to the entire range of emotional disorders.

4. People with learning disabilities can suffer from a psychiatric disorder without behavioural problems and, equally, can show behavioural problems without being mentally ill.
5. Psychiatric diagnosis and assessment is often difficult, especially with those with severe learning disabilities. One of the challenges is how to decide when a behaviour is symptomatic of a mental illness.
6. A comprehensive, multi-disciplinary approach to treatment—preceded by a comprehensive multi-disciplinary assessment—is most important.
7. There is a need to address prevention of emotional distress and disturbance, as well as assessment and treatment.

REFERENCES

Bender, M. (1993) The unoffered chair: the history of therapeutic disdain toward people with a learning disability. *Clinical Psychology Forum*, **54**, 7–12.
Benson, B.A. (1994) Anger management training: a self-control programme for persons with mild mental retardation. In N. Bouras (ed.), *Mental Health in Mental Retardation: Recent Advances and Practices*. Cambridge University Press, Cambridge.
Berg, J.M. and Gosse, G.C. (1990) Specific mental retardation disorders and problem behaviours. *International Review of Psychiatry*, **2**, 53–60.
Bicknell, J. (1994) Psychological process: the inner world of people with mental retardation. In N. Bouras (ed.), *Mental Health and Mental Retardation: Recent Advances and Practices*. Cambridge University Press, Cambridge.
Bicknell, J. and Conboy-Hill, S. (1992) The deviancy career and mental handicap. In A. Waitman and S. Conboy-Hill (eds), *Psychotherapy and Mental Handicap*. Sage, London.
Bouras, N., Drummond, K., Brooks, D. and Laws, M. (1988) *Mental Handicap and Mental Health: A Community Service*. NUPRD, London.
Brandon, D. (ed.) (1989) *Mutual Respect: Therapeutic Approaches to Working with People who have Learning Difficulties*. Good Impressions Publishing, Surrey.
Bregman, J.D. (1991) Current developments in the understanding of mental retardation, Part II: Psychopathology. *Journal of the American Academy of Child and Adolescent Psychiatry*, **30**, 861–872.
Emerson, E. (1995) *Challenging Behaviour: Analysis and Intervention in People with Learning Difficulties*. Cambridge University Press, Cambridge.
Fraser, W. and Nolan, M. (1994) Psychiatric disorders in mental retardation. In N. Bouras (ed.), *Mental Health and Mental Retardation: Recent Advances and Practices*. Cambridge University Press, Cambridge.
Gardner, W.I. and Cole, C.L. (1990) Aggression and related conduct difficulties. In J.L. Matson (ed.), *Handbook of Behaviour Modification with the Mentally Retarded* (2nd edition). Plenum, New York.
Holland, A.J. (1994) Down's syndrome and Alzheimer's disease. In N. Bouras (ed.), *Mental Health and Mental Retardation: Recent Advances and Practices*, Cambridge University Press, Cambridge.
Holland, T. and Murphy, G. (1990) Behavioural and psychiatric disorder in adults with mild learning difficulties. *International Review of Psychiatry*, **2**, 117–136.

Hollins, S. (1992) Group analytic therapy for people with a mental handicap. In A. Waitman and S. Conboy-Hill (eds), *Psychotherapy and Mental Handicap*. Sage, London.

Hollins, S. and Curran, J. (1995) *Feeling Blue*. Books Beyond Words, St George's Mental Health Library, London.

Hollins, S., Sinason, V. and Thomson, S. (1994) Individual, group and family psychotherapy. In N. Bouras (ed.), *Mental Health in Mental Retardation: Recent Advances and Practices*. Cambridge University Press, Cambridge.

Hollins, S. and Sireling, L. (1994) *When Mum Died or When Dad Died* (2nd edition). Books Beyond Words, St George's Mental Health Library, London.

Howlin, P. (1997) Interventions for people with autism: recent advances. *Advances in Psychiatric Treatment*, **3**, 94–102.

Hurley, A.D. (1989) Individual psychotherapy with mentally retarded individuals: a review and call for research. *Research in Developmental Disabilities*, **10**, 261–275.

Lindsay, W.R. (1991) Psychological therapies in mental handicap. In W. Fraser, A. Green and R. Gillvray (eds), *Hallas Handbook of Mental Handicap*. Butterworth, London.

Lindsay, W.R., Baty, F.J., Michie, A.M. and Richardson, I. (1989) A comparison of anxiety treatments with adults who have moderate and severe mental retardation. *Research in Developmental Disabilities*, **10**, 129–140.

Lindsay, W.R., Howells, L. and Pitcaithly, D. (1993) Cognitive therapy for depression with individuals with intellectual disabilities. *British Journal of Medical Psychology*, **66**, 135–141.

Ollendick, T.H., Oswald, D.P. and Ollendick, D.G. (1993) Anxiety disorders in mentally retarded persons. In J.L. Matson and R.P. Barrett (eds), *Psychopathology in the Mentally Retarded* (2nd edition). Allyn & Bacon, Massachusetts.

Paul, G. (1967) Strategy of outcome research in psychotherapy. *Journal of Consulting Psychology*, **31**, 109–118.

Reiss, S. (1994) Psychopathology in mental retardation. In N. Bouras (ed.), *Mental Health and Mental Retardation: Recent Advances and Practices*. Cambridge University Press, Cambridge.

Sinason, V. and Stokes, J. (1992) Secondary handicap as a defence. In A. Waitman and S. Conboy-Hill (eds), *Psychotherapy and Mental Handicap*. Sage, London.

Sovner, R. (1986) Limiting factors in the use of DSM-III criteria with mentally ill/mentally retarded persons. *Psychopharmacology Bulletin*, **24**(4), 1055–1059.

Stokes, G. (1995) Sleep disorders and learning disabilities. Paper delivered at BILD International Conference, 19 September 1995, Oxford.

Thompson, T., Axtell, S. and Schaal, D. (1993) Self-injurious behaviour: mechanisms and intervention. In J.L. Matson and R.P. Barrett (eds), *Psychopathology in the Mentally Retarded* (2nd edition). Allyn & Bacon, Massachusetts.

Turk, V. and Francis, E. (1990) An anxiety management group: strengths and pitfalls. *Mental Handicap*, **18**, 78–81.

Waitman, A. and Conboy-Hill, S. (eds) (1992) *Psychotherapy and Mental Handicap*. Sage, London.

8

PRACTICAL SUPPORT FOR PARENTS WITH LEARNING DISABILITIES

Susan McGaw

People with learning disabilities and borderline learning disabilities intend to have children at some time in the future and, for many, their wish will probably be fulfilled although it is less likely to happen for people with profound or severe learning disabilities. There are an estimated 250,000 parents with learning disabilities in the UK, based on families known to agencies (McGaw, 1996) and services report increasing involvement with families headed by one or both parents with a mild or borderline learning disability. Some of these parents require intensive support and guidance to assist them in their parenting, while others do not. Currently, services are attempting to respond to the multiple needs of these families despite a lack of training, service guidelines or funding designated for this purpose.

NEEDS OF PARENTS WHO HAVE LEARNING DISABILITIES

'Learning disabilities' describes a significant impairment of intellectual functioning on standardised intelligence tests of thinking skills and self-help skills (see Chapter 1). That is, a person's thinking ability and adaptive behaviour (demonstrated in everyday tasks such as shopping,

Adults with Learning Disabilities. Edited by J. O'Hara and A. Sperlinger.
© 1997 John Wiley & Sons Ltd.

washing, using public transport, telephone skills) are not developing at the same rate as those of people of the same age. However, people with learning disabilities *can and do learn, but need specialised help* so that they may acquire skills and live independently within the community.

Community Attitudes and Support

In order for parents to get on with the job of parenting, they need to live in a community which is not judgemental about their learning disabilities or entitlement to life experiences, including being a parent. However, the concept of people with learning disabilities becoming parents and being responsible for children tests the ideologies and philosophies of the most progressive services within our communities. Rightly or wrongly, service providers are setting standards regarding the quality of personal relationships and enforcing conditions which many non-learning disabled couples would consider to be an infringement of their civil rights. Any individual with a learning disability who is over the age of 18 years may marry, so long as the Registrar of Marriages is satisfied that the person understands the nature of what he or she is undertaking.

Sex Education and Pregnancy

Current family planning and contraceptive services do not meet the needs of people with learning disabilities. Studies of mothers with learning disabilities report that as few as 25% of pregnancies are planned. Across the general population, countries with the lowest teenage pregnancy rates are those which have more liberal attitudes to sex, easily accessible contraceptive services for young people, and effective programmes of sex education. There appears to be very little information for pregnant women and new mothers in general. Both the information provided and the format of the material are unsuitable for young women with learning disabilities. There is a pressing need to ensure that they are given information about family roles, parenting responsibilities and child development in clear, simple terms. Preferably, this will happen during adolescence. A common concern (voiced by teachers and support services) is that people with learning disabilities will fail to anticipate the demands that their children will make on them (as is, in fact, common for the general population) and they will treat their children 'like dolls'. In reality, this happens infrequently. Nevertheless, these fears and doubts might be abated if parenting education programmes were introduced to students at school as part of the national curriculum.

Rights to Service

Parents need to be informed of their rights in terms that they understand. Such information should include their rights as outlined in the Children Act 1989 presently in booklet form (DoH, 1991, 1995a).
    Parents are entitled:

- to receive agency support if they are deemed to be a family with 'special needs';
- to seek representation from the official solicitor in court matters;
- to have specialist support and individualised training programmes to enhance their parenting capabilities to the full. (Ideally, any specialist support should include expert assessment from learning disabilities services of their past, present and future capacity to parent.)
- to be informed about the conditions of admission to a service before entering any such programme. (Some parents, especially those who have learning disabilities within the borderline range, do not accept that classification and will not accept involvement from learning disability services or visits from professionals to their home.)
- to have their views respected and taken into account when decisions are made about their child.

PROGRAMMES OF SUPPORT
General Support

Often, when parents request support in their day-to-day parenting they simply require a friend, neighbour or relative with whom they can exchange ideas or from whom they can receive guidance on decision-making matters.

- Typically, such support is not available to parents with learning disabilities who report that they are socially isolated. Often, they cannot identify anyone who could help them. In our experience, social isolation and dysfunctional relationships are the most commonly reported problems cited by parents with learning disabilities.
- In particular, families report difficulties with the development and maintenance of relationships, and disengaging from inter-family fighting. Parents who describe being 'stuck' in family feuds or who are at odds with their neighbours or friends often resolve the situation by moving away from the source of the problem to live in another area. Often, this temporary resolution results in the family being cut off from

services for an interim period before they register with a new doctor, dentist, nursery and/or school in their new locality.

• Some parents are relocated in inferior housing because they were in a hurry to move. During this stressful period, children may stretch their parent's coping skills even further if they become distressed or anxious as a result of the disruption in care and change in routine. On reflection, many professionals recognise that family stresses could have been avoided, or the impact lessened in some situations, if only parents had been provided with some support and guidance at an earlier stage.

• Studies show that learning disabled parents are capable of acquiring effective interpersonal skills and alternative coping strategies (so crucial to family adaptation and day-to-day coping) if they are given training. Sadly, a major obstacle facing some parents is that they have been so 'bruised' by agency intervention in the past that they will not (or cannot) accept such help when it is available.

Specific Support

Families also benefit from intensive individualised instruction and help with nutrition, household management, and parenting skills along with persistent coordination of day-to-day routines. Simple, effective techniques developed by specialists from the learning disabilities and children's services are found to be the most beneficial in teaching parents with learning disabilities (Mandeville, 1992).

• Training needs to be set at the right level of comprehension and understanding. In many cases, parents seem to comprehend questions and advice, but their responses are biased towards answers in the affirmative. Often, parents have no understanding of the terms 'self-esteem', 'inoculations', 'child development' and 'routines'. Yet they appear to be familiar with terms such as 'respite care', 'supervision/care orders', 'child protection register' and 'freeing for adoption'.

• Training methods need to be based on task analysis, repetition, modelling, guided practice and the use of positive contingencies to reinforce learning. Verbal instructions will not be enough by themselves.

• Written instructions will need to reflect the reading age of parents (on average around the 7–9 year age level). A dictionary of commonly used words of terms, accompanied by symbols relevant to the parents' situation, can aid understanding.

• It is helpful to offer parents video- or audio-taped recordings of training sessions to enable them to play these back at their leisure to aid learning and to ensure that information is not lost or forgotten.

ASSESSMENTS OF PARENTING

Identifying Parents with Learning Disabilities

- Sometimes parents will let us know that they 'can't learn' or 'can't remember' simple information such as their child's birthday, address or doctor's name. More often than not, parents are reluctant to highlight their difficulties and avoid seeking help when they need it. Many parents have stored negative memories from their past when they were at school or receiving specialist services and they were made to feel bad about their learning disabilities.
- Mild learning disabilities are not easy to identify at first because the parent may seem to be managing. It may take some time before professionals realise that parents are experiencing difficulties in recognising their child's needs and that they do not have all the necessary skills to attend to their child appropriately. A simple screening tool is the Einstein Parent Screen Instrument (Kaminer and Cohen, 1983) and the Maternal Profile (Tymchuk and Keltner, 1991).

Where do we Start?

- It is most useful to help families by viewing the family as a system—made up of several people who interrelate and function well together (or not, as the case may be). We know that in order for the family to function effectively, most of the physical, emotional, cognitive and social needs of each individual and the family as a whole should be met.
- As we get to know the family better it becomes easier to carry out an assessment for the purpose of identifying the family's strengths and needs.
- Together with the family we can then develop a set of goals, both short term and long term, to improve their parenting skills and the quality of their family life (Heighway, 1992).
- Assessments need to be completed on parents and children individually as well assessing their total functioning as a family unit (McGaw and Sturmey, 1994).

Does IQ Determine the Quality of Parenting?

No, although the research literature indicates that above a critical level of 60, there is no clear relationship between parenting competency and IQ, but minimal levels vary across studies.

- Below IQ 60 there appears to be a positive correlation between parental competency and IQ although some studies have not supported this finding. In our experience (Special Parenting Service), parents with an IQ of 55/60 or below are less likely to succeed in their parenting than those parents functioning at a higher level.
- Other factors, such as the parent's education, their life-skills (practical and social skills in particular), their exposure to good parental role models during childhood, and their access to positive day-to-day support will be major contributors affecting their parental competency.

All assessments need to be carried out sensitively, at the pace of the client, using appropriate tests and methods. Many parents fear that failure on such tests will result in the removal of their children. They will require plenty of reassurance that this will not be the case.

DO STANDARD PARENTING ASSESSMENTS APPLY TO PARENTS WITH LEARNING DISABILITIES?

The same standards of parenting apply, as laid down by the Children Act 1989. When the local authority has reasonable cause to suspect that a child is suffering or is likely to suffer significant harm they (or the NSPCC) are duty bound to assess families at risk, in accordance with the Department of Health (DoH, 1988) 'orange book' guidance. Such assessments are complicated because no two families are alike in their structure, style of parenting and personality.

Often there exists a tension in deciding whether a child is in need (as defined in Section 17 of the Children Act) as opposed to in need of protection (as defined in Section 47 of the Children Act). A list of risk factors can give workers a false sense of security while failing to protect children whose families do not appear to exhibit these particular risk factors. Professionals involved in such an investigation should follow inter-agency child protection procedures (as laid down by the Area Child Protection Committee for their district). Guidance is offered within these procedures regarding the stages of investigation and the role of parents and should guide workers to:

- regularly discuss their actions with their line managers and colleagues as appropriate (seeking guidance from different specialisms as necessary);
- avoid managing suspected child abuse on their own;
- be aware that their own experiences and feelings will influence their work;

- keep contemporaneous records of their actions throughout the investigation and assessment process;
- ensure that the family receives appropriate information (level of understanding and format) and support, regarding the investigation, assessment and outcome.

In general (Dowdney and Skuse, 1993), assessments of parenting take the form of (a) global assessments, (b) observational assessments and (c) reports or indications of failures in parenting according to the current threshold criteria on abuse (DoH, 1995b). Confusion results from the proliferation of assessments and checklists used by professionals, many of which are not standardised on learning disabled populations and are therefore invalid and unreliable in their interpretation. Difficulties arise as to whether it is the *qualitative element* of a parenting task which is crucial or the *frequency of its delivery*. Standard assessments, even those adopted by professionals who take a holistic approach in the assessment of family relationships and functioning, often fail to answer the classic question asked of assessors: *'What is the capacity of parents to learn?'*

How do we Assess the Capacity of Parents to Acquire New Skills?

Intelligence assessments alone will not determine the quality of parental competence or a parent's capacity to acquire new skills. A practical approach to assessment is one involving a global assessment of parent's functioning including measurement of the parent's life skills, academic skills (numeracy, literacy) and decision-making/problem-solving skills. Currently, the Special Parenting Service is developing an assessment based on this approach (see Checklist 2, Part 1).

Decision-making and Problem-solving Skills

Parents are required to engage in multiple decision making and problem solving at a personal, interpersonal and community level each day. Typically, taking care of a child requires parents to make decisions involving child-care routines, household tasks, time-management, acquiring resources, developing relationships and making choices about general lifestyle. People with learning disabilities often struggle with:

- comprehending the requirements of a problem;
- isolating any relevant factors while disregarding irrelevant information and acquiring problem-solving strategies;

- dealing with problems in a random trial-and-error manner, rather than using systematic planning approaches;
- motivational, attentional and memory difficulties.

People with learning disabilities have shown that they *can acquire many of these skills after training*. However, they need to be offered the opportunity to engage in such training before judgements about their capacity to function at a higher level of parental competency are made. One approach which is useful involves assessing parental knowledge/skills/ practice. Not all parents understand the need to acquire and practice skills, or how such skills as those given below directly, or indirectly, affect their child's care, health and development.

Knowledge

For example, some parents are unaware that poor time-telling skills will mean that they may have difficulties working out feeding schedules with their baby; meeting their child from school on time; and organising their day efficiently. Assessments used for the purpose of establishing parental knowledge need to include responses to visually presented activities such as pictures, videos, vignettes or real-life situations. Teaching methods must be presented at an appropriate level of understanding for the parent.

Skills

Once parental knowledge has been established it cannot be assumed that such knowledge will necessarily transfer to skill acquisition without training. Studies have found that even when training did produce sizeable increases in knowledge this did not automatically transfer to increases in parenting skills in the home environment. Tymchuk and Andron (1992) provided training to three mothers with learning disabilities on categories of home dangers, ways to remedy those dangers and how to deal with emergencies with the eldest children in the family. Training increased knowledge of mothers and children regarding dangers and safety; however, no improvement in home safety was observed until specific training was provided. Evidently, generalisation of learnt skills to new situations needs to be assessed by direct observation on a day-to-day basis.

Practice

Maintaining and generalising skills at the right level of delivery and frequency is consistently reported as problematic for parents with learning disabilities. A common observation made of parents is that they do not practise a skill to the required frequency (e.g. feeding the child three meals a day, instead of one) and/or standard (the food is fed to the child in a rough, hurried manner). In order to promote generalisation, training programmes must include systematic strategies to enable the person to use the skills appropriately in everyday life. Considering the degree of similarity/dissimilarity between the teaching and living situations is essential. Emphasis should be placed on the variables affecting maintenance and generalisation, something which needs careful consideration (e.g. a parent is much more likely to continue preparing different foods and nutritious meals if the child enjoys it and tells her so). Often, when skills are not maintained or generalised, despite intensive training, it is because parents are expending time and energy on other problems in their lives which they are prioritising.

Other Factors Affecting Parental Practice

Many parents with learning disabilities suffer a multitude of problems in addition to their learning disability which might impede the parental practice. These problems often include drug/alcohol use, poor emotional and physical health, childhood history of abuse and neglect, relationship difficulties and bereavement (often following the loss of a child). Many of the problems also result from poverty: poor diet and nutrition, damp housing with inadequate heating and ventilation, inadequate clothing and no transportation. Assessing for parents' adaptation and general coping will be indicative of practical coping and the ability of parents to balance the needs of all family members. However, parents' ability to cope with stress and adaptation to new situations may be dependent upon mediating variables that buffer or exacerbate stress. Parents may need help to access counselling or therapeutic services before they are able to attend to the requirements of a training programme.

HOW TO MEET THE NEEDS OF BOTH THE CHILD(REN) AND PARENT(S)

Meeting the needs of both parents and children concurrently, is problematic. Difficulties about 'who is the client' perpetuates discussions among professionals and service managers. While the Children Act 1989 requires child protection and support services to work in partnership with families hand-in-hand, in reality, much depends upon the role of the individuals, the agency they work for and their remit. Some agencies (Social Services,

NSPCC, Police) carry statutory obligations under the Children Act 1989 to ensure that a child is not at risk from 'significant harm' from the parenting. *The greatest risk presenting children of parents with learning disabilities is that of unintentional neglect* (Tymchuk and Andron, 1992).

Many parents do not know what to do to improve their parenting. However, not all professionals approach the task in the same way across localities (Booth and Booth, 1994). An overzealous approach to child protection usually works to the detriment of the child and the family, often leaving feelings of hostility and animosity towards those involved. In contrast, adult services or advocacy services whose primary remit is to support the parent(s) first may feel obliged to place their client's needs first. Assumptions can be made erroneously by professionals that children need to remain with their natural family, whatever the cost. The risks to the children of parents with learning disabilities should not be underestimated, as was seen in the tragic case of Jasmine Beckford. In reality, there is often just a thin line dividing those professionals who, for whatever reason, prioritise the need of the child or parent before that of the other.

- Families fare best when all parties work towards the needs of the family as a whole, always bearing in mind that the health and safety of the child is paramount.
- The stage of engagement with families is crucial. Parents are much more likely to accept professional support during pregnancy or following the birth than later when parents' first experience of services will involve a formal assessment of parental competency because a crises has occurred and support is offered to them as part of case conference recommendations.

PARENTS WHO ARE UNABLE TO COPE

Occasionally, parents with learning disabilities feel overwhelmed by the demands of parenting, despite intensive support from services.

1. Many difficulties arise when children are around 7 or 8 years old and they start to challenge their parents' authority and decision making. This is most likely to occur when the older children are extremely intelligent and they attempt to parent their siblings (described as the 'Huck Finn Syndrome'). Families can benefit from therapeutic input from child and family guidance clinics or parenting services to help identify roles within the family and to give guidance on individual coping responses.

2. Sadly, some parents struggle on for some time, attempting to manage disruptive behaviours and the multiple demands of a family, before making the decision to place their child for long-term fostering or adoption. Other parents have this decision made on their behalf by the statutory agencies, for the same reasons. Sometimes parents appear relieved if the topic of alternative care is brought up in discussion as a possible option (after all else has been tried). Typically, parents will seek reassurance that they are not bad or unloving parents because they have decided to allow someone else to bring up their child.

3. Once a decision about long-term care of a child is made, professionals will consider the interests of the child to be paramount, before that of the parent. A welfare checklist will apply to check that the criteria for fostering or adoption is met and the courts and adoption agencies will strive to ensure that this process will not prejudice the welfare of the child in any way. However, a number of issues do arise:

(a) Children placed for adoption will either have the consent of the parent or guardian, or be under a placement order (DoH/DEE, 1996). Parents with learning disabilities may not fully understand this legal process and will benefit from counselling before giving parental consent to placement at two distinct stages, each requiring separate consent to be given. A placement order will be made in situations where the agency considers that adoption is in the child's best interests but the parents or guardian is not prepared to give his or her consent to placement.

(b) Court proceedings can become complex and lengthy before the case is finally heard. In part, the delay may arise because a parent is identified as having a 'learning disability' and a proliferation of expert assessments are sought to give opinion on
  - the parent's ability and standard of child care,
  - the appropriateness of past, present and future services, and
  - the capacity of the parent to raise his or her parental competency skills under the guidance of specialist services.

Often delays in the proceedings do impact on the child's health and well-being and this process can contravene the 'no delay principle'.

(c) Courts often seek expert opinion regarding the ability of parents with learning disabilities to engage in contact with a child who will be placed in long-term fostering or adoption. Where attachment and bonding between a child and his or her birth parent is already established, open contact (usually conditional) is recommended as a means of enhancing a child's sense of identity and emotional permanency. However, clinical judgements have to be made regarding the parent's ability to be altruistic during contact sessions when they need to reassure their child that it is okay for him or her to be loved by the new family. Most parents find this process exceptionally painful. Much will depend upon the coping strategies of parents and their ability to place their child's needs before their own. Some learning disabled parents are able to do this well after guidance and subject to careful monitoring of the situation during or after contact. Contact should not be recommended where there is considerable doubt voiced about the parents' integrity or understanding of their role during contact.

4. When it becomes evident to parents that they will not be caring for their children in the future they will be entitled to a counselling service and information regarding alternatives to adoption. They are also entitled to the support of a social worker (not previously allocated to their child) to advise on their options and role within the court proceedings. Learning disabilities services and citizens advocacy services are well placed for simplifying and structuring information passed to parents during this stressful situation.

ROLE OF HEALTH PROFESSIONAL, HOSPITAL STAFF AND PRIMARY HEALTH CARE WORKERS

Most health professionals, including nurses, have had no training about the needs of mothers with learning disabilities. Often interventions rely on the parent's ability to read and to apply instructions in various circumstances. Medical terminology such as 'sterilisation', 'obstetrics', 'forceps', etc., is an added barrier to understanding for many parents with learning disabilities. This situation has been recognised by some maternity services (National Childbirth Trust, 1995). While there is much variation in the quantity and intensity of public health services and primary care available to families across countries, common characteristics include the expectation that services will be specific and brief. Good practice occurs when:

* GPs, community midwives and health visitors work closely alongside parents (as part of a core team of professionals across learning disabilities and children's specialisms) especially during the early stages of pregnancy. Preparing the mother for the birth and encouraging her to attend ante-natal classes is vital. Research indicates that learning disabled mothers are poor attenders and vulnerable to hospital admission resulting from medical complications.
* An alternative approach is to offer parents pregnancy, babycare and parentcraft videos (which are available from most Health Promotion

Departments) for use in the privacy of their own home. *The Special Parenting Service found this approach particularly useful with one mother who had a history of poor bottle preparation and weaning skills who consistently failed to attend parentcraft classes when she was pregnant with her third child. The worker compiled different sections from several videos to illustrate the bottle feeding sequence and weaning tasks to the mother. We encouraged the mother to describe some of the frozen frames as a means of drawing her attention to each of these skills in turn. We used video to record the mother's progress as she learnt the necessary skills over a period of time and used this technique to provide positive feedback to her.* In general, commercial videos tend to be pitched at a 'middle-class' audience and need simplification in this way for parents with learning disabilities.

- Preparatory visits to the delivery suite can be useful so that parents might familiarise themselves with the equipment in advance of the birth. Couples will benefit from being given the chance to hold a real baby and to carry out a few simple tasks such as preparing bottles. Unfamiliar hospital rules and procedures need to be explained to them clearly. Many parents with learning disabilities have poor social skills and do not form friendships easily, which often results in a feeling of isolation during their stay in hospital (see Checklist 3).

MULTI-AGENCY APPROACH

Often when a parent asks for help or a need is identified, this results either in poor uptake by professionals or a proliferation of programmes resulting from multiple agency involvement. Confusion can arise from a lack of centralised service coordination across professionals whose roles and boundaries are unclear. Parents who receive contradictory information from 'over-servicing' may cease to participate in remediation plans. As a result, their children may miss the external support needed by the family to ensure adequate childhood development. Parents with learning disabilities are often interpreted as non-compliant or dependent, while their intellectual limitations are not always acknowledged or understood. In reality, the service system poses many potential obstacles. Providing help to parents in a way that is useful to them should be a requirement for the services families seek from any system. Characteristics of a more desirable system include:

- *Service coordination.* Barriers do exist between health professionals and other agencies on service delivery in part because of competition arising from resource constraints and the health/social care divide. Agencies can become so entrenched in their differing opinions on childcare matters and resource issues that the child almost appears to be forgotten in the legal battle and (in the most difficult situations) is eventually made a ward of court until the situation is resolved. Legal confrontations like this leave agencies feeling 'bruised' and tensions perpetuate between professionals for some time into the future.

- *Specialist multi-disciplinary teams.* Such teams help to override inter-agency differences as the same goals, philosophy, protocol and structure are adhered to by all, regardless of specialism. The Special Parenting Service comprises psychologists, occupational therapist, clinical nurse specialist and developmental psychologist. Each therapist manages his or her own case load, while also sharing specialist skills and knowledge in the running of groups, development of resources and across training.
- *Sensitive and informed professional/client relationships.* Communication between professionals and adults with learning disabilities needs to be a two-way process facilitated through regular core-group meetings involving parents and their children. Information needs to be worded (and recorded) in terms that are understandable to the parents. No one agency should take on all of the work and no one voice should become persistently dominant. The rights of parents and children need to be observed throughout this process. Where there are difficulties, parents should be represented or supported by an advocate, friend or relative upon their request.
- *Service information.* Services need to advertise what they do in terms that are understandable to parents with learning disabilities (e.g. video, leaflets, posters). Parents need the opportunity to refer themselves and to choose between the services on offer (in terms of practical help) and the specialisms (statutory agencies, learning disabilities teams, children's services, adult mental health services). Studies indicate that many parents with learning disabilities have either been court referred, referred after leaving an institution, or school referred after completion of a special education class.
- *Range of services.* Ideally a range of comprehensive, individualised, and continuing services should be provided to families across different settings.
  - Group work is often the most common form of service delivery in community-based mainstream family support services for parents with learning disabilities.
  - Service providers need to also offer home-based programmes for many parents who require a different (or additional) approach to training.
  - Some parents require programmes to include specific task analysis, with longer and more frequent training sessions in order to acquire, maintain and generalise new skills. Such training needs to include

instruction adapted to the individual learning style of the parent, problem-solving support, and organisational and instrumental help with tasks that the parents cannot master independently.

- *Community support.* A concern often voiced by families is their sense of social isolation. Parents want their children to have playmates in the neighbourhood, they want the acceptance and friendship of their neighbours, and they want a valued role in their extended family. While these issues have been identified as important to families, their formal support services are not set up to help with this concern. Multi-agencies need to identify who among them are best placed to help parents build bridges with their family, neighbourhood and community systems as outlined in Checklist 2 (Part 2).

Evidently, the needs of parents with learning disabilities and their families are multi-complex and changeable. As their children's needs change, so do the demands on the parents. While the move away from institutionalised living has brought a catalyst of opportunities and change for people with learning disabilities, there remains a 'tendency . . to present independent living as a miraculous formula for all persons with (mild) mental retardation asking for help' (Van Hove and Broekaert, 1995). In reality, families often report that independent living means that they are marginalised from mainstream services which they then have difficulties accessing. Providing the appropriate services to families who have long-term multiple needs remains a challenge which still needs to be addressed.

KEY POINTS

1. There are an estimated 250,000 parents with learning disabilities in the UK. These families have multiple needs and services lack the training, guidelines or funding required.
2. Many parents with learning disabilities need specialised help to acquire parenting skills and live independently in the community.
3. Programmes of support must be tailored to the individual needs of the parent(s) and must use specialised training strategies.
4. Assessment of parenting must view the family as a whole as well as the individual needs of parents and children. Checklist 2 (Part 1) shows the main areas of a global assessment of a parent's functioning.
5. Meeting the needs of both parents and children concurrently is problematic and requires close working between all professionals involved.
6. The needs of parents who are unable to cope, despite intensive support, must be identified and met in the long and very painful process of court proceedings, long-term fostering and adoption.

7. Most primary health care professionals have no training with parents with learning disabilities. Examples of good practice are described for ante-natal preparation and early parenting.
8. Parents with learning disabilities are marginalised in mainstream services. A multi-agency approach which provides accessible help, training and support to these parents is essential.

REFERENCES

Starred entry indicates recommended reading

Booth, T. and Booth, W. (1994) *Parenting under Pressure.* Open University Press.
Department of Health (DoH) (1988) *Protecting Children: A Guide for Social Workers undertaking a Comprehensive Assessment.* HMSO, London.
Department of Health (DoH) (1991) *The Children Act and Local Authorities: A Guide for Parents.* HMSO, London.
Department of Health (DoH) (1995a) *The Children Act and The Courts: A Guide for Children and Young People.* HMSO, London.
Department of Health (DoH) (1995b) *Child Protection: Messages from Research.* HMSO, London.
Department of Health and Department of Education and Employment (DoH/DEE) (1996) *Children's Services Planning: Guidance and Interagency Working.* HMSO, London.
Dowdney, L. and Skuse, D. (1993) Parenting provided by adults with mental retardation. *Journal of Child Psychology and Psychiatry,* **34**(1), 25–47.
Heighway, S. (1992) *Helping Parents Parent.* Wisconsin Council on Developmental Disabilities, USA.
Kaminer, R. and Cohen, H. (1983) Intellectually limited mothers. In *Developmental Handicaps, Prevention and Treatment.* American Association of University Affiliated Programs for Persons with Developmental Disabilities, Washington, DC.
Mandeville, H. (1992) *Building the Foundation: Public Policy Issues in Supported Parenting.* Wisconsin Council on Developmental Disabilities, USA.
McGaw, S. and Sturmey, P. (1994) Assessing parents with learning disabilities. The Parental Skills Model. *Child Abuse Review,* **3**, 36–51.
McGaw S. (1996) Services for parents with learning disabilities. *Tizard Learning Disability Review,* **1**, 1.
National Childbirth Trust (1995) *Birth Words: Some Pregnancy and Childbirth Words and What they Mean.* NCT Maternity Sales.
Tymchuk, A.J. and Andron, L. (1992) Project parenting: child interactional training with mothers who are mentally handicapped. *Mental Handicap Research,* **5**, 1.
Tymchuk, A.J. and Keltner, B. (1991) Advantage profiles: a tool for health care professionals working with parents with mental retardation. *Comprehensive Pediatric Nursing,* **14**, 155–161.
Van Hove, G. and Broekaert, E. (1995) Independent living of persons with mental retardation in Flanders: a survey of research data. *European Journal of Mental Disability,* **2**(8), 38–46.
*Whitman, B. and Accardo, P. (1990) *When a Parent is Mentally Retarded.* Paul Brookes, Baltimore.

9

CULTURAL ISSUES

Zenobia Nadirshaw

This chapter offers a framework for understanding the lives and experiences of black and minority ethnic people with learning disabilities as an oppressed and doubly disadvantaged group in society—in terms of the processes by which these groups and their carers find themselves in subordinate positions and at the receiving end of little or no appropriate services. It also offers a series of recommendations and the way forward.

THE LANGUAGE OF RACE, CULTURE AND ETHNICITY

There has been a marked increase in use of the terms 'race', 'culture' and 'ethnicity' in the health literature. However, there is evidence of a progressive lack of understanding of these concepts and inconsistency in the way these terms are used. It is essential to clarify these concepts from the start, and helpful definitions are provided by Fernando (1991).

- The term *race* was used in the sixteenth century as a sense of lineage. In the nineteenth century, race as lineage referred to groups of people connected by common descent or origin. Later, with the onset of Darwinism, race was seen as subspecies and, finally, sociological theories of race led to the notion of races as populations. Today, all these ideas exist together, creating confusion in current thinking about race.

Adults with Learning Disabilities. Edited by J. O'Hara and A. Sperlinger.
© 1997 John Wiley & Sons Ltd.

- *Culture* may be described as the shared history, practices, beliefs and values of people constituting a social group. Because of its lack of precision, culture is often confused with race. These two concepts are combined and absorbed into that of ethnicity, which is seen as a term which avoids the pejorative meaning attributed to the word race and the limitations implicit in using the term culture.
- *Ethnicity* is a term which lacks precision but alludes to the definition of both cultural and racial groups. The members of an 'ethnic group' are thought by themselves, and/or others, to share a common origin and to share important segments of a common culture. The bonds that bind together people of an ethnic group are often not clear cut. They are not definable in terms of physical appearance (race) or social similarity (culture) alone. The overriding feature of an ethnic group is the sense of belonging together that the individuals feel. It is, basically, a psychological feeling.

'Race', 'culture' and 'ethnicity' are difficult to disentangle in practical situations and there is great confusion in many areas of thought—from politics to scientific research. As Table 1 shows, race is primarily physical, culture is sociological and ethnicity is psychological.

Table 1:   Race, culture and ethnicity

	Characterised by	Determined by	Perceived as
Race	Physical appearance	Genetic ancestry	Permanent (genetic/ biological)
Culture	Behaviour attitudes	Upbringing choice	Changeable (assimilation) acculturation
Ethnicity	Sense of belonging Group identity	Social pressures Psychological need	Partially changeable

From Fernando (1991); reproduced with the permission of Macmillan Press Ltd.

THE BLACK AND MINORITY ETHNIC COMMUNITY OF GREAT BRITAIN

The presence of black and minority ethnic communities in the UK has a long history. Recent research has shown that these communities face inequalities, discrimination and disadvantage in almost every aspect of their lives. For example, they are more likely to: live in run-down inner city areas and in substandard housing; be found in semi-skilled and unskilled jobs; be disproportionately affected by unemployment; and be economically worse off than their white peers. There is also evidence of discrimination in education and in health, where black and minority ethnic people have poorer health experiences and less access to health care (DES, 1985; Pearson, 1985; McNought, 1984; Ahmed and Atkin, 1996). There is a danger of emphasising people's needs in terms of religion, customs and traditions and overlooking their basic needs for decent housing, access to health care and assistance to claim benefits.

According to the 1991 Census (see Table 2), black and minority ethnic people constitute just over 3 million (6%) of the total population of the United Kingdom. The 1991 Census 'missed' about one million people, half of them young adults (Soni-Raleigh, 1995). Under-numeration was proportionally greater among multi-ethnic populations, particularly among young, black men.

Table 2: The ethnic composition of the population of Great Britain (not allowing for the under-numeration)

Ethnic group	Number (000s)	%
White	51 874	94.5
Black Caribbean	500	0.9
Black African	212	0.4
Black other	178	0.3
Indian	840	1.5
Pakistani	477	0.9
Bangladeshi	163	0.3
Chinese	157	0.3
Other Asian	198	0.4
Other	290	0.5
Great Britain	54 889	100.0

Source: 1991 Census

PREVALENCE OF LEARNING DISABILITIES IN BLACK AND MINORITY ETHNIC PEOPLE

There is no national information on the prevalence of learning disabilities among black and minority ethnic communities. Local studies, however, have provided some useful but controversial information.

In a study of Asian learning disabled people living in two metropolitan boroughs of north-west England, Azmi et al. (1996) found the prevalence of severe learning disabilities in children and young adults between 5 and

34 years of age to be approximately *three times greater* in the Asian community than in the non-Asian community. This picture is consistent with the relatively young age profile of the Asian population as a whole. Comparing these figures with the Sheffield case register confirms, at least on a small scale, an increased prevalence of learning disabilities (including severe learning disabilities) among the Asian communities. Need and demand for services for adults with learning disabilities will sharply increase, as the population of Asian adults is expected to more than double over the next 10 years. No such figures exist nationally for the Black, Afro-Caribbean communities in Britain.

Baxter *et al.* (1990) documented the long-running debate about the causes of the apparently higher prevalence of learning disabilities in these communities. Factors which have been suggested as specifically relevant are a higher incidence of congenital rubella syndrome and a higher frequency of first cousin marriages within the Asian communities. The latter is particularly emotive and controversial. First cousin marriages may increase the risk of autosomal conditions, but many of these conditions are rare, so that 50% consanguinity would be required before a significant number would appear in the population. Furthermore, in the few studies which have carefully explored the association between consanguinity and the incidence of congenital malformations, a significantly high correlation has not been established.

Other factors which have been used to explain the relatively higher than expected proportion of black and minority ethnic infants, young children and young adults with learning disabilities include the general effects of social and educational deprivation which are known to be associated with the prevalence of mild and moderate learning disabilities. For example: poverty, diet, effects of poor housing, environmental pollution, lack of knowledge about, and unfamiliarity with, methods of genetic counselling and ante-natal services, and poorer maternal health care.

HEALTH AND SOCIAL CARE POLICIES AND PRACTICES AND BLACK AND MINORITY ETHNIC PEOPLE

Both the Government White Paper *Caring for People* and *The Health of the Nation* document clearly recognise the importance of race, ethnicity and culture. However, the impact of these policies on black and minority ethnic people with learning disabilities is negligible. Their needs are still being classified as 'special' requiring 'specialist' and segregated services which remain marginalised from mainstream services, policy making and discussion.

Black and minority ethnic people with learning disabilities using health care services are disadvantaged as a result of discrimination and culturally inappropriate forms of care and service provision. They are *doubly disadvantaged* by:

- The *interchangeable use of the terms race, culture and ethnicity*, which leads to either the perception of black culture, ethnicity and race as unitary, or an assumption that knowing about these different cultures and races solves the problem of equity, fairness and availability of services to this client group (Smaje, 1995).
- The *'colour-blind' approach*, which implies that everyone—irrespective of race, colour, class, ethnicity and religious background—should receive similar services. As a result, the needs of black and minority ethnic people with learning disabilities are either ignored, or unacknowledged, or assumed to be the same as their white peers.
- The *prevailing cultural bias of services*, which influences practices, procedures and policies. These may be very obvious and include a mission statement from a particular religious perspective or political belief. Rather than have their specific cultural, ethnic and religious diversity respected and enhanced by services, black and minority ethnic people with learning disabilities often have other people's values imposed on them. This alienates people who do not 'fit' and the unmet needs of these people are then classified as 'special'. The needs of black learning disabled groups are not special, only different. Services must recognise and positively value this 'different-ness'.
- The *'victim blaming' approach* by service providers locates the problem in the client and/or the culture and results in the creation of a black pathology (Rocheron, 1980). The view is taken that it is not the services that are inadequate, it is the people.
- The *unresponsiveness of community care legislation* to black and minority ethnic communities has led to an increasing dissatisfaction and cynicism about the helping professions by black and minority ethnic people with learning disabilities and by their carers. This is particularly so of assessment and care management (Nadirshaw, 1991, and in press). Lack of information about the process, total dependence on professionals to complete the needs assessment, and little knowledge about their rights to satisfactory alternatives (including the complaints procedures and appeals process) are common.
- The *perpetuation of concepts of 'differences' and 'different-ness'* based on the visible difference of colour. This results in: being seen and treated as of 'less value' than their white counterparts with learning disabilities; being subjected to negative and discriminatory attitudes and beliefs;

rejection and stigmatisation within both health care services and the general community; and denial of a positive black racial and cultural identity (Downer, personal communication).

CHARACTERISTICS AND CIRCUMSTANCES OF BLACK AND MINORITY ETHNIC FAMILIES WITH LEARNING DISABLED PEOPLE

No national data are available about the characteristics and circumstances of black and minority ethnic families in Britain. Azmi *et al*'s (1996) study provides a picture of Asian families caring for a learning disabled person of 14 years or older in two metropolitan boroughs in north-west England. A similar profile was found in a survey in Bradford (ADAPT, 1993) and reflects a national picture of a significant amount of 'hidden' need among Asian communities. In the 54 families studied, almost all the main carers were mothers, but in two families the main carer was the spouse of the person with learning disabilities. Ten families (19%) contained two, three or four people with learning disabilities, almost always siblings. The main findings were:

- *Significant language barriers to communication between Asian carers and English-speaking services.* Ninety-five per cent of the carers had been born outside the UK, and only a minority could speak or write English.
- *High levels of economic hardship and social deprivation.* Sixty-nine per cent of families had no full-time wage earner, and half of the 54 families studied were on income support.
- *Little evidence to suggest that informal networks were available to meet the considerable support needs of families.* When asked to whom they would turn in a crisis, twenty-one per cent of carers did not know of anyone.
- *Despite the need for formal support, it was not readily available.* Fifty-three per cent of the people with learning disabilities had challenging or 'problem' behaviours and one in four displayed seriously challenging behaviour (physical aggression to others or self-injury). Asked to comment on the quality of services received, forty-one per cent of carers reported that they were not receiving enough services to be able to comment.
- *The lack of either formal or informal support had overstretched the resources of many mothers.* Many carers reported substantial stress-related health problems and eighty per cent reported such high levels of stress that they were at risk of developing mental health problems. This degree of

stress is higher than that reported in any other study of carers for people with learning disabilities.
- *The experience of racial abuse* from either people in the local neighbourhoods, other service users or staff.

ACCESS TO, AND UPTAKE OF, SERVICES FOR PEOPLE WITH LEARNING DISABILITIES BY ASIAN COMMUNITIES

Information from a range of studies has shown that:

- The majority of services are taken up by only a small percentage of Asian service users. Most are not aware of what is available. Residential and respite services are markedly under-used.
- There is a lack of interpreting services or staff who speak the family's first language.
- Services are culturally inappropriate, with a lack of understanding of cultural and dietary needs.
- Racial discrimination exists within services.

When asked what they need in services, Asian carers and service users identify the following:

- The need for services to reflect the importance of gender with Asian cultures. For example, ensuring that personal care tasks are conducted by someone of the same gender, providing appropriate day services (which are accepted by their community) for Asian women.
- Services which ensure that staff are sensitive to cultural issues and Asian staff at all levels within all agencies.
- Services which are culturally appropriate—for example, meeting dietary needs, or acknowledging religious festivals and holidays.
- Flexible and sensitive support to Asian carers, including siblings or relatives of the person with learning disabilities.

It is a curious comment on our services that the preference of same gender staff to carry out intimate forms of personal care and support—a moral code which exists to a large extent in all communities—is portrayed as a religious and cultural requirement when working with black and minority ethnic people. This approach is unhelpful as it suggests 'different' or 'special' needs and the impression of an additional burden on existing resources (Baxter, 1996).

ACCESS TO, AND UPTAKE OF, PRIMARY HEALTH CARE SERVICES BY BLACK AND MINORITY ETHNIC COMMUNITIES

Information from surveys suggest that:

• The majority of carers are aware of GPs, dentists, hospital services, opticians and social workers. In contrast, only a minority are aware of the services of specialist community learning disability teams or home helps.
• Approximately 80% of Indian, Pakistani and Bangladeshi adults are registered with an Asian GP (Rudak, 1994).
• There is evidence that black and minority ethnic communities have a higher rate of GP consultation than their white counterparts. GPs are seen as the linchpin of health care provision and the primary health care team are the most frequently contacted professionals by individuals with learning disability (Evans *et al.*, 1994).
• People from both Asian and Chinese communities tend to present to primary health care services with somatic symptoms of psychological distress. Evidence suggests that this is largely due to the cultural rules governing the expression of distress and that GPs may fail to recognise the psychological basis for the symptoms presented.
• Traditional healers are often consulted by some communities either in place of, or as well as, conventional medicine. The advantage for the patients include: freedom of communication; time in which to explain their symptoms; and treatment which accords with their own perceptions of ideal health care.

ATTITUDES AND BELIEFS ABOUT LEARNING DISABILITY IN BLACK AND MINORITY ETHNIC COMMUNITIES

Prejudiced ideas about black and minority ethnic parents give little attention to what is, in fact, a natural and universal response to having a child who is born with a disability (Shah, 1992). The way in which parents learn about their child's disability, and their knowledge of their child's condition, are important determinants of their attitudes and beliefs about learning disabilities. These attitudes and beliefs, in turn, influence their aspirations for their son or daughter and their expectations and use of services.

• Typically, parents have very little knowledge or understanding of their son's or daughter's disability and do not recall having a medical explanation of his or her condition. Most have had inadequate coun-selling at the identification of the disability, ineffective education about the prognosis for their son or daughter and little help or support.

- Many black and minority ethnic parents feel that their religion has something important to say about learning disabilities and that religious faith has helped them to cope.
- Parental religious involvement may provide an explanation of, and attitude towards, their son's or daughter's learning disabilities. For example: the Hindu belief in the concept of 'Karma' provides a way of understanding learning disabilities and a sense of resignation or acceptance (Fatimilehin and Nadirshaw, 1994); Chinese people appeal to fate and use a coping strategy of forbearance, seeking supernatural power, and praying to ancestors (Cheng and So-kum Tang, 1995); Middle Eastern cultures regard disability as punishment from heaven, emanating from the spirits or caused by an evil eye (Aminidav and Weller, 1995). People who hold these beliefs are less likely to expect progress from a person with a learning disability.
- The notion of curability and the search for a cure are important in some communities.
- Securing a marriage partner for a daughter or son with learning disabilities, in some Asian communities: serves to provide comfort to parents that, after their death, someone will look after their daughter or son; suggests that some parents are not fully aware of the degree of their daughter's or son's disability; or is part of a belief that marriage will alleviate the disabling condition.
- The stigma of having a learning disabled person in the family is important for some Asian communities, as it affects the marriage prospects of other siblings in the future.

WAYS FORWARD—AN AGENDA FOR ACTION

The majority of black and minority ethnic people with learning disabilities live in the community with their families. They are significant consumers of health care. It is incumbent upon health care services to provide coordinated services which are responsive to the needs of these groups.

Make Services Accessible and Responsive

- Services must enable black and minority ethnic learning disabled people to positively re-value and re-adopt their distinct different-ness (of diet, clothing, appearance, lifestyles, etc.) and relinquish the pressure to 'fit' into dominant cultural norms and value systems. This requires going beyond encouragement to dress according to stereotypes, to eat traditional foods, or to be surrounded by ethnic people and artefacts.

- Diversity of staff in services enhances the workforce and improves relations with service users from diverse communities. Black and minority ethnic staff can communicate with service users in their own languages and can identify gaps or inadequacies in services. However, they often become known as the 'race experts' (Malhotra and Mellan, 1996). This absolves white staff of their responsibilities to black and minority ethnic people, and can result in black staff feeling restricted to working with minority service users. The token black person with a different job description to his or her white peers must be avoided.

- Interpreters tend to be seen as a luxury for clients rather than as a necessity for professional practice. It is unethical and unprofessional to use children or other family members as interpreters (Shah, 1992). Both interpreters and staff working with them need to be adequately trained to ensure that *all* staff can communicate with *all* clients (see Box 1).

Box 1:   Using interpreters

Essential tasks to facilitate interpreting are:

- Agree a method of joint working with interpreter: e.g. literal translation or translation of the cultural context (idioms of distress, non-verbal communication).

- Insist on mutual briefing sessions between interpreter and worker before the interview with clients.

- Ensure that the interpreter is well versed in the information needed from the interview and in any specific concepts which may be used (e.g. home help, learning disability, respite care, depression, etc.).

- Check for compatibility and fluency in the use of language or dialect and other matching variables, such as religion, gender, age, class, etc., to create a comfortable atmosphere.

- Ensure that all information will be kept confidential. Fear of leakage of delicate matters is real to service users.

- Use clear language and avoid jargon during interviews.

- Use diagrams and other materials to make information more simple and avoid jargon.

- Do not be suspicious of the relationship between the client and the interpreter, or of the length of time they spend talking. Listen and observe carefully and, if in doubt, find out tactfully what is being said.

- Allow extra time for de-briefing with interpreter after the interview.

• Communities are not static and inflexible. The experience of growing up in the UK can be expected to have a significant impact on the aspirations and values of 'second generation' immigrants. As a result, services will need to ensure that they develop effective ways of listening to the needs and aspirations of different sections of the black and minority ethnic communities and continue to do so over time as these communities change.

Ensure a Better Understanding of, and Credibility with, the Local Black and Minority Ethnic Community (Adapted from Shah, 1992)

• *Identify the extent of need* and make sense of ethnic data to identify patterns and types of service use. Identify the incidence of learning disabilities in these groups.
• *Ensure that a senior member of staff* within the organisation or General Practice has responsibility for services to these groups.
• *Check the diversity and range of religious and cultural practices* which exist within the local communities. Familiarise yourself with them and learn to understand and respect them.
• *Find out the number of languages spoken and the dialects used.*
• *Make good links with, and develop an ongoing dialogue with,* local black and minority ethnic community groups and identify problems and issues of concern to them.
• *Make use of the local community organisations* to set up advice surgeries, thereby creating greater access to information about services and benefits.
• *Observe gender issues* and question the appropriateness of a male worker visiting a female Asian, or vice versa.
• *Observe religious and cultural events* and organise meetings to avoid these important days.
• Employ *professionally trained* interpreters and link support workers to offer better genetic counselling and understanding of the causes of learning disabilities, to assist in health checks and screening of black people with learning disabilities and their families and to act as a specific contact point for guidance and direction in accessing and explaining services. An excellent example of good practice is the Parent Adviser Scheme (Davis and Rushton, 1991).
• *Use the black Voluntary Sector.* The role and strengths of the black Voluntary Sector need to be seen against the background that the traditional white Voluntary Sector has failed to meet the needs of black and minority ethnic people. These organisations appear to be in

a stronger position to offer a 'whole/combined community care service' (Ahmed and Webb-Johnson, 1995). They offer flexible services, acknowledging the diverse and differing needs of this vulnerable group of people.

Increase the Accessibility and Uptake of Services

Lack of availability of services, lack of interpreting services, inappropriate existing services and racial attitudes and discrimination existing at the point of service delivery, appear to be major obstacles to service use. The following are suggestions to overcome these obstacles:

- *Provide information in appropriate language and formats.* For example: use audio or video tapes; present information through the national and local ethnic press and media or through the community and religious groups—including mosques, churches, gurdwara.
- *Use simple translated leaflets with the use of diagrams.* Many people may not readily understand new information, even if it is conveyed in their own language because they have no previous knowledge or experience of concepts such as respite care or Disability Allowance.
- *Employ black and minority ethnic staff* throughout mainstream service provision rather than 'specialist', 'segregated' posts.
- *Increase respite care* and *domiciliary support* when families go on extended holidays to their country of origin.
- *Provide culturally sensitive services* including single sex day services; same gender carers—particularly in personal care tasks and functions; appropriate food and diet; respect for religious holidays.
- *Increase communication* between service providers and carers about assessment and care management systems and individualised packages of care.
- *Ensure that care plans* reflect individuality and personal differences, equal respect and value about people's religious wishes and cultural needs. Translate assessment procedures into relevant languages with the use of audio and visual media including the use of ethnic press, if necessary. Employ black trained advocates.
- *Provide anti-racist training and support* to all staff as part of mandatory training, with senior management taking overall responsibility. This should include the development of an action plan with clear targets and delegated responsibilities for the development of an anti-racist and race equality strategy in employment and service provision for black and

minority ethnic people with learning disabilities (Ferns and Madden, 1995).

Inequity in health care for black and minority ethnic people with learning disabilities cannot be justified. It is essential that services become more responsive to the cultural and religious needs of these people who are vulnerable and doubly disadvantaged. It is government policy to support carers. The needs of black and minority ethnic carers have been over-looked, partly because of the myth that they are part of a large, informal network of support. These carers desperately need information and ac-cess to appropriate services and should be consulted about their needs.

KEY POINTS

1. It is important to clarify the terms 'race', 'culture' and 'ethnicity'.
2. There are just over three million black and minority ethnic people in the UK (6% of the population).
3. Black and minority ethnic groups face inequalities, discrimination and disadvantage in almost every aspect of their lives. There is a danger of emphasising people's needs in terms of religion, customs and tradi-tions and overlooking their basic needs for decent housing, access to health care and assistance to claim benefits.
4. Evidence suggests a higher prevalence of severe learning disabilities in children and young adults in the Asian community, but no figures exist nationally for black, Afro-Caribbean communities.
5. Despite formal health policy statements, black and minority ethnic people with learning disabilities are *doubly disadvantaged* as a result of discrimination, racism and culturally inappropriate forms of care and service provision. The unmet needs of these groups are not 'special', only different. Services must recognise and respond to this 'different-ness'.
6. Studies of Asian families with a person with learning disabilities reveal a deprived, isolated group who have little formal or informal support, have significant levels of stress, have language barriers and suffer racial abuse. Typically, parents have little knowledge or understand-ing of their son's or daughter's disability.
7. Health care services need to have a better understanding of their local black and minority ethnic communities and to provide more respon-sive services.
8. Services will need to continue to listen to the needs and aspirations of different sections of the black and minority ethnic communities as they are not static, but will change over time.

REFERENCES

ADAPT (1993) *Asian and Disabled. A Study into the Needs of Asian People with Disabilities in the Bradford Area.* Asian Disability Advisory Project Team, The Spastics Society and Barnardos, West Yorkshire.

Ahmed, W.I.U. and Atkin, K. (eds) (1996) *'Race' and Community Care.* Open University Press, Buckingham.

Ahmed, T. and Webb-Johnson, A. (1995) Voluntary groups. In S. Fernando (ed.), *Mental Health in a Multi-ethnic Society: A Multidisciplinary Handbook.* Routledge, London.

Aminidav, C. and Weller, L. (1995) Effects of country of origin, sex, religiosity and social class on breadth of knowledge of mental retardation. *British Journal of Developmental Disabilities,* XLI(80), 48–56.

Azmi, S., Emerson, E., Caine, A. and Hatton, C. (1996) *Improving Services for Asian People with Learning Disabilities and their Families.* Hester Adrian Research Centre/The Mental Health Foundation, Manchester.

Baxter, C. (1996) Sex education: ethnically sensitive services to people with learning disabilities. *Tizard Learning Disability Review,* 1, 1–6.

Baxter, C., Poonia, K., Ward, L. and Nadirshaw, Z. (1990) *Double Discrimination. Issues and Services for People with Learning Difficulties from Black and Ethnic Minority Communities.* King's Fund Centre/Commission for Racial Equality, London.

Cheng, P. and So-kum Tang, C. (1995) Coping and psychological distress of Chinese parents of children with Down's Syndrome. *Mental Retardation,* 33(1), 10–20.

Davis, H. and Rushton, R. (1991) Counselling and supporting parents of children with developmental delay: a research evaluation. *Journal of Mental Deficiency Research,* 35, 89–113.

DES (1985) *Education for All. The Report of the Committee of Enquiry into the Education of Children from Ethnic Minority Groups.* Department of Education and Science, London.

Evans, G., Todd, S., Beyer, S., Felce, D. and Perry, J. (1994) Assessing the impact of the All Wales mental handicap strategy: a survey of four districts. *Journal of Intellectual Disability Research,* 38, 109–133.

Fatimilehin, I. and Nadirshaw, Z. (1994) A cross cultural study of parental attitudes and beliefs about learning disability (mental handicap). *Mental Handicap Research,* 7(3), 202–227.

Ferns, P. and Madden, M. (1995) Training to promote race equality. In S. Fernando (ed.), *Mental Health in a Multi-ethnic Society: A Multidisciplinary Handbook.* Routledge, London.

Fernando, S. (1991) *Race, Culture and Mental Health.* Macmillan Press Ltd, London.

McNought, A. (1984) *Race and Health Care in the United Kingdom.* Centre for Health Service Management Studies. Polytechnic of South Bank, London.

Malhotra, S. and Mellan, B. (1996) Cultural and race issues in sexuality work with people with learning disabilities. *Tizard Learning Disability Review,* 1, 7–12.

Nadirshaw, Z. (1991) Gearing up for good practice. Implications in the assessment and care management of black and minority ethnic people with learning difficulties and their carers. Occasional Paper No. 2. London Boroughs Disability Resource Team, London.

Nadirshaw, Z. (in press) Learning disabilities. In D. Bhugra, S. Shashidharan and R. Cochrane (eds), *Transcultural Psychiatry.* Gaskell Publication/Royal College of Psychiatrists, London.

Pearson, M.A. (1985) *Equal Opportunities in the NHS. A Handbook*. National Extension College/Training in Health and Race, Cambridge.

Rocheron, Y. (1980) The Asian mother and baby campaign: the construction of ethnic minorities' health needs. *Critical Social Policy*, **22**, 4–23.

Rudak, K. (1994) *Black and Minority Ethnic Groups in England: Health and Lifestyles*. Health Education Authority, London.

Shah, R. (1992) *The Silent Minority: Children with Disabilities in Asian Families*. National Children's Bureau, London.

Smaje, C. (1995) *Health, Race and Ethnicity: Making Sense of the Evidence*. King's Fund Institute, London.

Soni-Raleigh, V. (1995) *Mental Health in Black Minority Ethnic People: The Fundamental Facts*. The Mental Health Foundation, London.

10

VULNERABILITY ISSUES

Hilary Brown

This chapter explores issues of vulnerability as they affect adults with learning disabilities and seeks to clarify the role of the different health professionals in addressing these through prevention, recognition and response to concerns or allegations (see also Checklist 10). Until recently the service community has often acted as if adults with learning disabilities were immune from abuse or exploitation, even when other adults were addressing issues of personal safety for themselves. So an important place to start is to acknowledge that adults with learning disabilities are not alone in having to recognise their vulnerability to personal violence, bullying or sexual assault: these are issues faced to some extent by *all* women and men in their neighbourhoods, families and relationships.

However, research suggests that both children and adults with learning disabilities may be more at risk not only because of their own difficulties in understanding or communicating but also because of the way they receive services and the fact that they may be actively targeted or taken advantage of. Moreover, risk is extenuated by:

- the congregate settings in which adults with learning disabilities live and work—in group homes and day centres;
- their needs for support and assistance—often provided by people who do not know them well or remain long in their lives;
- and the fact that, all too often, they lack independent advocacy.

Adults with Learning Disabilities. Edited by J. O'Hara and A. Sperlinger.
© 1997 John Wiley & Sons Ltd.

TAKING THE RISK OF ABUSE SERIOUSLY

In this chapter you are challenged to take a proactive stance to abuse and vulnerability—in other words, to adopt an appropriate level of suspicion on behalf of your patients. This does not mean over-reacting by seeing abuse everywhere or assuming malicious motives behind every situation in which care is less than perfect. But it does mean keeping that possibility in the back of your mind in relation to individuals who give rise to concern and to care agencies and their managers or proprietors who seem to be failing or to be overly defensive.

By taking the risk of abuse seriously, services should aim to protect people without disempowering them. To do this professionals have to walk a tightrope between acknowledging vulnerability and individual needs while enhancing the status of adults with learning disabilities as a group. Talking about 'vulnerability' can seem to cut across the language of rights, choices and normalisation which services have worked hard to establish. But the 'duty of care' has to include appropriate protection from harm and to be based on a clear assessment of the options open to individual service users and their understanding of the risks and implications of a particular course of action.

Although it may *sound* 'valuing' to act as if a person is fully in charge of his or her life, it can be very *dis*empowering if the person is actually being exploited or hurt. A 'hands-off' approach on the part of service workers can leave people feeling undermined or unsupported in situations in which they really are 'out of their depth'. Moreover, the risk of abuse is inherent to the care task—ordinary common sense dictates some lines over which service workers should not step. But some judgements are complicated by the fact that carers and workers do have a legitimate right to cross *some* boundaries for *some* people at *some* times—for example, in the context of intimate care—to protect them from risk or to restrain them if they pose a risk to others.

Increasingly these issues are being addressed through explicit policies and procedures which formalise some aspects of the decision-making process. Your first impression of this may be that it is cumbersome or bureaucratic and it certainly limits your discretion to some extent, as child protection procedures do, by mandating the sharing of information and setting out deadlines and structures for action. For example, you are probably required to report concerns even if they have been told to you in confidence. But there are very good reasons for not 'going it alone'. Evidence of the risk of repeated abuse to an individual or to other vulnerable adults justifies such caution.

WHAT DO WE MEAN BY THE TERM 'ABUSE'?

Abuse is a rather loose term and one which has been criticised from opposing points of view. Williams (1993) has argued that it minimises the impact of incidents which are often serious offences, such as theft, assault or rape: while others (Biggs, 1996) have argued that it is too heavy handed and might be used as the basis for unwarranted surveillance of informal carers. Often it is used only to refer to harm caused or sustained within an ongoing relationship marked by dependency and other inequalities. But this focus on family or other 'carer' relationships draws attention away from the abuse and exploitation which vulnerable adults experience in day and residential services or in their neighbourhoods and communities (see Flynn, 1987).

Consensus is beginning to emerge in relation to which *categories* of abuse should be covered within generic Adult Protection procedures (i.e. overarching policies which include older people, people with mental health problems and disabled people, alongside adults with learning disabilities) and these are usually cited as

- physical abuse
- sexual abuse
- psychological abuse (sometimes called emotional, or social abuse)
- financial or material abuse and
- neglect (see Brown and Stein, forthcoming).

If we take each of these types of abuse in turn, we can see that there are some special issues which arise for adults with learning disabilities in relation to each category of abuse and some potential omissions from this list. Also, practitioners are very clear that it is not the *category* but the *threshold of seriousness* which they find difficult to interpret.

Physical Abuse

Physical abuse includes hitting and rough handling and manifests itself as bruising, finger marking and so on. It is more likely to occur in settings where carers (whether family members or paid staff) have little understanding of challenging behaviours, or assume that any difficulties are directed at them personally (see Chapter 6). Although it is important to treat adults distinctly from children, if you have training in recognising non-accidental injury in children or in older people, you should use this as a rule of thumb and act on any evidence of such injuries (however minor), so that it can be followed up in an appropriate multidisciplinary forum. Overmedication or misuse of medical procedures might also fall within this category (for example, the use of enemas without sound medical reasons or safeguards in their administration).

Sexual Abuse

Sexual abuse occurs whenever anyone is subjected to a sexual act to which they do not or cannot consent or where they have been unduly pressured (see Chapter 11). Any sexual behaviours, whether they involve direct contact or not, can be abusive in the absence of valid consent or in the presence of force or intimidation. Even non-contact abuse such as voyeurism, involvement in pornography, indecent exposure, harassment, serious teasing or innuendo, can be experienced as seriously abusive, especially if it takes place in a threatening atmosphere. We usually think of abuse as acts done *by* the abuser *to* the person who is abused but sometimes they involve situations where the abuser forces or persuades the abused person to do things to them. The act(s) might have happened once only or be part of an ongoing sexual relationship. Consent is dealt with in Chapter 11, but as a shorthand formulation there are three issues (see Brown and Turk, 1992):

1. Whether the person *did* give his or her consent, because if the person did not, he or she has been raped or assaulted like any other woman or man.
2. Whether the person *could* give his or her consent; that is, if the person understood enough about sexual behaviour and knew what was happening. At law, adults with severe learning disabilities are deemed not to be able to give consent to sexual acts.
3. A judgement has to be made as to whether the person with learning disabilities was *under undue pressure* in this particular situation—for example, due to an authority or caregiving relationship, as might be the case if sex is initiated by a staff or family member, or where force, trickery or exploitation is used. Physical force or the threat of violence or reprisals also cut across any meaningful consent.

Because the law specifies a distinction between adults with severe intellectual impairments and those with milder degrees of disability, it would be wise for professionals to undertake, or draw on, clear assessments of the capacity of individual service users who are engaging in sexual activities (see Chapter 11). When adults with severe learning disabilities are sexually active you should enquire what evidence there is that they have mutual or reciprocal relationships. In respect of adults with mild learning disabilities, questions should hinge upon whether the relationships appear to have exploitative or threatening elements. Services sometimes opt out, taking a laissez-faire stance to *all* service users, regardless of their ability to understand risk or to protect themselves within, and from, unequal relationships.

For adults with learning disabilities, sexual abuses often take place against a background of negative expectations about their sexual options. People may have little in the way of credible or reliable sex education, have few opportunities to make friends or be private and always be swimming against the tide if they wish to establish an independent sexual life. Unfortunately this kind of protective veneer does not keep people safe, merely ignorant. It means that they are often ill equipped to make a complaint, to appreciate when they might be putting themselves at risk, or to have their problems recognised through routine health checks. Because people often assume that adults with learning disabilities are asexual their sexual health needs are not routinely addressed. They may not be offered smear tests, ordinary help with menstruation (as opposed to more drastic measures like hysterectomy) or safer sex education. Where these interventions are attempted, they may collapse at the first hurdle because no one is willing to put the necessary effort or ingenuity into making them appropriate or acceptable to the particular individual. There are many instances of excellent practice on the part of health visitors, psychologists and other professionals (see, for example, Flynn *et al.*, 1996; Carlson *et al.*, 1994; Baum, 1994; and Cambridge and Brown, 1997). Health visitors, in particular because of their unique work with parents who have learning disabilities, are attuned to the importance of positive sexual health and the investment required to ensure that mothers with learning disabilities have safe pregnancies and supportive relationships if they are to manage. They have learned that they need to be explicit in their guidance to, and close work with, these women and their relatives (see Chapter 8).

As a practitioner you may uncover sexual abuse through offering such routine health screening or interventions yourself. Certainly, if you are faced with evidence of sexual activity, such as a sexually transmitted disease, anal or vaginal tearing, or pregnancy, in someone who cannot legally give valid consent, you should explore the situation further. Until recently, requests for sterilisation of adults with learning disabilities who cannot give their own consent to such an intervention, were made and agreed to by parents, but these now have to be referred for judicial review. However, women with learning disabilities are routinely referred for contraceptive advice, or may find themselves in long-term receipt of injectable or oral contraceptives, without the kind of sex that they are thought to be involved in being questioned. It is a widespread myth that the pill offers protection from sexual abuse. Nor are they given space to ask their own questions. For example, they may be very confused about terms such as 'coil' and 'smear' but feel unable to ask when everyone around them seems to know what everything means (see Chapter 4).

Psychological Abuse

Psychological abuse is often wrapped up in these situations but obscured because the mental health needs of adults with learning disabilities are overlooked. Difficulties tend to be explained away as part of the person's condition, rather than an expression of distress or outrage at what might be happening to him or her. As a category of abuse this is often used as something of a 'catch-all' (the equivalent term in child protection is 'failure to thrive'). It has been pinned down, in a recent research study on elder abuse, to consist mainly of verbal assault, threats and insults, including humiliation in relation to bodily functions such as incontinence and threats to abandon the vulnerable person. Pillemer and Finkelhor (1988) term this 'chronic verbal aggression'.

Financial or Material Abuse

Financial, or material, abuse is also an issue for adults with learning disabilities, although one which is not often reported within the framework of abuse policies. Practitioners who participated in the adult abuse work described above (Brown and Stein, forthcoming) were aware that adults with learning disabilities on their case loads had such restricted access to money and property that they considered it abusive. It is, however, striking that this did not lead to reports under the policies in the way that more tangible or fraudulent transactions involving older people did. Families may subsume benefits into the family income, and irregularities in managing personal moneys in residential services are also commonplace (Davis et al., 1995). Single transactions require professionals to satisfy themselves about valid and uncoerced consent in the same way as the sexual interactions outlined above. Occasionally, formal measures are taken where individuals lack capacity. More often, people make informal arrangements which are condoned by those around as long as they seem to work in the interests of the person concerned. Health professionals may be aware of these arrangements and should be alert to problems, especially when the care provided is in other ways inadequate, or bordering on neglect. In this case, financial motivation may be at the root of a particular care arrangement, or an unwillingness to 'allow' a learning disabled adult to leave home.

Neglect

Neglect is also difficult to determine but is commonly used to describe those situations and relationships within which an individual's basic physical, social and health care needs are not being met. For example, Beverley Lewis died because her mother, who suffered from mental health problems, was unable to take physical care of her. Her death and the subsequent inquiry led to inter-agency guidance in Gloucestershire which has served as a model for policies on vulnerable adults. Failure to access proper medical or dental care, to give prescribed medication or pain relief reliably, or to enable someone to use services (such as a day centre or leisure group) could all be considered neglectful. Sometimes *negligence* is included under this heading, although it implies a more active failure to take risks into account. For example, when someone is encouraged to engage in high-risk activities without proper planning or consultation (such as the use of dangerous equipment without any training or supervision, or involvement in a road safety programme which has not been carefully considered). In relation to sexual health issues, services often face difficult decisions about whether to intervene in situations where a service user is engaging in high-risk sex (see Cambridge and Brown, 1997) and a balance has to be achieved between negligence and respect for his or her sexual rights.

DOUBLE STANDARDS, COMPLEX DYNAMICS AND ABUSIVE REGIMES

These definitions are not inclusive but they do provide a framework within which you can begin to address the risks which are faced by vulnerable adults in their day-to-day lives and service settings. An important part of any definition is the extent to which the harm was intentionally caused, but this should not confuse or cut across the right of a *victim* to receive help.

Double Standards

Using generic labels for abuse is helpful in that it challenges us as to why we apply different standards to people in particular settings or relationships. Why, for example, is it less of a shock for a service user to be assaulted by another service user with 'challenging behaviour' than for any member of the public to be assaulted in his or her home or place of work? Yet these different situations would almost certainly lead to different sanctions and interventions. Nor would most women choose to live with a man who had a previous history of sexual offending, and yet a woman with learning disabilities might well find herself in this position without either her knowledge or assent. Moreover, if she were then the victim of such an assault, she would probably not wish to continue to live or spend time alongside the person who had harmed her—but again, might have no option. Accessing help for victim *and* perpetrator in such situations is an important measure of good practice.

Complex Dynamics

Also, such a typology may obscure the complex dynamics which exist in abusive relationships and tend towards seeing abuse as a single act rather than an ongoing process which usually includes some elements of a 'cover-up'. In practice the types often overlap—in a recent study of cases reported in two authorities over one year, multiple abuses were documented in at least one-fifth of cases (Brown and Stein, forthcoming). For example, a member of staff might use physical violence or the threat of it to coerce an adult with learning disabilities to engage in, or maintain secrecy about, sexual abuse and it is hard to see how such an act could fail to cause psychological harm.

Abusive Regimes

When abuse takes place within a service, it is important to be alert to the nature of the whole regime rather than just the behaviour of an individual abuser. If the abuse is the act of a lone worker, the management should deal with it openly and summarily. But it could also be a reflection of negligence on the part of management in the form of lack of knowledge, support and resources. Workers in abusive regimes are often underpaid, untrained, and insecure. They may be afraid of the proprietor, management or union and unable to 'blow the whistle'. For example, in two recent cases which were the subject of action under the Registered Homes Act, illegal immigrants were employed in one home and young women on social security in another. None was in a position to question practice or to formalise a complaint. A further dynamic to take into account in both institutional and informal settings is the distortion of behavioural programmes or sanctions. Occasionally serious assaults are carried out under the guise of punishment or control. For example, in this home, which was eventually closed by the Residential Homes Tribunal, a man who had epileptic fits was dealt with by being sent outside in all weathers:

How they dealt with his challenging behaviour was to punish him by send-ing him outside whatever the weather, where he would stay for long periods. . . . On a particular occasion [he] had refused a group activity, went to attack a computer, [whereupon he] had been wrestled to the ground, and self-abused himself, by biting his arm until it bled and [he was then] put out of the house in his slippers in wintry weather. At 19.45 he had been repeat-edly refused entry, despite his requests to come in. He was still there at 21.00 and when he asked for his drugs, which he normally had at this time, they were refused him. He was still outside at midnight and told that he was no longer wanted at the home. He set off down the road and was returned by the Appellant's son at 01.00 having promised to behave in the future. Another form of punishment . . . was to have his meal removed and put in the wastebin, and to be put outside. He also had records from his much loved record collection deliberately broken . . . as a punishment.
(Registered Homes Tribunal, 1993, Decision 221, p. 1184)

Comments

- As an outside professional, it is important to be able to sympathise with the difficulties a family or staff group may encounter and point them to additional resources or input such as a specialist team or psychologist, without condoning such responses.
- You may have to make a judgement about whether a service has done enough to seek outside expertise or if they have been negligent in tackling aspects of their work such as dealing with challenging be-haviour, difficulties in communication or feeding.
- As independent professionals we must collectively make a judgement about the roots of the response in the intentions and personality of the per-son responsible for it. Is it that the person lacks knowledge or skills, or is it a matter of judgement, or lack of self control? Misuse of alcohol or misuse of other substances on the part of the alleged abuser is sometimes implicated.
- Where you are concerned that practice is well outside standards com-monly agreed within the professional community, you have a duty to alert social services or the inspection unit, as well as to design and monitor new interventions.

INDICATORS OF ABUSE

We have seen that there are social as well as medical/physical indicators of abuse to which, as independent practitioners, you should be alert. By their very nature the cards are stacked against abusive incidents coming to light.

- They 'leak' out sometimes through the distressed, angry or sexualised be-haviour of a victim or the sexualised, authoritarian, or persecutory behaviour or views of the perpetrator. Many 'text book' lists alert practitioners to *sudden* changes of mood or behaviour but even this can be misleading since abuse is often long-standing and/or introduced gradually.

- Nonetheless such changes, along with newly sexualised language or dislike for particular individuals or activities, should always be taken seriously.
- Cycles of weight loss or gain, gagging and (dramatically) elective mutism are among the disguised ways in which some people communicate their distress (Flynn and Brown, in press; and Vizard, 1989).
- Otherwise, you should be alert to agencies which are characterised by closed systems and rigid hierarchies (Wardhaugh and Wilding, 1993).
- But by far the most common route for discovery is disclosure or partial disclosure (Turk and Brown, 1993). Practitioners are often reluctant to listen or to ask (Rose *et al.*, 1991) as acknowledgement that one is willing to hear, and believe, a disclosure of abuse would allow a person to say what is happening to them.

If someone you are working with does disclose abuse, you should follow the guidance set out in the *Memorandum of Good Practice* (HO/DoH, 1992),[1] see Box 1.

This allows the initial disclosure to be followed up with a more formal and evidentially sound interview as soon as practicable.

Box 1:   Responding to a disclosure of abuse

If someone discloses abuse:

1. Listen, rather than directly question.
2. Don't stop someone who is freely recalling importance events, he or she may not tell you again.
3. At the first opportunity, make a note of what the person said, exactly in the person's own words wherever possible, noting especially details about the time, setting and any witnesses who might have seen what happened.
4. Date and sign the record.

PREVALENCE AND INCIDENCE OF ABUSE

Systematic research into abuse has been patchy and is rife with methodological difficulties. The very fact that abuse is hidden and that there

---

[1] The guidance in this document is specific to *child* protection, but a similar standard in relation to vulnerable adults is recommended for those cases in which disclosure may eventually lead to prosecution.

are barriers to reporting means that all samples are biased towards those cases which do not come out into the open. Knowledge about single cases which come to court or to other forms of inquiry needs to be added to that which is drawn from surveys and case note reviews. Moreover, far more work has been done on sexual abuse, than on other types of abuse, perhaps because there *is* more consensus about how serious it is and less ambiguity about defining a threshold. Studies have 'plugged in' to different layers of the services and used a range of data-gathering techniques (Brown, 1994). The studies reported below relate primarily to sexual abuse.

Of the *prevalence studies*, the study by Hard and Plumb (1987) is the only one which gathered data about a wide range of non-consensual sexual contact—including vaginal and anal intercourse—directly from those service users who were able to answer questions themselves (65 of 95 attendees at a day centre). Overall, 38 of the 65 (58%) reported sexual abuse, 83% of whom were women and 32% men. Buchanan and Wilkins (1991) sought their information from front-line staff working with children and adults aged 8 to 45 and arrived at a figure of 8% prevalence. Cooke (1990) surveyed psychiatrists and estimated a prevalence of 4.5%. These figures illustrate how cases are edited out of awareness as an individual moves between different sources of professional help, and also shows that the initial stage of finding staff who can hear and validate the experiences of adults with learning disabilities is the greatest hurdle.

Incidence surveys similarly log into reports at different stages. Dunne and Power (1990) gathered data through a retrospective review of case notes of adults with learning disabilities seen by a community service over a 3-year period, augmented by interviews with clinicians, and arrived at a figure of 2.88 per 1,000 adults with learning disabilities. Turk and Brown (1993)—based on reports filed through statutory agencies, and assuming 3% prevalence of learning disability within the general population—estimate approximately 0.5 per 1,000 adults with learning disabilities, of which 1 in 10 led to prosecutions.

Clearly, it is difficult to make authoritative claims from comparison of studies with different methodologies and parameters, but there are clues to what happens to reports of sexual abuse involving adults with learning disabilities in these figures. For every 5 or 6 cases acknowledged by clinicians and/or documented in case records, only 1 would be recalled in a retrospective review or available to the statutory agencies for service development or planning purposes. These more conservative figures yield an estimated 1,250 cases of sexual abuse involving adults reported annually in England and Wales, increasing to 1,400 if Scotland and Northern Ireland cases are included (Brown *et al.*, 1995).

A clear picture does emerge from these studies about *patterns of abuse and abusing* in which men are the predominant perpetrators, abusing both women and more vulnerable men as victims. Perpetrators include other service users, staff/volunteers, family members and other known and trusted adults, many of whom were referred to as 'pillars of the community' in separate written reports. This does not mean that all 'pillars of the community' are suspect, but workers should be alert to the fact that potential abusers do actively attend to their own credibility (as one strategy for avoiding detection) and be careful of being drawn into collusive networks.

Recording in relation to other kinds of abuse may well follow these same patterns, demonstrating a filtering out of knowledge by those who work at 'arm's length' from service users and the necessity for clear channels of reporting which can bypass a manager or homeowner who has a vested interest in keeping allegations about abuse under wraps. Where sexual abuse may differ is in its tendency to be repeated, often against serial victims, and this warrants the most stringent safeguards.

WHAT TO DO IF YOU HAVE CONCERNS

'Adult abuse' or 'vulnerable adult' policies, whether these are generic or refer to adults with learning disabilities as a specific group, or to specific forms of abuse, should set out routes for referral and consultation to assure that adults with learning disabilities are neither denied assistance in their sexual lives nor confined within 'closed' systems. A model policy produced by ARC/NAPSAC (1993) with support from the Social Services Inspectorate, outlines *key features of a sound response to allegations about abuse of vulnerable adults* (see Box 2).

Social Services is the lead agency for adults with learning disabilities so, even if abuse takes place within a health service provider unit, they

---

Box 2:   Responding to an allegation of abuse

The response to allegations of abuse of vulnerable adults should include:

- Action to promote positive practice and safeguards.
- Preventative steps taken routinely, such as take up of references and proper supervision.
- Separation of the initial alert from subsequent interagency consultation and investigation.
- Clear decision making through a formal case conference.
- Intensified individual planning for the victim (and perpetrator if that person is another service user) in the form of an Adult Protection Plan.
- Sharing of information on a 'need to know' basis.

---

should be informed under these procedures. Health professionals may be involved at any, and indeed at several, of the stages within this sequence of activities. They may:

- be responsible for raising an initial alert;
- be contacted to share information or provide a specialist assessment for, or support to, the investigation; or
- be part of the case conference and protective planning process and subsequent treatment.

Psychologists, for example, are often asked to provide an assessment of capacity and decision-making skills for the investigation. Afterwards, they may provide direct treatment such as post-traumatic stress counselling or cognitive treatment related to sexual offending. A speech therapist may be asked to provide input into a formal interview (Brown et al., 1996). Community nurses may become involved in monitoring medication or mental health needs, while health visitors are often asked to work around family planning issues. Investigations should always be coordinated by someone who is sufficiently senior and independent to command respect and be able to access and manage information from a number of sources. This role is usually carried by a team leader or care manager within social services who will work alongside the police in relevant cases.

If individuals are abused or exploited, the legacy for them can be very long-standing and this may affect the way you work with them as a clinician for many years to come. Again, as an outsider you may be the only source of continuity as residential staff often change, and you may have a responsibility to interpret back the special needs of an individual to direct care staff. You may also have a role in accessing immediate or long-term support from other agencies because help is not easy to locate or provide. Generic agencies, which provide services for other people who have been victimised or subjected to trauma—such as women's refuges, victim support, rape crisis or other counselling services—are often unable or unwilling to provide services to adults with learning disabilities. They have their own training needs (Simpson and Bull, 1994) as do the staff of some of the newly formed specialist services and the many workers who become involved in supporting particular individuals through difficult times. One woman who had been severely abused throughout her childhood looked upon her support worker as a life saver as well as lifeline (Stein and Brown, 1996) but this can be a demanding role to find yourself in and one in which the workers can come to feel isolated and unsupported.

KEY POINTS

1. Adults with learning disabilities are vulnerable to a range of exploitative and abusive experiences.
2. You should be alert to signs of distress or to any hints from service users that something is wrong.
3. Maintain a stance that is appropriately independent of service providers.
4. Work alongside social services staff by
   - passing on initial referrals and concerns
   - supporting them in investigating and following up specific allegations.
5. Workers who 'go it alone' risk becoming a weak link in supportive networks and this may not only allow the abuse to continue but to be extended to other potential victims.
6. Concern for personal safety should be at the core of quality assurance systems. If people are not safe, what quality of life is there?

ACKNOWLEDGEMENT

The author would like to thank Dr Margaret Flynn for comments and suggestions on this chapter.

REFERENCES

Starred entries indicate recommended reading.
*ARC/NAPSAC (1993) It Could Never Happen Here: The Prevention and Treatment of Sexual Abuse of Adults with Learning Disabilities in Residential Settings. ARC/ NAPSAC, Chesterfield.
Baum, S. (1994) Interventions with a pregnant woman with severe learning disabilities: a case example. In A. Craft (ed.), Practice Issues in Sexuality and Learning Disabilities. Routledge, London.
Biggs, S. (1996) Elder abuse and the policing of community care. Generations Review, 6(2), 2–4.
Brown, H. (1994) Establishing the incidence of abuse in services for people with learning disabilities. In J. Harris and A. Craft (eds), People with Learning Disabilities at Risk of Physical or Sexual Abuse. BILD Seminar Papers No. 4, Kidderminster.
*Brown, H. and Turk, V. (1992) Defining sexual abuse as it affects adults with learning disabilities. Mental Handicap, 20, 44–55.
*Brown, H., Stein, J. and Turk, V. (1995) The sexual abuse of adults with learning disabilities: report of a second two-year incidence survey. Mental Handicap Research, 8(1), 3–24.
Brown, H. and Stein, J. (forthcoming) Implementing adult protection policies in Kent and East Sussex. (Submitted to Journal of Social Policy.)

Brown, H., Egan-Sage, E. with Barry, G. and McKay, C. (1996) *Towards Better Interviewing: A Handbook on the Sexual Abuse of Adults with Learning Disabilities for Police Officers and Social Workers*. NAPSAC/Pavilion Publishing, Brighton.

Buchanan, A.H. and Wilkins, R. (1991) Sexual abuse of the mentally handicapped: difficulties in establishing prevalence. *Psychiatric Bulletin,* **15**, 601–605.

Cambridge, P. and Brown, H. (eds) (1997) *HIV and Learning Disabilities*. BILD, Kidderminster.

Carlson, G., Taylor, M., Wilson, J. and Griffin, J. (1994) *Menstrual Management and Fertility Management for Women who have Intellectual Disability and High Support Needs: An Analysis of Australian Policy*. Department of Social Work and Social Policy, University of Queensland, Australia.

Cooke, L.B. (1990) Abuse of mentally handicapped adults. *Psychiatric Bulletin,* **14**, 608–609.

*Davis, A., Eley, R., Flynn, M., Flynn, P. and Roberts, G. (1995) To have and have not: addressing issues of poverty. In T. Philpot and L. Ward (eds), *Values and Visions: Changing Ideas in Services for People with Learning Difficulties*. Butterworth Heinemann, Oxford.

Dunne, T.P. and Power, A. (1990) Sexual abuse and mental handicap: preliminary findings of a community-based study. *Mental Handicap Research,* 3(2), 111–125.

Flynn, M. (1987) Independent living arrangements for adults who are mentally handicapped. In N. Malin (ed.), *Reassessing Community Care*. Croom Helm, London.

Flynn, M., Howard, J. and Pursey, A. (1996) *GP Fundholding and the Health Care of People with Learning Disabilities*. National Development Team, Manchester.

Flynn, M. and Brown, H. (in press). The responsibilities of commissioners, purchasers and providers. In J. Churchill, H. Brown, A. Craft and C. Horrocks (eds), *There are No Easy Answers: Working with Service Users who Sexually Abuse*. ARC/NAPSAC, Chesterfield.

Hard, S. and Plumb, W. (1987) Sexual abuse of persons with developmental disabilities: a case study. Unpublished manuscript.

Home Office in conjunction with the Department of Health (HO/DoH) (1992) *Memorandum of Good Practice: Video Recorded Interviews with Child Witnesses for Criminal Proceedings*. HMSO, London.

Pillemer, K. and Finkelhor, D. (1988) The prevalence of elder abuse: a random sample survey. *The Gerontologist,* **28**(1), 51–57.

Registered Homes Tribunal (1993) *Decision no. 221*, Registered Homes Tribunal, London, pp. 1179–1202.

Rose, S., Peabody, C. and Stratigeas, B. (1991) Undetected abuse amongst intensive case management clients. *Hospital and Community Psychiatry,* **42**(5), 499–503.

Simpson, D. and Bull, N. (1994) *Sexual Abuse and People with Learning Difficulties: Developing Access to Community Services*. Family Planning Association, London.

Stein, J. and Brown, H. (1996) *'A Nightmare I Thought would Never End'*: a tape made for staff by service users who have been sexually abused. Pavilion, Brighton.

Turk, V. and Brown, H. (1993) The sexual abuse of adults with learning disabilities: results of a two year incidence survey. *Mental Handicap Research,* **6**(3), 193–216.

Vizard, E. (1989) Child sexual abuse and mental handicap: a child psychiatrist's perspective. In H. Brown and A. Craft (eds), *Thinking the 'Unthinkable'*. Papers on Sexual Abuse and People with Learning Difficulties. Family Planning Association, London.

*Wardhaugh, J. and Wilding, P. (1993) Towards an explanation of the corruption of care. *Critical Social Policy*, Summer 1993, 4–31.

*Williams, C. (1993) Vulnerable victims? A current awareness of the victimisation of people with learning disabilities. *Disability, Handicap and Society*, 8(2), 161–172.

11

CONSENT ISSUES

Glynis H. Murphy and Isabel C.H. Clare

Historically, adults with learning disabilities have often been thought unable to make decisions for themselves. Indeed, during this century, very large numbers have been subjected to medical interventions or interventions involving medical practitioners (including segregation in hospital, gynaecological experimentation and sterilisation) against their will, as though they were not even entitled to the right to make such decisions (Fennell, 1996).

With the introduction of normalisation (Brown and Smith, 1992), it was increasingly argued that it was unacceptable to *assume* that adults with learning disabilities did not have the capacity to make decisions about their own lives (Law Commission, 1995). Nevertheless, it may be difficult to help adults with learning disabilities make decisions for themselves, including decisions about medical treatment. Increasingly, methods are being developed both to assess the individual's capacity to consent and to maximise that capacity.

PSYCHOLOGICAL FUNCTIONING IN ADULTS WITH LEARNING DISABILITIES

The standard definitions of learning disabilities in the *International Classification of Diseases* (ICD, 10th Edition, World Health Organisation) and the *Diagnostic and Statistical Manual* (DSM-IV, American Psychiatric Association) refer to the appearance, in the developmental period, of a significant impairment of intellectual functioning together with a significant

Adults with Learning Disabilities. Edited by J. O'Hara and A. Sperlinger.
© 1997 John Wiley & Sons Ltd.

impairment of adaptive behaviour or social functioning. The most recent definitions proposed in the USA are similar (see Chapter 1).

The relative prevalence of mild and severe learning disabilities (see Chapter 1) means that, numerically, GPs and health care professionals are more likely to meet people with mild learning disabilities than those with severe learning disabilities. Frequently, those with mild learning disabilities will be living in the community with little or no support and may come to the GP's surgery unaccompanied. They may appear at first to have no special difficulties and they may not tell health care staff that they have a learning disability. In contrast, those with severe learning disabilities are more likely to be living with families or in supported living schemes and will probably be accompanied by family members or support staff when they attend the surgery. Very often the GP will have no information on the intellectual ability of the person with learning disabilities attending the surgery. Even if this information were available, it would not be very useful in this context because it is known that intellectual ability is not a good predictor of capacity to consent to treatment (Murphy and Clare, 1995).

While it is now clear that, with support, many adults with learning disabilities are able to express their views on a wide variety of issues, the most obvious difficulties in a GP's surgery concern communication (see Chapter 4). Any information given to people about health promotion or about their own health problems, in the context of consent or in other contexts, will therefore need to be extremely carefully planned and, preferably, be available in several different forms (see Chapter 4).

Less obviously, adults with learning disabilities tend to have a number of other disadvantages which may impair their capacity to consent (see Chapter 4). Intellectual and language problems are often accompanied by limited memory and problem-solving skills, the extent of which will vary between individuals and be more pronounced in those with more impaired intellectual ability (Murphy and Clare, 1995).

There are also some specific cognitive and social difficulties which, though by no means obvious, may crucially affect the capacity to consent of adults with learning disabilities (Clare and Gudjonsson, 1993). In certain contexts, they may be particularly acquiescent and suggestible (see Chapter 4). Evidence from research on interviewing (Gudjonsson, 1992) indicates that—especially when faced with a powerful person in society, like a GP—adults with learning disabilities are particularly likely to:

- acquiesce (say 'yes') to 'yes/no' questions, especially when they do not understand what they have been asked;
- be misled by leading questions or the presentation of misleading information;

• comply with ('go along with') ideas, requests or instructions with which they do not really agree because they feel intimidated.

This means that if a GP, or anyone else, is seeking a person's consent, it is very easy to obtain the desired decision rather than the decision the person really wishes to make, by the use of leading questions, confusing information, or suggestions about the 'correct' decision. The GP must therefore be very careful about how he or she interacts with a person with learning disabilities, and this may require some advance planning (see Chapter 4).

Finally, it is worth noting that adults with learning disabilities are at increased risk of other mental health problems which may impair their capacity to make decisions (see Chapter 1). For example, people with Down's syndrome are vulnerable to early dementia from Alzheimer's disease. Similarly, as a group, adults with learning disabilities are at increased risk of mental illness (such as schizophrenia or severe depression—see Chapter 7).

MENTAL CAPACITY

According to the law in England and Wales, once a person has reached adulthood (i.e. 18 years of age), he or she is presumed to have the capacity to make decisions, including legally significant decisions. Whether a particular decision seems sensible to other people is considered irrelevant. This is clearly illustrated by the judgement in a recent case (*Re T* [1992] 4 All E.R. 649) relating to consent to treatment (a woman's wish to refuse life-saving blood products):

> An adult patient who . . . suffers from no mental incapacity has an absolute right to choose whether to consent to medical treatment, to refuse it or to choose one rather than another of the treatments being offered. . . . This right of choice is not limited to decisions which others might regard as sensible. It exists, notwithstanding that the reasons for making the choice are rational, irrational, unknown, or even non-existent.
> (Quoted in Fennell, 1996, p. 250; Jones, 1996)

Even when a person has a mental disorder, he or she is not necessarily considered unable to make decisions about his or her life. In a recent case (*Re C* [1994] 1 W.L.R. 290), the Court upheld the right of a patient with paranoid schizophrenia and diabetes, detained in Broadmoor Hospital, to make an advance refusal of treatment to amputate his gangrenous foot (for details, see Fennell, 1996; Jones, 1996).

However, inevitably, there will be some individuals at some times who are unable to make particular decisions. For these individuals, while it may have been widespread practice in the past to accept consent by a proxy (such as a relative or carer), recent case law has made it absolutely clear that proxy consent has no legal standing (Fennell, 1996, p. 261). Acknowledgement of the unsatisfactory, and piecemeal, legal provision for situations involving "mental incapacity" (i.e. involving the making of decisions for those unable to do so) led to an inquiry by the Law Commission of England and Wales, and, following consultation documents, a final report (Law Commission Report No. 231, 1995) was produced, accompanied by a draft bill (a draft bill has also been produced in Scotland, see the Scottish Law Commission (1995), Report No. 151, following a similar process). The draft bill made wide-ranging recommendations for decision making for an individual who is 'lacking mental capacity' because, at the material time:

• he is unable by reason of mental disability to make a decision for himself on the matter in question; or
• he is unable to communicate his decision on that matter because he is unconscious or for any other reason (section 2 of the draft bill).

In 1996, the government stated that it had no current plans to implement these recommendations or enact the legislation. What is described here is the present legal position in England and Wales, together with ideas of good practice (from the Law Commission documents, 1995, and the British Medical Association and Law Society Guidance, 1995).

Assessments of whether someone has the capacity to take a particular decision may be made in a variety of ways:

• In adopting a diagnostic approach (or a status approach, as the Law Commission, 1995, more correctly term it), a person's capacity to make any kind of decision is considered necessarily impaired simply because of a particular characteristic. At various times, and in various jurisdictions, characteristics such as age, religious belief, race, gender and clinical diagnosis have been used as criteria. This approach is not supported empirically (Murphy and Clare, 1995) and has not found favour in case law (for example, in Re C, described above).
• In adopting an outcome approach, a person's capacity is considered to be impaired simply because he or she makes a decision which appears unsound. This has not found favour in case law in England and Wales since it is clear that people have a right to take decisions which do not seem sensible to others (for example, the cases of Re T and Re C, described above).
• In adopting a functional approach, a person's capacity is judged on the basis of his or her ability to understand the information relating to the

decision in question, to weigh that information and to make a voluntary choice. One of the implications of this approach is that a person may be considered capable of making a decision in one set of circumstances (but not in another) and at one point of time (but not at another). Thus a person who has a diagnosis sometimes associated with a lack of capacity (such as schizophrenia) can be recognised as having the capacity to take a particular decision at a particular point in time, even if he or she was not able to take that decision at another time (cf. the diagnostic approach). Moreover, if a person makes an unusual decision, his or her right to do so is protected, provided he or she has the *capacity* to make the decision (cf. the outcome approach).

Despite the difficulties of the diagnostic and outcome approaches, it has sometimes been argued that they should not be entirely rejected: the existence of a particular diagnosis (for example, one of learning disabilities) can act as a signal to the GP that the person may not be able to understand as much as first appeared to be the case and that he or she may be especially vulnerable to acquiesce to the GP's suggestions. Similarly, if a person makes a very unusual decision (such as refusing to take an effective medication for a serious medical condition for which he or she has previously accepted medication), it may alert the GP to the need for more detailed questioning. Thus the occasional use of the diagnostic or outcome approach as a means of *alerting* the GP to the need for a proper assessment of capacity is not inappropriate (it does not imply that the person does not have the capacity to make the decision in question, only that his or her capacity may need to be assessed).

When it comes to assessing capacity, the functional method has been increasingly recognised as the most effective, accurate and empowering approach. It is also the approach which best reflects current law. The task for anyone consulted about a person's capacity to make a particular decision thus has become specific (i.e. specific to the decision in question) and complex (i.e. assessing capacity has now become a question of assessing the individual's understanding of the decision in question, rather than simply applying a diagnosis or evaluating the soundness of their decision). Ultimately, however, where a dispute about capacity arises, it is the court which will decide whether a particular individual has or has not the mental capacity to make a particular decision: it is not a conclusion which can be drawn only 'by the family; or the proprietor of a residential care home; or a social worker; or a solicitor; or even a doctor—although their opinions as to capacity may be of assistance in enabling a court to arrive at its own conclusions' (BMA/LS, 1995, p. 11). Nevertheless, it should be noted that millions of people make all kinds of decisions every day and, because of the presumption of capacity, these are not challenged in the courts.

There are a number of different kinds of decision, in relation to mental capacity, which can be described (BMA/LS, 1995):

- Capacity to deal with financial affairs.
- Capacity to make a will.
- Capacity to make a gift.
- Capacity to litigate.
- Capacity to enter into a contract.
- Capacity to vote.
- Capacity to enter personal relationships.
- Capacity to consent to and refuse medical treatment.
- Capacity to consent to research and innovative treatment.

It is not unusual for a medical opinion (often the GP's opinion) of capacity to be sought by solicitors for the decisions listed above, on the assumption that doctors are able to apply suitable tests of mental capacity in each case. In fact, this is sometimes very difficult and GPs should not be reluctant to seek advice from others (for example, from clinical psychologists, psychiatrists, speech and language therapists, community nurses or social workers on the local community learning disability teams) where they feel insufficiently expert.

Here capacity to consent to treatment and capacity to consent to relationships will be considered in detail as they are the most common decisions on which the GP's advice is likely to be sought (see Checklist 8 for a summary).

CONSENT TO TREATMENT

Adults (that is, people aged 18 years or more) are presumed to be able to consent to treatment ('treatment' is normally taken to include medical investigations, medical and nursing treatments, as well as rehabilitation). This is the case for all adults regardless of their level of disability (the situation for those aged 16–18 years is more complex—see Fennell, 1996—and will not be dealt with here). The doctor or other health care professional providing treatment is accountable in law for judging whether or not the person is able to consent to a particular treatment, and whether he or she gives or withholds that consent (BMA/LS, 1995, p. 66). According to the functional approach (see above), whether a person has the capacity to consent to a particular course of action will depend to some extent on the complexity of the decision to be made: for example, many people even with severe learning disabilities would be capable of making everyday decisions about what clothes to wear, what to eat or what to drink.

However, few would be able to consent to a complex series of treatments for a medical condition without at least considerable prior education about the issues involved.

Assessing capacity to consent to medical treatment is acknowledged to be difficult. In some other countries, for instance in many parts of the USA, there are guidelines about what should be considered in answering the question 'Can this person consent to this medical procedure?' In the USA, consent to treatment is only valid if it is 'informed consent'. This comprises three factors: knowledge relating to the particular decision to be made, the capacity to make decisions, and the voluntariness of the choice. Specific tests of the second element—the capacity to make decisions—have now been developed for people with mental disorders by Grisso and his colleagues (Murphy and Clare, 1995) and it has become clear that people with mental disorders, including those with learning disabilities, are sometimes perfectly capable of understanding medical information, weighing it up, reaching a decision and communicating that decision.

However, an individual's capacity to consent to medical treatment will need to be assessed anew for each occasion as the complexity of decisions (and the person's capacity) may vary. Based on recent case law it has been recommended (BMA/LS, 1995, p. 66) that to demonstrate capacity individuals should be able to:

- understand in simple language what the medical treatment is, its purpose and nature and why it is being proposed;
- understand its principal benefits, risks and alternatives;
- understand in broad terms the consequences of not receiving the proposed treatment;
- retain the information for long enough to make an effective decision;
- make a free choice (i.e. free from pressure).

Most medical treatment involves touching the person. Any intentional touching of a person, regardless of the fact that it is intended to be for his or her benefit, is a civil wrong and may constitute a criminal offence *unless* the person has given consent. Where a person is unable to consent, no one can consent on his or her behalf. At the same time, however, doctors and other health care professionals have a common law duty of care, and may be negligent if they withhold treatment. The decision to provide treatment to a person who is unable to consent can be defended if the doctor or other health care professional has carried it out because it was necessary. That is:

- It was required to preserve the life, health or well-being of the person. Such action is not limited simply to emergency situations but 'may well transcend such measures as surgical operations or substantial medical treatment and may extend to include such humdrum matters as routine medical or dental treatment, even simple care such as dressing and putting to bed' (the judgement in *Re F* [1990] 2 A.C.1, quoted in BMA/ LS, 1995, p. 69).

and

- It was in the person's 'best interests' because the particular treatment was in accordance with a practice accepted by a responsible and competent body of relevant *professional* opinion (BMA/LS, 1995; Gunn, 1994).

Where the person is unable to consent, it is important to document the reasons for proceeding with treatment.

There are special considerations in some cases (for example, advance refusals—BMA/LS, 1995—which limit the justification for proceeding with treatment, even in an emergency). For adults with learning disabilities, the most important of these relates to the sterilisation of women. Where the woman does not have the capacity to consent, it is expected that treatment providers will seek a declaration from the Court about the lawfulness of the proposed operation (BMA/LS, 1995; Gunn, 1996). Similarly, withdrawal of artificial hydration and nutrition from people who are considered to be in a persistent vegetative state requires a declaration from Court (as in the case of *Airedale NHS Trust* v. *Bland*) and tissue donation from a person who is unable to consent is also likely to do so (BMA/LS, 1995, p. 70). Such a declaration is not required from the Court for termination of a pregnancy, on the grounds that abortion is already closely regulated by statute (*Re SG* [1991] 2 F.L.R. 329).

With certain other exceptions (for example, treatment for a mental disorder under Part IV of the Mental Health Act 1983 (Jones, 1996 and Checklist 9) the individual must personally consent to treatment.

Case Example

Mr A is 35 years old. He has a profound disability and no apparent understanding of language or other forms of communication. He lives with his parents who carry out all aspects of his care, including feeding him, bathing him and changing the pads he wears because of his incontinence. However, in law, neither Mr A's parents (nor anyone else who knows him, such as his key-worker at the day-centre he attends) is empowered to make decisions on his behalf. If Mr A went to the GP for medical examination or a nursing procedure (such as having his ears syringed), it would not be possible for the GP (or the nurse) to obtain consent from him because of the extent of his disabilities. Any examination or treatment would therefore have to be done without Mr A's consent. The GP's defence to any challenge would be that the examination and treatment were necessary for his life, health or well-being and in his best interests. Other health care professionals (e.g. nurses) would be in exactly the same position as the GP and would need to argue similarly, if challenged.

Comments

Parents often find the fact that they are not able to make decisions for their son or daughter surprising, incomprehensible and personally insulting: they may feel that the law is implying that they are mistreating their relative in some way. This means that, where capacity to consent to treatment is an issue, an important first step for the GP or health care professional is likely to be to explain the law to the carers and to make it clear that carers are neither able to consent to treatment nor to withhold consent on behalf of their adult son or daughter.

Case Example

A GP's advice was sought by the mother of Mr B, an adult with severe learning disabilities living with his parents. He had very long-standing difficulties at night. His mother, who had recently been unwell, wanted medication for a short period to help him sleep. The GP wanted to see Mr B before prescribing, so arranged to visit him at home.

On visiting, the GP found the parents exhausted. Apparently, Mr B wandered about the house, making a good deal of noise, until the early hours of the morning. He then normally returned to his bedroom to sleep, although he awoke quite early. He was often restless in the day.

Mr B seemed to understand some signs which his parents made but used neither words nor signs himself. The GP observed while Mr B's parents tried to explain the proposed treatment to their son, but she did not feel that he understood. The GP concluded that Mr B did not have the capacity to give or withhold consent on this matter. Nevertheless, the GP wrote a prescription because she felt this could be defended on the grounds that it was necessary and in Mr B's best interests because his health would be improved by having more sleep, and he would be adversely affected if his parents became so exhausted that they could not care for him. The GP documented her decision fully in Mr B's notes.

Mr B took the medication on the first night, and slept well. The next day, he was a little less restless than usual. On the second night, he would not accept the medication, so his parents crushed it in a drink. Mr B drank it and he slept well. On the third night, Mr B's parents tried the same tactic but Mr B refused the drink, poured it in the sink and threw the cup at the wall, smashing it. Later, Mr

B's parents tried to mix the medication in his food but again Mr B, after tasting it, refused to eat it. That night he slept poorly.

His mother approached the GP again for advice. She was advised that, given that Mr B did not have the capacity to consent, he was probably objecting just to the taste of the medication (rather than to the principle of having medication to improve his sleep). An alternative was prescribed, which he accepted, and seemed effective. However, the GP remained concerned: she did not feel it was appropriate for Mr B to be on long-term medication. With the agreement of the parents, she therefore made a referral to the local specialist team for adults with learning disabilities (community team for people with learning disabilities—CTLD) for advice about other strategies and support for his parents (including possible respite), with the aim of reducing or eliminating the medication altogether as soon as possible.

CONSENT TO SEXUAL RELATIONSHIPS

In England and Wales, sexual relationships are lawful if the partners are able to consent and have given their consent (Gunn, 1996). Women aged 16 years or more are presumed to be able to consent to heterosexual or lesbian relationships. For men, there is no age of consent for heterosexual relationships; men aged 18 years or more are presumed to be able to consent to homosexual relationships. Where there is sexual activity and consent is disputed, an offence (such as rape, indecent assault, buggery) may have taken place. At such times, a GP may be asked whether, in his or her opinion, a particular individual could have given consent; whether or not he or she did so is ultimately a matter for a court to decide.

According to the British Medical Association and the Law Society (BMA/LS, 1995, p. 59), the common law test of capacity to consent to sexual relations implies that the person understands what is proposed and its implications, and is able to make a free choice. Strictly applied, however, this means that consent to sexual relationships requires good sexual knowledge (about sexual touching, intercourse, pregnancy, contraception, sexually transmitted diseases and safer sex) and good social and communicative skills (to understand what was proposed, to express a wish and to be able to assert the right to decide without undue pressure).

In practice, neither the GP nor other health professionals may ever know for certain whether the particular person with learning disabilities in their care is sexually active or not. This is often only known to the carers, and they are therefore the people who most often may need to consider whether the person has the capacity to consent to sexual relationships and whether he or she did consent in any particular case. In fact, individuals living in staffed residential accommodation are often at the mercy of their carers' attitudes to sexuality. These attitudes can vary from extreme liberalism, where everyone is thought to have the right to a sexual life regardless of the risks, to the very repressive, where sexual activity of any kind, particularly between two persons of the same gender, is actively discouraged. Neither of these extremes is acceptable, however, and ideally, for each individual:

- information should be gathered and recorded about the level of his or her sexual knowledge
- all individuals should be offered sex education to improve their sexual knowledge and understanding of their sexual rights (see Chapter 10; Murphy and Clare, 1995; and McCarthy and Cambridge, 1996)
- staff and carers should be alert to the possibility of sexual abuse, should have sexual relationship policies in place (see Chapter 10) and should consider seriously whether the rights of individuals are being properly protected if they acquire a sexual partner (see Chapter 10; Murphy and Clare, 1995).

Commonly, the carers are first to have concerns about adults with learning disabilities whom they think may be engaged in abusive relationships, and the carers are usually the first to approach the Adult Protection Teams in the local social services departments for advice. Nevertheless, it sometimes comes to the GP's notice that a person with learning disabilities is sexually active (see case example below) and at such times he or she needs to know how to proceed.

Despite the general presumption of competence to consent to sexual relationships in law, some protection does exist for those considered vulnerable to abuse (Gunn, 1996):

- It is an offence for a man to have sexual intercourse with, or procure, a woman who is a 'defective' (Sexual Offences Act 1956). The word 'defective' is outmoded and offensive; in today's terminology, this means a woman with a severe learning disability.
- Until 1994, it was clear that a man with 'severe subnormality' (in today's terminology, a severe learning disability) could not consent to homosexual acts (Sexual Offences Act 1967), even those which would not be an offence in the general population, such as acts in private when both partners are 18 years or more. It has been argued (Gunn, 1996) that the Criminal Justice and Public Order Act 1994 has been drafted in such a way that a man with a severe learning disability might be able to consent to anal intercourse, though not to other homosexual activities (for details, see Gunn, 1996, p. 42).
- It is an offence for a man who is a member of staff at, or employed by, a hospital or residential home to have sexual intercourse with a woman

with a mental disorder (other than his wife) who lives there or attends for treatment (Mental Health Act 1959, not repealed by the Mental Health Act 1983). Equivalent legislation exists relating to anal intercourse and other sexual acts by male staff and men with mental disorder who are in their care (Sexual Offences Act 1967).

The implications of this legislation are that adults with learning disabilities cannot consent to sexual relationships with members of staff and, therefore, where the GP or other health professionals think that such a relationship may have occurred, they do not need to assess capacity to consent; this is irrelevant. Instead, they should immediately contact the local Social Services Department and ask for the Adult Protection Team, who will deal with the concerns under the local guidelines for the protection of vulnerable adults from sexual abuse (see Chapter 10). Similarly, under the current law, people with severe learning disabilities are not considered able to consent to sexual relationships with others (see above). So, for example, if someone with a severe learning disability appears to be having a sexual relationship with a member of the public, it is very likely that an offence is taking place and, if approached for advice, the GP should again contact the local Adult Protection Team through the Social Services Department. They will normally wish to involve the police.

However, where two people with severe learning disabilities develop a sexual relationship and appear to show a real affection for each other, provided there is no evidence of exploitation (Brown and Craft, 1994), many professionals would consider that it would not be reasonable to interrupt the relationship, despite the fact that it may be difficult to establish capacity to consent. Nevertheless, this is a difficult decision in which all those involved with the couple need to consider the risks to the individuals as well as their rights. The local Adult Protection Team should at least be informed and those involved with the people should document their decisions carefully.

Case Example

Ms C, a 25-year-old woman with learning disabilities and autism, came to the GP's surgery with a member of staff from her residential placement. It transpired that Ms C had developed a sexual relationship with a man with learning disabilities who was resident in the same house (the staff member was pleased about this as the service emphasised opportunities for an 'ordinary life' for adults with learning disabilities). She asked the GP to prescribe Ms C the contraceptive pill.

With the help of a book (Hollins et al., 1996) designed for this purpose, the GP explained to Ms C that he needed to examine her. He was confident that Ms C had the capacity to consent to his examination and that she did so.

It appeared, from the physical examination and from what Ms C was able to convey to the GP, that she had had sexual intercourse in the past with the co-tenant at her house, but it was not clear when this had taken place.

[Note: Some GPs might have gone on simply to establish consent to the contraceptive pill at this stage. This would have been wrong as consent to a medical procedure was not the only issue here: Ms C might have been being sexually abused and the GP needed to ensure this was not the case (i.e. that Ms C could legally give consent to sexual relationships and that she had done so).]

The GP felt that he needed further advice before prescribing the contraceptive pill. He referred Ms C to the local specialist team for adults with learning disabilities (community team for adults with learning disabilities—CTLD), requesting an assessment of the extent of her learning disability, her capacity to consent to sexual relationships, and whether, if she was able to consent, it was likely that she did so with this partner. The GP also requested advice about the likelihood that Ms C would become pregnant with her partner and the likelihood that the partner could, or would, use a barrier form of contraception (which would also protect Ms C from sexually transmitted diseases).

The results of the assessment by the CTLD suggested that:

- *Ms C did not have a severe learning disability (i.e.* in law *she could give consent);*
- *her understanding of sexual matters was so limited that, at present, she could probably not give consent to sexual intercourse (so the question of whether she did do so with this particular partner was therefore premature);*
- *her partner did appear to have a severe learning disability and it seemed unlikely that, without a great deal of help, he could be responsible for contraception or for practising 'safer sex';*
- *the likelihood of pregnancy was thought very low because the cause of the man's learning disability meant he was probably not fertile.*

However, the assessment also suggested the possibility of sexual abuse, since the man had a long history of unacceptable sexual behaviour with previous co-residents. A multi-disciplinary case review was set up (to include the GP, professionals from the CTLD and the local Adult Protection Team) to discuss the best way forward. This was not a simple matter since it was not clear that Ms C rejected, or was distressed by, contact with the partner. However, given the young woman's vulnerability, it was decided that it would be better for the sexual relationship to be suspended (through close supervision) until the possibility of abuse had been ruled out. This necessitated some explanations with Ms

C (and her partner). Ms C was also offered sex education (by the CTLD) to improve her capacity to consent to sexual intercourse. After that, the possibility that she did consent had to be established. In the meantime, the GP did not prescribe the contraceptive pill.

KEY POINTS

1. In general, adults with learning disabilities have the same rights as other adults to choose for themselves whether to give or withhold consent to medical treatment and sexual relationships, and to make other decisions affecting their lives.
2. Adults with learning disabilities are at risk of not being offered any choices, being given inadequate information about possible choices, and being pressurised to decide in particular directions.
3. Wherever possible, adults with learning disabilities should be empowered to make choices for themselves even though this will sometimes involve GPs, carers, and members of specialist services for adults with learning disabilities in considerable work.
4. There will be a very small number of people who will not be able to make decisions for themselves and the current legal provision is unsatisfactory in these cases. (Recommendations have been made for changes in the law and it is possible that new legislation will be enacted.)
5. The British Medical Association and the Law Society (BMA/LS, 1995) offers very helpful advice in dealing with what are often difficult situations to which there are no easy solutions.
6. In assessing an adult's capacity to decide, GPs and other health care professionals need to understand the law in relation to consent, know the person's level of cognitive and social skills and his or her understanding of the particular decision at issue. This will often require the assistance of carers and of other professionals (such as those on the local community team for people with learning disabilities).
7. GPs and other health care professionals should always be prepared to consult specialists in making decisions and should document the decision-making process very carefully.

ACKNOWLEDGEMENTS

We are very grateful to Dr Marie Bambrick, Dr John Crichton, Professor Michael Gunn and Dr Tony Holland for helpful discussions about the issues in this chapter and for their comments on previous versions.

REFERENCES

Starred entries indicate recommended reading

*British Medical Association and the Law Society (BMA/LS) (1995) *Assessment of Mental Capacity: Guidance for Doctors and Lawyers*. BMA, London.

British Psychological Society (1991) *Mental Impairment and Severe Mental Impairment: A Search for Definitions*. British Psychological Society, Leicester.

Brown, H. and Craft, A. (1994) Personal relationships and sexuality: the staff role. In A. Craft (ed.), *Practice Issues in Sexuality and Learning Disabilities*. Routledge, London, pp. 1–22.

Brown, H. and Smith, H. (1992) *Normalisation: A Reader for the Nineties*. Routledge, London.

Clare, I.C.H. and Gudjonsson, G.H. (1993) Interrogative suggestibility, confabulation and acquiescence in people with mild learning disabilities (mental handicap): implications for reliability during police interrogations. *British Journal of Clinical Psychology*, **32**, 295–301.

Fennell, P. (1996) *Treatment Without Consent: Law, Psychiatry and the Treatment of Mentally Disordered People since 1845*. Routledge, London.

Gudjonsson, G.H. (1992) *The Psychology of Interrogations, Confessions and Testimony*. Wiley, Chichester.

Gunn, M. (1994) Competency and consent: the importance of decision-making. In A. Craft (ed.), *Practice Issues in Sexuality and Learning Disabilities*. Routledge, London, pp. 116–134.

Gunn, M. (1996) *Sex and the Law* (4th edition). Family Planning Association, London.

*Hollins, S., Bernal, J. and Gregory, M. (1996) *Going to the Doctor* (illustrated by B. Webb). Books Beyond Words, St. George's Mental Health Library, London.

Jones, R. (1996) *Mental Health Act Manual* (5th edition). Sweet & Maxwell, London.

Law Commission (1995) *Mental Incapacity (Report No. 231)*. HMSO, London.

Murphy, G. and Clare, I.C.H. (1995) Adults' capacity to make decisions affecting the person: psychologists' contribution. In R. Bull and D. Carson (eds), *Handbook of Psychology in Legal Contexts*. Wiley, Chichester, pp. 97–128.

McCarthy, M. and Cambridge, P. (1996) *Your Sexual Rights*. BILD Publications, Clevedon, Avon.

Scottish Law Commission (1995) *Report on Incapable Adults (Report No. 151)*. HMSO, Edinburgh.

12

THE MULTI-DISCIPLINARY AND MULTI-AGENCY APPROACH

Margaret Macadam and Jackie Rodgers

Adults with learning disabilities have individual needs, and it may not be possible for all their needs to be met successfully by one professional or agency. Learned debates have taken place about the difference between health and social care, but demarcations are most relevant for administrative and service purposes, not from the perspective of service users. Adults with learning disabilities need access to both specialists and general health services. Joint working—multi-disciplinary and multi-agency collaboration—is therefore an important approach to ensuring that adults with learning disabilities receive high quality services and health care. This chapter explores some of the reasons for, and conflicts in, pursuing a collaborative approach, and looks at the example of community learning disability teams as one model of joint working.

POLICY IMPERATIVES FOR JOINT WORKING

Collaboration was one of the main themes of the Government's White Paper, *Caring for People* (DoH, 1989). Before outlining the responsibilities of different agencies in the proposed reforms, the paper stressed:

Adults with Learning Disabilities. Edited by J. O'Hara and A. Sperlinger.
© 1997 John Wiley & Sons Ltd.

... it is essential that the caring services should work effectively together, each recognising and respecting the others' contribution and responsibilities. It will continue to be essential for each of the relevant services to keep in mind the interests and responsibilities of the other; to recognise that particularly at the working interface, there is frequently much common purpose; to cross refer cases when appropriate; and to seek and share advice and information when relevant. There is no room in community care for a narrow view of individuals' needs, nor of ways of meeting them.

The notion of a *'seamless service'* continued to be a key aim when the White Paper became law, through the NHS and Community Care Act 1990. The accompanying guidance emphasised that the boundaries between primary health care, secondary health care and social care, should not form barriers seen from the perspective of the service user. Similarly, *The Health of the Nation* strategy for people with learning disabilities (DoH, 1995), emphasised that collaboration and partnership form an important means of reducing gaps in meeting people's needs and using resources effectively. It called for every agency responsible for an aspect of a service to improve joint working.

Such calls for collaboration arose within a context of important changes in the way health and social care are organised and delivered, namely *care in the community* and the *purchaser–provider split*. Some consideration of these is helpful to understand the opportunities for, and barriers to, joint working.

CARE IN THE COMMUNITY

The move away from institutionalised care for people with learning disabilities began well before the NHS and Community Care Act was drafted, but the principles embodied in the Act continued to emphasise the need for re-integration. People with learning disabilities have always lived in the community, the majority with their families. The closure of large institutions and subsequent resettlement of their residents into community provision, put a spotlight on the support services which people with learning disabilities need generally, whether or not they have recently moved out of an institution. With a dispersed population, the need for close collaboration across services is self-evident.

The aims of Care in the Community include:

• user choice and empowerment
• a needs-led approach through assessment of care needs
• effective targeting and use of resources (money and multiple providers)

- planning and ensuring delivery of 'seamless services'
- monitoring the quality of care
- review of clients' and family carers' needs.

The NHS and Community Care Act brought with it the principle of *care management:* individuals would have their needs assessed *(community care assessments)* and packages of care developed to meet those needs. A care manager would be responsible for designing and purchasing packages of care, identifying potential providers from statutory and voluntary agencies, and ensuring their delivery. The care management approach would, in theory, facilitate cross agency cooperation.

However, basic tensions and contradictions underlie these systems (Elwell *et al.*, 1995; Waddington, 1995). Issues such as child protection, services for elderly people and intense budgetary pressures mean that 'person-centred planning' will always be constrained by the political, organisational and social environment into which it was introduced.

PURCHASERS AND PROVIDERS

Central to the NHS reforms is the separation of the commissioning and purchasing of care from its provision, in both health authorities and social services departments.

- *Self-governing NHS Trusts* were set up to provide health services, while health authorities have retained the overall responsibility for commissioning and purchasing services from these and other providers, including the voluntary sector.
- *GP fund-holding* allows certain GPs to purchase a range of services directly from providers. The significance of this reform for people with learning disabilities became most apparent when the fund-holding scheme was extended in 1993 to cover community services, including specialist learning disability provision. At the time of writing, most fund-holding GPs are not taking an active role in purchasing such services, preferring instead, to arrange fixed price non-attributable block contracts. In the future they could pursue a 'cost per case contract', rather like those for acute hospital services. If this type of contract were used for specialist learning disability services, GPs would need to be knowledgeable about the special heath care needs of people with learning disabilities on their list, in order to make and monitor appropriate referrals within their overall budget. However, recent research (Langan *et al.*, 1993) found that many GPs did not have this knowledge, and that their communication with specialist secondary

health care providers, in the form of community teams for people with learning disabilities (CTLD, described below) is limited. This is not a desirable situation. It becomes even more serious if a lack of collaboration affects the adult with learning disabilities being able to access important services such as speech and occupational therapy. If GPs are to become more actively involved in purchasing these services in the way that the fund-holding scheme intended, then a prerequisite must be a closer working relationship between fund-holders and specialist service providers.

• *Social services departments* have a commissioning, purchasing and provider function. They may be responsible for providing respite services, residential facilities and day centres. They are also the lead agency for services to people with learning disabilities, and are responsible for community care assessments, and eligibility criteria for services. Traditional social worker roles have been almost superseded by the care manager role; some work within their own organisation, and others are placed as members of CTLDs.

JOINT COMMISSIONING

The purchaser–provider relationship has been complicated by an increasing recognition that health authorities (HAs) and social services departments (SSDs) need to work in partnership at a higher, organisational level, via joint commissioning and purchasing to ensure that the experience of delivery of health and social care is as seamless as possible. Joint commissioning is . . . 'joint commitment at an inter-agency level, leading to shared responsibilities . . .' (DoH, 1993a). As such, it depends on the recognition by local and health authorities that they have a *shared responsibility* for the provision of health and social care for people with learning disabilities in a style which reflects 'ordinary life' principles.

Progress towards joint commissioning can only be made where local conditions allow (Waddington, 1995). The mismatch of roles and styles between HAs' pure purchasing role, and the 'hybrid' role of SSDs, where they are major providers as well as purchasers, continues to be a source of misunderstanding and difficulty. The increasing numbers of GP fund-holding practices, and the merger of DHAs with FHSAs will inevitably add to existing differences.

It is important that HAs and SSDs work together to plan, formulate strategies, set priorities, allocate resources and establish a framework for jointly purchasing services. However, this approach is not well established in many authorities, and professionals are unlikely to be experiencing its benefits directly.

THE NEED TO WORK TOGETHER: THE VALUE OF JOINT WORKING

Research evidence has given us a good idea of the set of circumstances which are most effective in promoting health. These include:

- The provision of effective and appropriate health care, with all types of health professionals having a part to play, including dentists, hospital ward and outpatients staff, opticians and audiometrists.
- The person's health-related patterns of behaviour: notably smoking, diet, drinking and exercise. Health promotion departments and colleges, as well as the Primary Health Care service, will have a role to play in providing information and advice on healthy lifestyles. There may also be opportunities to collaborate with local authorities to ensure that appropriate opportunities for exercise, for example, are available to adults with learning disabilities.
- The person's economic circumstances: a range of agencies have a role to play. These may include housing departments and associations, job centres, employers, voluntary organisations facilitating supported employment, benefit advisers such as social workers and citizens' advice agencies.
- The person's social circumstances: social care agencies will clearly be important, and so will voluntary organisations that provide support to families and individuals.

It should not be forgotten that adults with learning disabilities, and carers who support them, have an important role to play both in defining their health needs, and in expressing preferences about how they should be met. Increasing emphasis on consumer involvement in health care means that it is no longer appropriate for professionals to make decisions, even collaboratively, that do not involve the person concerned.

It is worth remembering, however, that adults with learning disabilities may rarely or never have been consulted about their needs and wishes. They may need a supporter or advocate to help them speak up for themselves or to speak on their behalf. Schemes that develop such skills (known as self-advocacy and citizen advocacy) are well established throughout the country, and could be the first point of contact for health professionals who wish to adopt this approach.

Bearing in mind the range of people who have a role to play in improving the health of people with learning disabilities, a creative approach to collaboration can make best use of existing facilities and opportunities and create them where they previously did not exist.

CTLD: A MODEL FOR JOINT WORKING

The community team for people with learning disabilities (CTLD) is a model for multi-disciplinary and multi-agency working, spanning health and social services and including such professionals as: community learning disability nurses, clinical psychologists, psychiatrists, speech and language therapists, occupational therapists, physiotherapists and social workers. Such teams have existed for nearly 20 years. The original impetus for forming what were then known as Community Mental Handicap Teams arose out of concerns expressed by the National Development Team, about the fragmented nature of services for people with learning disabilities (Brown, 1990). The spread of these teams was quite dramatic. In a survey conducted in England in 1987, some 350 CTLDs were identified (Brown, 1990). In just 10 years, a new model of working was well and truly established.

CTLDs have several roles to play in meeting the health needs of their client group. Brown (1990) found that as well as being responsible for direct service delivery, many teams take on a service development role, in which they liaise with other professionals and agencies with a view to identifying any gaps in the range of services available, and work together to try to fill these gaps. This is often facilitated by individual programme planning, where a particular client's needs are identified, and a package of care designed which spans statutory, voluntary and private agencies, including health, housing and social services. CTLD members also take on coordinating roles, in which they attempt to ensure that the individual's identified programme of care is put into practice (now an integral part of care management process).

DIFFICULTIES AND TENSIONS IN JOINT WORKING

The structure and roles of CTLDs do not themselves guarantee effective collaboration between different professionals and agencies. The creation of a team does not necessarily mean the creation of team work.

Policy Tensions

The introduction of competition between providers, and the contractual relationship between purchasers and providers, has added complexity to the environment in which collaboration is supposed to take place. In theory, at least, different providers are 'rivals', competing to provide services to purchasers. A market system relies on the ability to cost services and buy and sell them at appropriate rates. An increasing awareness of the financial repercussions of calling in another professional may reduce the incentive to do so. Fund-holding GPs may be tempted to limit the number of 'costly' or time-consuming patients, including people with learning disabilities, on their list (see *The Independent*, 9.10.93). Such a system, with increasing complexity and a greater emphasis on budgetary considerations, cannot be ignored. It can serve as a barrier to joint working, while providing an even greater necessity that it should be achieved. The effects of policy are experienced at local and individual level, and can interact with other, less structural barriers to collaboration.

Ideologies and Cultures

One such barrier arises from the tendency of professionals and organisations to take on their own ideologies and cultures, holding set values and attitudes, which have developed through their training and practice, and coming to see the group or agency to which they belong as having distinctive characteristics. Once established, these cultures become recognisable to other groups of workers and some sense of opposition can develop (Dalley, 1989). Shared models of care, language, priorities and perspectives can arise within a group, and these may be different from those of the professional or agency with whom collaboration is sought.

For example, a referral letter can speak volumes, simply in the terms used to describe the person concerned (e.g. 'mentally subnormal'). Professionals can help overcome the difficulties that arise from this by trying not to pre-judge other workers for what appears to them to be inappropriate use of terminology. The terminology used is likely to be the result of that person's training and experience, and does not necessarily indicate that he or she will work in inappropriate ways. Personal contact and joint working can allow a non-threatening discussion; it can be enjoyable and stimulating to have your own ideas and ways of working questioned, as this can encourage a more thoughtful and open-minded approach.

Professional Roles

Even within shared organisational cultures, problems can arise around perceptions of professional roles. Professionals are trained to practise distinctive skills, which can be important to their status and identity. If these skills are not recognised, or if they overlap with the expertise of another professional, conflicts can result (Ovreveit, 1986). If the under-lying tensions of inter-professional working are not recognised, conflicts such as these can be experienced personally, making them harder to tackle. The skills and roles of each professional need to be known to everyone concerned, and equally valued.

Overlap can be avoided where this is unnecessary and inefficient, and managed where it is valuable and effective. Professionals can understand their own place in working towards a 'common purpose', and share in the achievements of all the workers who contribute to the development, care and support of a service user. They can see the value of their own work amplified and consolidated by the work of others.

Perceived differences in power or status can be apparent and are not easily overcome. It is important to understand and acknowledge why joint working can be difficult. Some strategies to help include: avoid personalisation of any problem that does arise; be clear about profes-sional roles and areas of expertise and experience; have a common system of documentation, referral, review and closure, agreed team protocols and time to communicate with one another.

Confidentiality Principle vs 'Team Confidentiality'

Although 'absolute' confidentiality is preferred by some professionals, confidentiality is never absolute. It makes it impossible to involve others properly in assessment, treatment or care. Teams need to clarify what type of confidentiality they observe in different situations, and make this clear to service users and other providers (Ovreveit, 1993).

Finding the Time

Joint working does involve some investment in time. It can be difficult for any individual to make this investment when time is limited and demands are high. It may seem that time spent pursuing joint working (including attending case conferences and reviews, informing, consulting and nego-tiating with others) is time away from direct work with service users and, therefore, less important. However, joint working can ultimately save time and allow more direct contact with service users. Unnecessary overlap can be avoided, information can be shared and working life can be made considerably easier if a contact in another profession or agency has been cultivated. A quick phone call to someone known personally over a long period of time, can help to bypass obstacles to effective care.

One particular difficulty can be that time spent in facilitating joint working is not recognised as an integral part of a particular worker's responsibilities. Time spent on collaborative working can be identified in supervision sessions, and 'time management reports', emphasising the value of this approach. Then, if the work of professionals is costed as part of the contracting environment, joint working can be identified and legitimated, instead of being squeezed into an already busy schedule. This needs to be understood and addressed by managers and purchasers of services. Time needed for casual contact and the everyday interaction that makes joint working so much easier can be reduced if working premises are shared, and again this is an issue for managers to consider.

The Way Forward

Recognition of the problems that can be encountered when attempting multi-disciplinary and multi-agency collaboration need not lead to inertia. We can be realistic without being intimidated. It may help to think in terms of small, achievable goals. For example, if professionals and agencies are faced with an individual whose particular needs are beyond their capacity to meet unaided, collaboration may take place on a 'needs must' basis, with immediate and clear benefits that outweigh any problems that might be encountered (see Box 1).

• Jointly agreed protocols, such as for hospital admission and discharge (Checklist 3) ensures a smoother transition from community to hospital, and vice versa. For example, in the Avon Health Authority area, the specialist learning disability trust has created guidelines for the care of people with learning disabilities who are admitted to hospital. The guidelines provide information about the range of living circumstances which people with learning disabilities may experience, and highlight issues such as the importance of easy to understand information, informed consent, and appropriate discharge procedures. It also outlines the role that other professionals, friends, advocates and families may have to play, in making hospital admission a satisfactory experience. The guidelines have been adopted as policy by the acute trusts in the area.
• Information sharing is particularly important if the service user cannot readily communicate details of the care and support he or she receives. For example, a psychologist working with a person with learning disabilities will be less able to help if he or she does not know that the person is receiving psychotropic medication prescribed by the GP.

Box 1:   Examples of effective milti-disciplinary, multi-agency working

Case vignette

Mr A is a 26-year-old man with multiple disabilities: severe learning disabilities, cerebral palsy, spastic quadriplegia, communication problems, recurrent aspiration pneumonia and swallowing difficulties. He attends day care in the neighbouring district, purchased for him by his care manager. The host district's specialist learning disability team agrees to provide a package of care to meet his health needs at the day centre: this includes support and advice to staff, management of health problems, and sensory work. Eventually, Mr A required a major surgical intervention because of his swallowing difficulties. Effective multi-disciplinary and multi-agency collaboration, coordination and communication, at the individual 'case level' was essential in order to meet Mr A's complex needs.

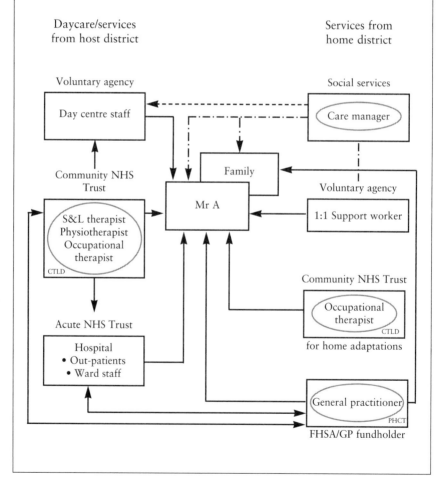

- Specially designed records, held by the service user, could provide a way of exchanging the information needed to coordinate the efforts of everyone involved. They would also emphasise the central role that the service user, with appropriate support, has to play in influencing the assessment and meeting of their needs.
- Community learning disability nurses could work alongside the Primary Health Care Team at the GP's surgery, helping adults with learning disabilities to attend for health screening and appointments, reinforcing information and advice in more appropriate ways, ensuring that health needs are identified and met, and helping general health care staff to develop their skills in working with adults with learning disabilities.

One way of dealing with the barriers to multi-disciplinary collaboration might be to focus on the service user's perspective. If professionals and agencies concentrate upon the needs and wishes of individual service users, it may be possible to marginalise issues that arise as a result of the different professional ideologies and organisational cultures. Recognition of the benefits of joint working can give us optimism that it can be more widely achieved, and provide the motivation to attempt it.

Joint working takes time to develop successfully. Professionals and agencies may well experience difficulties as they attempt to achieve it. However, if these challenges can be managed to the extent that they are not problems for the service user, the most important measure of success will have been achieved.

KEY POINTS

1. There are many challenges to collaborative working within the complex, market environment of health care. Joint commissioning and joint purchasing may ultimately provide a way forward to ensuring the delivery of a seamless service.
2. Barriers to multi-disciplinary and multi-agency collaboration could be lessened if professionals and agencies concentrated upon the needs and wishes of individual service users.
3. All professionals and agencies involved can be perceived as part of a team: a team designed to offer appropriate care and support to the person concerned.
4. Care management involves the identification and assessment of individual needs. The person with learning disabilities has a central role to play in influencing this assessment, and in having his or her needs met.

5. Care packages involve services from a variety of statutory and voluntary agencies. It requires effective monitoring, review, coordination and collaboration if high quality services are to be received by the person with learning disabilities and his or her family.
6. Joint working takes time to develop successfully. It needs to be identified and costed, and not squeezed, unrecognised, into an already busy schedule.

REFERENCES

Starred entries indicate recommended reading

Brown, S. (1990) *CMHTs: Variations on a Theme*. Practice Paper Series, No. 1. Centre for Research in Social Policy, Department of Health, London.
Dalley, G. (1989) Professional ideology organisational tribalism? The health service social work divide. In R. Taylor and J. Ford (eds), *Social Work and Health Care*. Jessica Kingsley, London.
Department of Health (DoH) (1989) *Caring for People: Community Care in the Next Decade and Beyond*. CM 849. HMSO, London.
Department of Health (DoH) (1993a) *Joint Commissioning for Community Care: A Slice Through Time*. HMSO, London.
*Department of Health (DoH) (1993b) *Working Together for Better Health*, HMSO, London.
Department of Health (DoH) (1995) *The Health of the Nation: A Strategy for People with Learning Disabilities*. HMSO, London.
*Elwell, L., Platts, H. and Rees, G. (1995) Putting people first? Assessment and care management. In T. Philpot and L. Ward (eds), *Values and Visions: Changing Ideas in Services for People with Learning Difficulties*. Butterworth Heinemann.
*Higgins, R., Oldman, C. and Hunter, D.J. (1994) Working together: lessons for collaboration between health and social services. *Health and Social Care*, **2**, 269–277.
Langan, J., Russell, O. and Whitefield, M. (1993) *Community Care and the General Practitioner: Primary Health Care for People with Learning Disabilities*. Norah Fry Research Centre, Bristol.
Ovreveit, J. (1986) *Organisation of Multidisciplinary Teams*. Health Services Working Paper, Brunel University.
Ovreveit, J. (1993) *Coordinating Community Care: Multi-disciplinary Teams and Care Management*. Open University Press, UK.
*Waddington, P. (1995) Joint commissioning for services for people with learning disabilities: a review of the principles and the practice. *British Journal of Learning Disabilities*, **23**, 2–10.

Part II
Checklists

A GP's ASSESSMENT
AND EXAMINATION

Gywn Howells

People with learning disabilities are a vulnerable group and warrant careful medical monitoring. The Royal College of General Practitioners recommends that they should be regularly assessed to identify their high morbidity and mortality rates, and produced a protocol designed to meet their special health care needs (Howells and Barker, 1990). The Department of Health (DoH, 1992) emphasised the continuing responsibility of health authorities and GP fund-holders to ensure provision of health care for this group, and *The Health of the Nation* strategy (DoH, 1995) focused on the particular needs of people with learning disabilities and their carers.

GUIDELINES FOR ASSESSMENT

Routine medical consultations should provide adequate time to talk to the patient (alone if possible) and then with the principle carer. The assessment should establish the following:

Social Situation

- Who are the primary carers and what is their relationship?
- What services, such as respite care, holiday relief and recreational activities, are being provided?

Adults with Learning Disabilities. Edited by J. O'Hara and A. Sperlinger.
© 1997 John Wiley & Sons Ltd.

- What are the hopes and aspirations of the patient and his or her carers?
- What social factors—employment, housing, family circumstances—adversely affect the physical and emotional health of the patient with learning disabilities? How can these be minimised?
- Do carers show the strains of constant caring? Are they getting all the support that they need?

Medical Assessment

The clinical history

In taking a detailed medical and family history the following are particularly important:

- Lifestyle in relation to diet, exercise, smoking, alcohol consumption, contraceptive and sexual practice.
- Immunisation history (with a plan to rectify any omissions).
- Drug therapy. Why is a drug prescribed? Review medication taken, enquire about administration difficulties, and consider possible interactions and side-effects.
- Dental hygiene and disease (including gum hypertrophy and gingivitis).
- Communication difficulties—level of understanding and ways by which the patient communicates in general, and with specific relation to health issues, e.g. pain.
- Problems with dysphagia, and possible recurrent respiratory infections.
- Orthopaedic problems and others associated with mobility.
- Epilepsy and its management.
- Incontinence. Can management be more effective? Is it of recent onset?
- Behavioural problems, especially changes in behaviour.
- Symptoms suggestive of mental health problems—e.g. changes in sleep pattern, appetite, weight, concentration, interest, motivation, mood and behaviour.

The physical examination

Fear and embarrassment, the need for privacy or for help with undressing may be issues to consider. Be aware of patients who willingly acquiesce, especially to more intimate examinations as this may be an alerting sign of abuse. Consider consent and ethical issues especially if the patient has difficulty cooperating, but simple, clear explanation and reassurance may be all that is needed. The examination should be as full as necessary with special attention to the following:

- height, weight and blood pressure
- detection of visual and hearing impairments
- orthopaedic problems, including spinal deformities and contractures
- mobility
- skin and pressure areas
- undescended testes and hernias
- special risks of any identified syndrome (e.g. congenital heart disease, obesity, hypothyroidism, and atlanto-axial instability in Down's syndrome; obesity and hypogonadism in Prader-Willi syndrome).

Investigations

- Routine urine testing and a full blood count are often productive.
- A cervical smear and breast examination, including mammography, should be carried out where appropriate.
- Consider need for monitoring serum levels of medication (e.g. lithium, carbamazepine) as well as associated side-effects (e.g. liver and renal function).

The Needs of Carers

The simultaneous assessment of family carers, who are often also on the GP's list, is a valuable undertaking. They may have increased risks of some health problems because of their role:

- stress and demands of caring for the person with learning disabilities
- implication of disability on the family and for the individual carer
- cause of the learning disability may also contribute to their health problems, e.g. dietary deficiencies, infections, deprivation
- inherited causes and the need for genetic counselling.

Meeting their needs is of vital importance not simply to their own sense of well-being, but also the patient with learning disabilities.

REFERENCES

Department of Health (DoH) (1992) *Healthcare for People with Learning Disabilities.* Department of Health Guidance HSG (92) 42.

Department of Health (DoH) (1995) *The Health of the Nation: A Strategy for People with Learning Disabilities,* HMSO, London.

Howells, G. and Barker, M. (1990) A protocol for primary health care. In *Primary Care for People with a Mental Handicap.* Occasional Paper 47. Royal College of General Practitioners.

PARENTING ASSESSMENT

Susan McGaw

1. PARENT PROFILE

Main Areas of Assessment

(Extract from *Special Parenting Service Assessment Manual*)

Intellectual functioning	IQ
	Reading
	Writing
	Numeracy
	Decision making
	Logical sequencing
	Organisational skills
	Problem solving
Independent living skills	Time telling
	Telephone skills
	Travel skills
	Budgeting
	Employment

Adults with Learning Disabilities. Edited by J. O'Hara and A. Sperlinger.
© 1997 John Wiley & Sons Ltd.

Homecare	
Domesticity	Cooking
	Washing
	Shopping
Cleanliness and Safety	Kitchen
	Living room
	Bedroom
	Bathroom
Safety	Outside of home
Health	Mental health
	Physical health
	Self-care
Support and Resources	Relationships
	Family
	Professional
	Community

2. COMMUNITY RESOURCE CHECKLIST

- Family Planning Associations (Brooks Advisory)
- Ante-natal Classes/Parentcraft Classes
- Well Woman Clinic/Well Men Clinic
- Adult Mental Health: MIND, Psychiatric Services, Independent Therapies
- Mother & Baby Group/Toddler Groups/Playschemes/Nurseries
- Child Health Clinics
- Child Guidance Clinics
- Child Assessment Units
- Parenting Programmes: Special Parenting, Elfrida Rathbone, Parent–Link, Under 8's, Parent Network, etc.
- Family Units/Centres: residential, day care, parenting programmes, home-help, family aides
- Churches: tea treats, residential services, therapeutic groups
- Toy & Equipment Libraries
- Councils: housing, benefits
- Housing Associations: accessing repairs, accommodation, equipment
- Public Transport: accessing service time-tables, cost, location
- Public Libraries

- Further Education Colleges:
  Lifeskill Courses: literacy, numeracy, cooking, sports
  Vocational Courses: office work, computing, catering, etc.
- Doctors/Dentist/Optician: registration/access
- Family Support Services: National Children's Homes, Echo, etc.
- Crisis lines: Cry-sis, MAMA, Relate, Samaritans, etc.
- Women's Refuge
- Citizens Advice Bureau
- Advocacy; Values into Action, Mencap, BILD, People First, etc.
- Legal Representation: Voice, etc.
- Adoption and Family Finding Unit.

PEOPLE WITH LEARNING DISABILITIES IN HOSPITAL

Heather Hogan and Peter Martin

People with learning disabilities may need to use hospital services like anyone else; or, they may have additional health problems associated with particular syndromes or additional disabilities which will necessitate regular contact with hospitals and specialist services. It is important to consider and prepare for the difficulties that may be experienced by patients, carers and staff, particularly when a hospital admission is necessary.

PLANNING AN ADMISSION

- Prepare the patient as much as possible, and try not to alter an admission date.
- The admitting hospital should nominate a named person to be responsible for planning and coordinating the admission.
- The named person should gather and share information about the patient (including medical, social and treatment history) with key staff. Involve carers, community services, general practitioner and specialist learning disability services as appropriate.
- Advise ward staff on key issues such as how best to communicate with the individual, the need for consistency, the need to use clear and simple language and the need for verbal or physical prompts.

Adults with Learning Disabilities. Edited by J. O'Hara and A. Sperlinger.
© 1997 John Wiley & Sons Ltd.

- Discuss with ward staff how the person communicates basic needs (hunger, thirst, pain, the need to use the toilet); particular behaviours, rituals and anxieties, sleeping habits and abilities for self-care and eating.
- Plan for appropriate staffing and skills to be available to meet any special needs identified. Consult with carers and specialist learning disability teams.
- Arrange a pre-admission visit if this is appropriate and feasible.
- Consider issues of consent.

THE ADMISSION

- Identify a named person responsible for coordinating care.
- Ensure communication boards, hearing aids, etc., come with the patient and that he or she is encouraged to use them.
- Encourage the patient and carers to make the environment as comfortable and as familiar as possible (e.g. personal items, comfort objects, familiar possessions).
- Check again how the patient communicates, and his or her level of understanding.
- Use simple, plain language. Avoid jargon, long words, euphemisms and complex sentences. Use pictures and images to back up information. Check that what is said has been heard and understood.
- Try to establish a good rapport with the patient and remember that extra time, skill and care are often required.
- Prepare a Care Plan in collaboration with the patient, carers and ward staff.
- Seek relatives' and carers' advice, support and involvement. Do not assume or expect them to provide care to the patient while on the ward unless this has been negotiated beforehand.
- It is often helpful to establish routine, regular and reliable visiting for the benefit of patient and staff. Ensure that the patient is aware of planned visits.
- Avoid isolating the person with learning disabilities from others unless it is essential for his or her care, treatment or comfort. The patient has already been removed from familiar routines and surroundings and should be made to feel as safe and secure as possible.
- Consider the emotional and psychological impact of being in hospital, of being ill, of frightening investigations, procedures and treatments. Remember, this may be the person's first time away from home or from his or her carers.
- Warn and explain before starting contact. Start with the least threatening contact. Explain and demonstrate in a calm, simple and unhurried

manner each procedure to be carried out and piece of equipment to be used. Be prepared to repeat yourself. Avoid keeping the patient waiting.
- Involve carers where appropriate in supporting the patient through invasive procedures and/or investigations.
- Relatives and carers often require special time and consideration too.

PLANNING A DISCHARGE

- Identify a named person responsible for coordinating the patient's discharge.
- Consider and arrange the support networks that will need to be in place for discharge.
- Ensure effective verbal and written communication with all those involved in the patient's after-care.
- Ensure that the patient and carers know and understand what follow-up medication and convalescent arrangements have been made. For example, who will receive and read appointment letters, and should they be copied to any one else?
- Who will be available for further advice and support after hospital discharge? Ensure that the patient and carers know who this person is and how to make contact. Who will arrange transport to appointments, if needed?
- Involve the local specialist learning disabilities services in providing additional help and support to the patient and his or her carers.

RECOMMENDED READING

Donaldson, J. (1980) Changing attitudes towards handicapped persons. A review and analysis of research. *Exceptional Children*, **46**, 504–514.

Kelly, M.P. and May, D. (1982) Good and bad patients: review of the literature and a theoretical critique. *Advance Nursing*, **7**, 147–156.

Lindsey, M., Singh, K. and Perrett, A. (1993) Management of learning disabilities in the general hospital. *British Journal of Hospital Medicine*, **50**(4), 182–186.

PRESCRIBING MEDICATION

Heather Hogan and Peter Martin

People with learning disabilities have higher than average health needs (Howells, 1986; Wilson and Haire, 1990) and are often on multiple drug regimes. How drugs (especially psychotropics) affect them is not well understood. Many never have their medication reviewed. Often they are reliant on others to administer medication, to observe ill effects and to summon help. It is therefore important to include carers when thinking about prescribing medication, or when it is being reviewed, changed or stopped.

PRESCRIBING

- Explain why the drug is being prescribed or changed, and how and when to use it. Check to make sure that instructions are understood and easily remembered. Use pictorial aids and reminders if necessary.
- Check any other medication the person is taking, and consider possible drug interactions. Use this opportunity to review all medication.
- Is the administration regime suitable? The person may be attending several day centres where inconsistent practice may result in variable compliance. Can the drug be taken once a day?
- Consider the most appropriate formulation: a slow release preparation, a liquid, capsule, tablets, powder?

Adults with Learning Disabilities. Edited by J. O'Hara and A. Sperlinger.
© 1997 John Wiley & Sons Ltd.

- Explain common side-effects, what to expect and how they may be helped.

ADMINISTRATION

- Check whether or not the patient is going to self-administer his or her medication and consider ways of facilitating this (e.g. dispensing packs, bubble packs, a dosette box or more appropriately designed labels on the bottle).
- Similar considerations may need to be given to non English speaking families. Use a professional interpreter instead of a family member.
- Try to avoid the need for tablets to be broken in half.
- Consider the ability of the patient or elderly carer to open 'child proof' bottles.
- If possible, avoid differing dose intervals of different drugs as this can be confusing. It is easier to remember to take the prescribed drugs at set times in the day.
- If a liquid is being used, check the concentration. Often patients and carers learn to administer medication by volume.
- Check that the appropriate storage of medication is understood.
- Ensure that the patient and carers know how to dispose of unwanted medication.
- If proper administration of medication is an issue, seek the help and advice of the community pharmacist and/or community nurse for learning disabilities.

MONITORING

- How will efficacy and side-effects be monitored? (For example, individual's self-reporting, or by carers reporting changes in behaviour?)
- Make sure that carers know what you will be looking for, and involve them. It may be helpful to set up a diary to help this monitoring process.
- How will the patient be reminded to have serum levels of medication checked? Will the support of a community nurse be helpful? Refer if needed.

REFERENCES

Howells, G. (1986) Are the medical needs of mentally handicapped adults being met? *Journal of the Royal College of General Practitioners*, **36**, 449–453.

Wilson, D. and Haire, A. (1990) Health care screening for people with mental handicap living in the community. *British Medical Journal*, **301**, 1379–1381.

5

EPILEPSY IN ADULTS WITH LEARNING DISABILITIES

Mohammed K. Sharief

For many people, epilepsy is a long-term condition affecting every area of their lives, and it is itself affected by many factors in their lives (Bird and Ovsiew, 1996). One in three adults with learning disabilities has epilepsy, and often seizures are complex and difficult to control. Epilepsy and its treatment can worsen cognitive function by impairing attention and the capacity to process incoming information. Seizures may be caused by the same cerebral insult that is associated with the learning disability. However:

- Epilepsy arising in adults over the age of 30 with Down's syndrome should alert the clinician to the possibility of dementia.
- Infantile seizures can persist into adult life. In West's syndrome this is often severe, reflecting the degree of brain damage. In Lennox-Gastaut syndrome it is particularly resistant to drug therapy; and a protective helmet may be necessary to avoid serious injury.
- Metabolic abnormalities, prenatal and postnatal infection and spastic cerebral palsy are regularly associated with epilepsy.

HOW SEIZURES MIGHT PRESENT

Epilepsy is a clinical diagnosis. It is reliant on a good history. This may prove difficult to elicit from adults with learning disabilities and/or their

Adults with Learning Disabilities. Edited by J. O'Hara and A. Sperlinger.
© 1997 John Wiley & Sons Ltd.

carers. It is important, but not easy, to distinguish between behaviour that is caused by the seizure (including pre- and post-ictal), by the treatment or unrelated to either (Kerr, 1996). EEG recordings may be distorted by movement artefacts and mild sedation may be needed.

The following types of seizures are commonly encountered:

- *Prodromal (pre-ictal) stage* may precede seizures by several hours with changes in behaviour or mood (e.g. anxiety, agitation, depression).
- *Partial seizures:* the onset of automatic behaviour, alteration of consciousness, confusion, intense fear and, occasionally, hallucinations. There are no falls, and the risk of serious injury is small.
- *Absence seizures:* sudden impairment of consciousness. The person is motionless and unresponsive for a few seconds. Recovery is prompt without serious injury.
- *Generalised seizures* may start with a cry. The person falls and stiffens and convulsive movements follow, often with incontinence and tongue-biting. Serious injuries can be sustained.
- *Status epilepticus:* a prolonged series of seizures, usually more than 30 minutes, without complete regaining of consciousness between them. It is regarded as a medical emergency.
- *Post-ictal state* follows seizures and may last for a few hours with prolonged confusion, agitation and, sometimes, aggressive behaviour.
- *Pseudo-seizures* are non-epileptic and precipitated by emotional stress. The onset is gradual, often with vocalisation. During attacks it is possible to communicate with the person, who may resist physical restraint.

MANAGEMENT

Seizure control is usually incomplete and multiple drug therapy may be necessary. It is important to balance the degree of control required with the possibility of side-effects which impair the individual's quality of life. In deciding on the drug of choice:

- Choose one with a broad spectrum of action if the type of seizure is unknown.
- Use a drug with few side-effects (avoid those which cause mental dysfunction and drowsiness) and one which does not require serum monitoring, as many people with learning disabilities (and their carers) find blood tests traumatic.
- Phenobarbitone and phenytoin are best avoided as they are associated with behavioural and cognitive disturbances, unsteadiness and gum hypertrophy.

- Carbamazepine and sodium valproate provoke minimal cognitive dysfunction, but the latter is less effective in partial seizures.
- Newer drugs cause relatively mild cognitive impairment. However, vigabatrin may cause behavioural disturbances in persons with a history of psychiatric disorders. Lamotrigine may cause agitation, sleep disturbances and skin rash. Gabapentin in high doses can result in headache and dizziness.
- Be aware of potential drug interactions, and drugs which lower seizure threshold such as concurrent use of neuroleptics (e.g. chlorpromazine).
- Improve compliance by ensuring the most appropriate formulation (e.g. slow-release, liquids or suspensions), memory aids and reminders (e.g. dispensing wallets), counting remaining tablets and the correct level of supervision.

INFORMATION AND ADVICE TO THE INDIVIDUAL AND CARERS

Measures to reduce anxiety in the individual and overprotection by carers include:

- Simple, clear explanations of what seizures are and their likely prognosis.
- Discuss implications for everyday life, including work and leisure activities.
- Discuss what to do in the event of a seizure and how to prevent injury.
- Show carers how to handle prolonged seizures—protection of airways, the recovery position and the possible need for rectal diazepam.
- Educate on monitoring seizure type and frequency (i.e. keeping a diary).
- Identify possible triggers: e.g. stress, excitement, infections, metabolic disturbances.
- Offer guidance on the importance of regular medication and potential side-effects.
- Give addresses of the British Epilepsy Association and the National Society for Epilepsy for advice and support.

People with learning disabilities and epilepsy have a dual disability and must be managed in that light, with easy access to specialist hospital and community services. Expertise in both learning disabilities and epilepsy is essential to successful management.

REFERENCES

Bird, J. and Ovsiew, F. (1996) Epilepsy: the quintessential neuropsychiatric disorder. *Current Opinion in Psychiatry*, **9**, 77–80.

Kerr, M. (1996) Epilepsy in patients with learning disability. *Aspects of Epilepsy*, Issue 3, *February*. LibraParm Ltd, UK.

6

CHALLENGING NEEDS AND PROBLEMATIC BEHAVIOUR

John Clements

1. **Does the behaviour of concern pose significant social problems?**
   Is the behaviour imposing, or likely to impose:
   - a significant 'cost' on the person, *and/or*
   - a significant and unreasonable 'cost' upon others?

   If **YES**, proceed to 2. If **NO**, focus on those expressing concern.

2. **Does the behaviour present a physical risk to the person or to others?**
   If **NO**, go to 3. If **YES**, either:

   - devise management guidelines to prevent incidents and specific drills (reactive strategies) to reduce risk when incidents occur;

   or, in extreme cases:

   - seek advice as to the appropriateness of detention under the Mental Health Act.

3. **Are there some basic contributors to the behaviour which have not yet been considered?**
   Screen for such obvious contributors as:

   - Physical health problems
   - Personality clashes

Adults with Learning Disabilities. Edited by J. O'Hara and A. Sperlinger.
© 1997 John Wiley & Sons Ltd.

- Lack of positive social support
- Lack of structure and consistency in service delivery
- High staff turnover
- Considerable amounts of time spent with nothing to do.

4. **What might be the more specific needs being expressed by the behaviour of concern?**
To establish such needs:

- Define the specific behaviours of concern: prioritise for investigation.
- Establish a behaviour monitoring system for prioritised behaviours.
- Collect information on prioritised behaviour(s)—contexts for incidents, contributing factors from current living environments, personal characteristics and personal history.
- Work to achieve empathic reflection.
- Summarise factors identified (formulation).

5. **What are we going to do to meet the needs identified in 4?**
To develop action plans derived from the formulation:

- Ensure engagement in the decision making of all those likely to be involved in programme implementation.
- Develop menu of relevant interventions—'If this is the need, what has to happen for this need to be met?'—for each need identified.
- Prioritise menu items for implementation (in terms of importance, feasibility and competence to deliver).
- Select interventions that will be actioned.
- Record needs and interventions identified that will not be actioned and reasons (for example, lack of resources, lack of available competence).
- Implement selected interventions (GO FOR IT!!).
- Monitor effects of action plans on behaviour via the already established behaviour monitoring system (4 above).

6. **And, depending upon the effects of intervention . . .**

- Celebrate or
- Persist or
- Implement further action plans or
- Reassess.

THE PSYCHIATRIC ASSESSMENT

Jean O'Hara

There is a growing awareness of the mental health needs of adults with learning disabilities. However, their ability to identify and verbally report symptoms of emotional and psychological distress is limited; often they rely on their carers and families to recognise their distress and to solicit help. Commonly this occurs when there are changes in behaviours which are experienced as problematic or challenging while the significance of less disruptive symptoms may go undetected. The GP is usually the first health professional to be consulted and the immediate response is often one of prescribing medication. However, it is important not to rush into drug treatments to 'manage a problem' but to assess it within the framework of general psychiatric practice.

1. The GP may not have knowledge of the patient or his or her family or situation. Indeed, carers may seek the GP's intervention without bringing the person with learning disabilities to the surgery.
   - It is important to assess the patient's mental state through direct observation and examination.
   - The GP will need to pay attention to:
     - environmental factors affecting the interview, e.g. background noise;
     - attention span: use frequent re-caps, if necessary arrange to see the patient for a number of short consultations, target interview to specific areas of interest;

Adults with Learning Disabilities. Edited by J. O'Hara and A. Sperlinger.
© 1997 John Wiley & Sons Ltd.

— his or her own body language, gestures and communicative skills
— the patient's non-verbal communication (e.g. behaviour, appearance, mood).

2. In adults with mild learning disabilities it is possible to adapt general psychiatric questioning to elicit a range of symptoms. However, be aware of:
   - jumping to premature conclusions as the person may be suggestible, and will often acquiesce when asked leading questions;
   - the significance of symptoms as they may be different from that of the general population—for example, self-injurious or aggressive behaviours, often considered a key feature of personality disorders, must be seen as a means of communicating distress;
   - language and form of questions used:
     — make sure the person understands what you are asking
     — structure questions to avoid 'yes/no' answers
     — the person's ability to label different emotional states is often limited
     — relate timing of symptoms to events (e.g. before you went on holiday?).

3. In adults with severe learning disabilities, look for:
   - behavioural equivalents—for example, physical symptoms, exacerbation of existing behaviours, onset of new behaviours;
   - biological features—for example, changes in sleep patterns, weight, appetite, concentration.

4. Try to gain an understanding of the person's life experiences and circumstances, through talking to him or her, gathering information from reliable informants who know the person well, and documented notes. Consider:
   - The person's views of his or her disability, problem, situation
   - The family's views, relationships and culture: 9% of adults with learning disabilities have a positive family history for learning disability, and 26% have a positive family history for mental illness (Bouras et al., 1988)
   - Birth and developmental history, including developmental milestones, language and communication development, social interactions
   - Educational/employment/daily living skills, including ability to self-care, travel independently, money skills. Do not assume that the current level of functioning is due to learning disabilities.

- Social history, including living circumstances, leisure opportunities, social supports
- Life events, losses, anniversaries, worries, changes in environment (including staff)
- Changes in behaviours and level of functioning
- Medical and psychiatric history: including previous interventions and outcomes, current medication and possibility of side-effects.

5. In the physical examination, exclude the possibility of underlying physical disorders such as acute confusional states due to drug toxicity or infections, epilepsy, biochemical or endocrine abnormalities such as thyroid disease.

6. In deciding on treatment, all the factors which are thought to be important in the causation, precipitation and maintenance of a psychiatric disorder need to be considered. Often it needs a thorough multidisciplinary assessment before a proper plan of treatment and intervention can be formulated, implemented and monitored. Refer to the local CTLD.

REFERENCE

Bouras, N., Drummond, K., Brooks, D. and Laws, M. (1988) *Mental Handicap and Mental Health: A Community Service*. NUPRD, London.

RECOMMENDED READING

Anness, V. (1991) A multi-aspect assessment for people with mental handicap. *Psychiatric Bulletin*, **15**, 146.

CONSENT ISSUES

Glynis H. Murphy and Isabel C.H. Clare

1. In England and Wales, all adults (that is, everyone aged 18 years or more) are presumed to be able to make their own decisions, both about everyday matters and more unusual events, including:
   - medical and other treatments such as nursing care, psychological interventions
   - dealing with personal relationships
   - dealing with financial affairs
   - entering into a contract
   - voting
   - taking part in research.

2. There is a presumption of capacity. A person does not lack capacity to make a particular decision *just* because he or she has a learning disability *or* because he or she makes a different decision from other people.

3. There is no global concept of 'capacity', so a person may be able to make some decisions but not others. The 'capacity' required will depend on the complexity of the decision and the legal test (if one exists—see BMA/LS, 1995) to be applied. Capacity applies to *this* particular decision in *these* particular circumstances.

4. If someone has capacity in relation to a particular decision, then his or her decision must be respected.

5. No one can consent on an adult's behalf. *Parents, carers, or partner/ friends cannot make the decision for the person.* Terms such as 'proxy consent' have no legal meaning and will not be accepted by a court.

Adults with Learning Disabilities. Edited by J. O'Hara and A. Sperlinger.
© 1997 John Wiley & Sons Ltd.

6. For health care professionals, consent to treatment (which includes investigations and other procedures) is particularly important. The *treatment provider*, whether he or she is a doctor, nurse, physiotherapist, clinical psychologist, speech and language therapist or any other health care professional, is accountable in law for judging whether the person is able to consent and whether he or she does so.

7. If the person appears to lack capacity to make a particular decision, health care professionals need to ask:
   • Have I assessed this person in relation to this particular decision, taking into account the legal test where this exists?
   • Can the person be helped to have the capacity to make this decision?
   • Is there any one else (other health care professionals, significant others in the person's life) who can give advice or help?
   • Are all my actions documented fully?

8. If a person has the capacity to consent to treatment, but withholds it, giving treatment can be a criminal offence!

9. Where a person is *unable* to consent, the decision to treat can be defended if treatment is necessary to preserve life, health or well-being *and* is in the person's best interests according to an accepted body of opinion of professionals skilled in that treatment. Always ask:

   • Is there a less intrusive alternative?
   • Would I give this treatment to someone who did not have a learning disability—am I discriminating against him or her?
   • Does this treatment respect the person's dignity and privacy?
   • Even though the person does not have capacity, have I sought his or her views? Have I asked others who know the person well about his or her likely wishes?

10. Some treatment decisions, (such as sterilisation, which is not carried out as an emergency) require that the court should always be involved.

11. If in doubt, consult the British Medical Association and the Law Society *Guidance*; seek legal advice.

REFERENCE

British Medical Association and the Law Society (BMA/LS) (1995) *Assessment of Mental Capacity: Guidance for Doctors and Lawyers*. BMA, London.

THE MENTAL HEALTH ACT 1983*

Jean O'Hara

1. *All sections of the Mental Health Act can apply to people with learning disabilities, and the Code of Practice is applicable to all.*

2. *'Medical treatment'* includes nursing, care, habilitation and rehabilitation under medical supervision. *Such treatments are for mental disorders and do not apply in other contexts.*

3. *Compulsory admission to hospital ('Sectioning')* applies only if the following are met:
   - The patient has a mental disorder (as defined by the Act).
   - It is of such severity that the patient requires and refuses treatment.
   - Hospital admission is in the interest of his or her own safety and/or for the protection/safety of others.

4. *Definition of 'mental disorder'.* Mental disorder means mental illness, mental impairment, severe mental impairment, psychopathic disorder and any other disorder/disability of mind. It excludes promiscuity, immoral conduct, sexual deviancy and dependence on alcohol or drugs. [Severe] Mental impairment is defined as 'a state of arrested or incomplete development of mind which includes significant [severe] impairment of intelligence and social functioning *and* is associated with abnormally aggressive or seriously irresponsible conduct'. (Only

*Provisions under The Mental Health Act may be different in Scotland and Northern Ireland

Adults with Learning Disabilities. Edited by J. O'Hara and A. Sperlinger.
© 1997 John Wiley & Sons Ltd.

a minority of people with learning disabilities will fall into this definition.)

5. *Consent to treatment for mental disorder.* Treatment orders (such as Section 3) allow for medication to be given in the first three months without the patient's consent. After this time, either the patient must consent to medication or there must be a second opinion from the Mental Health Act Commission. A second opinion is also required if ECT is recommended. Some treatments, such as psychosurgery, require *both* the patient's consent *and* a second opinion, regardless of whether the person is a detained or informal patient.

6. *Section 117 (Aftercare)* is now linked with the *Care Programme Approach* (CPA). It requires aftercare provision to be provided for all those detained for treatment, in cooperation with statutory and relevant voluntary agencies, until such time as the services are no longer required.

7. *Section 25 (Supervision Orders/Supervised Discharge), Mental Health (Patients in the Community) Act 1995, amends the 1983 Act.* For a limited number of patients with long-term enduring mental illness who have been detained for treatment, formal supervision on discharge may help to ensure that appropriate aftercare is provided, through a process of planning and review, and the specific roles assigned to the community responsible medical officer (CRMO) and the nominated supervisor. It has no power to enforce treatment, but is intended to operate as an integral part of CPA. It specifically excludes those with psychopathic disorders but can be used for those adults who are, or are likely to be, exploited. The application is made to the health authority.

8. *Sections 7 and 8 (Guardianship Order)* enable the establishment of an authoritative framework for working with a patient to achieve as independent a life as possible in the community. The application is made to the local authority. It requires the patient to reside in a specified place, to attend for purposes of medical treatment, occupation, education or training, and allows access to specified persons (such as the doctor or social worker).
   - It has no power to give consent to treatment.
   - At present it is used mainly for the protection of adults with learning disabilities in environments of inadequate care or where they are in an exploitative relationship.
   - It is doubtful whether guardianship can be used in the absence of 'abnormally aggressive or seriously irresponsible conduct'. Recent proposals call for an extension in eligibility criteria, to cover those at risk of sexual abuse.

9. *Court of Protection (Part VII of the Mental Health Act)* gives authority to make orders and give direction in relation to the estate of a person who, because of a mental disorder, is incapable of managing and administrating his or her property and affairs. It applies mainly to those with dementia, severe brain damage and severe learning disabilities.

- *Enduring Powers of Attorney* is a practical way in which the elderly/ infirm can anticipate and nominate a person to act on their behalf.
- *Appointment and supervision of Receivers*: usually a relative or friend, but may be a solicitor or someone from the local authority.

RECOMMENDED READING

Ashton, G.R. and Ward, A.D. (1992) *Mental Handicap and the Law*. Sweet & Maxwell, London.
Mental Health Act (1983) HMSO, London.
Mental Health (Patients in the Community) Act (1995) HMSO, London.

VULNERABILITY, EXPLOITATION AND SEXUALITY

Hilary Brown

1. Always familiarise yourself with locally agreed policies, guidance and procedures in relation to:
   - abuse of all vulnerable adults
   - sexual abuse specifically both of, and by, other vulnerable adults
   - sexuality and personal relationships
   - intimate care
   - control and restraint
   - confidentiality and sharing of information on a 'need to know' basis.

   In all these areas practitioners should be sure they understand the *values* expressed in the policy, the channels for *communicating* concerns, the forum and mechanisms for *decision making* and the extent of their *discretion* in making decisions without reference to other practitioners or agencies.

2. Remember that abuse often takes place in circumstances of intimidation and secrecy: do not take a patient's assurance that everything is all right or that they don't want you to proceed with any action at face value . . . always explore the possibility that they are afraid and that other people may also be at risk.

3. Keep an open mind and an independent position in relation to providers of residential and domiciliary care or to family members. Your

Adults with Learning Disabilities. Edited by J. O'Hara and A. Sperlinger.
© 1997 John Wiley & Sons Ltd.

value to vulnerable adults derives partly from the fact that you can stand outside the immediate situation and advocate for them. If you come 'alongside' the other professionals or carers in the person's life you may not be able to question what these more powerful people are doing or to challenge their assumptions about, or methods of, care. There may be *real* conflicts of interest and you need to be independent in order to ensure that individuals are safe.

4. Don't be afraid to make decisions: it is better to develop a view about whether someone can or cannot give their consent to a particular relationship or a financial transaction and be open to changing your mind if the evidence warrants it than to hide behind phrases like 'individual choice' or 'rights' when these notions are not really being put to the test. Support people with learning disabilities in making their own choices as much as possible but only when you have satisfied yourself that they understand what they are deciding and are not being coerced or unfairly persuaded into a course of action for someone else's benefit.

5. Always check out and properly record:
   - any bruises, cuts, abrasions, burns, or finger marks;
   - evidence of sexual trauma such as bruises around and/or tears to vagina or anus, sexually transmitted disease, pregnancy in someone who could not give their consent to intercourse, disclosures or partial disclosures;
   - financial transactions above an agreed limit;
   - risk assessments arising in the course of individual planning or skills teaching;
   - difficulties encountered in dealing with any difficult behaviour which may have necessitated physical restraint.

   You may only have partial or disjointed information but do record and date it and sign the record: it may help you to build up a picture over time and ensure that lack of continuity as a result of staff turnover does not lead to individual or institutional abuse continuing over time.

6. Abuse will rarely stop unless action is taken: it is not usually a one-off event or a single lapse but signals ongoing problems with sexuality, respecting others or managing aspects of care or challenging behaviour. If you have concerns do not take 'no' for an answer. If you cannot verify your concerns enough to take *formal* action, find another way of protecting the individual or of monitoring the situation.

USEFUL ADDRESSES

BILD (British Institute for Learning Disabilities)
Wolverhampton Road
Kidderminster
Worcs DY10 3PP
Tel.: 01562-850251
Fax: 01562-851970

Carers National Association
20–25 Glasshouse Yard
London EC1A 4JS
Tel.: 0171-4908818

Down's Syndrome Association
155 Mitcham Road
London SW17 9PG
Tel.: 0181-6824001
Fax: 0181-6824012

Family Planning Association
(Education Unit: training courses for staff in health, social and educational services who work with people with learning disabilities; publishes training handbooks on sex education and counselling)
2–12 Pentonville Road
London N1 9FP
Tel.: 0171-8375432

NAPSAC
(National Association for the Protection from Sexual Abuse of Adults and Children with Learning Disabilities)
Department of Learning Disabilities
Floor E, South Block
University Hospital
Nottingham NG7 2UH
Tel.: 0115-9709987

National Society for Epilepsy
Chesham Lane
Chalfont St Peter
Bucks SL9 0RJ
Tel.: 01494-873991

People First
(Advocacy for People with Learning Disabilities)
207–215 Kings Cross Road
London WC1X 9DB
Tel.: 0171-7136400
Fax: 0171-7135826

Respond
(Individual and group psychotherapy and counselling for adults with learning disabilities who have been sexually abused, and/or who abuse others)
3rd Floor
24–32 Stephenson Way
London NW1 2HD
Tel.: 0171-3830700

MENCAP (Royal Society for Mentally Handicapped Children and Adults)
123 Golden Lane
London EC1Y 0RT
Tel.: 0171-4540454
Fax: 0171-6083254

VOICE UK
(A support and action group for people with learning disabilities who have been abused: aimed at supporting families and gaining awareness)
PO Box 238
Derby DE1 9JN
Tel.: 01322-519872
Fax: 01332-521392

INDEX

Index compiled by Liz Granger

Related titles of interest...

Psychology in Counselling and Therapeutic Practice

Jill D. Wilkinson and Elizabeth A. Campbell, with contributions by Adrian Coyle and Alyson Davis

Throughout the book, case material, examples and discussion are used to demonstrate the synergy between psychological processes and therapeutic practice. By bringing psychology into the consulting room, the authors ensure that psychological theory and research are accessible and applicable to the therapist's work with clients.

0-471-95562 0   286pp   February 1997   Pbk

Brief Rational Emotive Behaviour Therapy

Windy Dryden

Practitioners will find useful insights and guidance on applying brief therapy methods throughout the process of therapy, including building the working alliance, assessment, formulation, and work in sessions and outside the sessions. The whole process is illustrated by a case study which reflects the problems of real life work with a client.

0-471-95786 0   244pp   May 1995   Pbk

Cognitive Developmental Therapy with Children

Tammie Ronen

This book is a concise, simple guide to the application of cognitive therapy to child problems, with particular focus on self-control methods, and on the author's model for working with children, in family and school settings.

"I think it is an <u>excellent</u> book and that it will make a significant contribution to continuing developments in the conceptualization and practice of child psychotherapy..."

Professor Michael J. Mahoney, Department of Psychology, University of North Texas, USA

0-471-97006 9   224pp   April 1997   Hbk
0-471-97007 7   224pp   April 1997   Pbk

Culture and the Child
A Guide for Professionals in Child Care and Development

Daphne M. Keats

This first book in the new Wiley Series in Culture and Professional Practice is intended to be a handy practical guide for those professionals dealing with children whose cultural backgrounds differ from those of the mainstream of the society in which they live.

0-471-96625 8   200pp   December 1996   Pbk

Visit the Wiley Home Page http://www.wiley.co.uk